I REALLY
SHOULD BE
PRACTICING

I REALLY SHOULD BE PRACTICING

Gary Graffman

DOUBLEDAY & COMPANY, INC.
GARDEN CITY, NEW YORK

ISBN: 0-385-15559-X
Library of Congress Catalog Card Number 80–1119

For my mother, who sincerely believes that playing the piano in public is far more perilous than pleasurable; and for the memory of my father, who (as usual) thought exactly the opposite.

I gratefully acknowledge the help of friends concerning this book. Eugene Istomin, although he regarded the entire project with more than his usual skepticism, was unstinting with his time and energy. Simon Karlinsky most generously answered my plea for guidelines in the transliteration of Russian words and phrases. Ellen Roddick sifted patiently through sandpiles of excess verbiage, which she tried valiantly to pat down to size. (If the reader feels that I did not follow enough of her advice, the reader is correct.) Constance Shuman and Harry Beall also waded through this stream of consciousness; Piero Weiss made many valuable suggestions and fished out a few bloopers. Of course, my wife, Naomi (without whom there would be no book), is responsible—as always—for any mistakes that remain.

Every author has an editor. I, however (for reasons perhaps best left unexplored), have been blessed with two. All my thanks go to them both—to Susan Schwartz and Kenneth D. McCormick—for their good-natured encouragement of an amateur in a professional's world. Should either of them contemplate making a Carnegie Hall piano recital debut, I'll be glad to reciprocate.

CONTENTS

CHAPTER ONE

The Devil Made Me Do It

THE FIRST TIME I played at the Hollywood Bowl, it was Tchaikovsky. The second time, two years later, it was the same Tchaikovsky. The third time, two years after that, I was once again told, "Tchaikovsky."

"Ummmm, maybe you've forgotten," I said meekly to Jaye Rubanoff, the gentleman from the Los Angeles Philharmonic management who had given me this information, "but that's what I played here the last two times."

"Yup," agreed Jaye, frowning at me sternly as he growled out the old gag, "and what's more, you'll keep on playing it until you get it right."

Some improvement must have been noted at that performance, for the following summer I found myself scheduled to play Prokofiev. On the morning of the concert I remember arriving at the Bowl for rehearsal feeling very exhilarated. This was not so much because of the new repertoire but rather for the achievement of just being in Los Angeles. It was the last stop on a three-month tour that had taken me, by some freakishly alliterative coincidence, from Baden-Baden to Bora-Bora, and although I was incubating a typhoid bug picked up in the latter, I didn't know that yet. So nothing spoiled my delight at having proved once again that the world was indeed round. I greeted the conductor, André Previn, exultantly:

"And to think that only yesterday I was driving in Papeete!"

André didn't miss a beat. Looking up from the score he was studying, he merely nodded sagaciously and observed, "Boy! Ya musta made all the lights."

A young pianist sitting at my knee seeking enlightenment would undoubtedly ask at this juncture, "O Master, I have heard what it is you said, but could you please tell me now just what it all means?" After a suitable amount of thought, I guess I'd reply, "My child, the first thing to remember is that you'll *never* get it right. And even if every now and then you think you're doing fine, there'll always be someone who disagrees. As the saying goes, that's what makes horse races. And, ultimately, it means that it's you who must be your own judge."

"And the second parable? What does that teach?"

"Item Number Two," I would tell him, "is that a conductor is not, generally, terribly interested in where you've been, just as long as you come in on time."

Perhaps this explains why not too many young pianists sit at my knee. On the other hand (or knee), probably it's just as well. Certain things can only be learned, as my unsinkably philosophical manager Harry Beall is fond of saying, by "sliding down the razor blade of life." And besides, nowadays things are different.

I first began to give concerts around 1947. Suddenly that seems like a long time ago. I meet adults—responsible, tax-paying citizens with kids in school and condominia in Florida—who weren't even born then, and sometimes they ask me, "What was it like in those days?" and I am reminded of the story about Sibelius.

It seems that when he was very young he met an old, old

man who, when *he* was very young, had worked as a messenger for Beethoven's publisher. Sibelius was, of course, fascinated by the possibility of learning something about Beethoven from someone who had actually known him. He pestered the old man endlessly. "What was he like? Surely you must have some recollection . . . after all . . . Beethoven!" The old man thought and thought. He tried to visualize those long-gone days. "*What was he like?*" Sibelius persisted. The old man finally dredged up the scenes of his encounters at Beethoven's door, picking up or delivering manuscripts, brightened, and replied, "Well, he had awfully hairy hands."

Although I can endeavor to give only a messenger's-eye view of some of the great musicians with whom I've come in contact (my association with most of the legendary artists whose names I shall drop being peripheral or, at best, student-teacher), I do feel qualified to describe with total intimacy, if not reasonable accuracy, the life and times of an American concert performer in mid-century—as well as the pleasures and perils of playing the piano in public.

Kenneth D. McCormick, now Senior Consultant Editor at Doubleday, suggested this book. We have been friends for many years (he is an ardent music lover), and he has frequently been subjected not only to my playing but also to the recounting of my sagas. I never thought, however, that he would turn on me in this way. (This proves that nobody can be trusted.) The final straw, or actual genesis of this volume, was an article I wrote last year for the Sunday New York *Times* Arts and Leisure (ha!) Section about a trip to Egypt. Although that article got me in terrible hot water with the directress of the Cairo Conservatory, Ken liked it. *He* didn't especially care that my descriptive (as opposed to pejorative) term for the Cairo Conservatory—"dank"—rendered me the first Jew to become *persona non grata* in Egypt since the signing of the peace treaty. I, meanwhile, having enjoyed enormously the visit to Egypt and thus infinitely regretting my inadvertent affront, had resolved never to put pen to paper again. But Ken is extremely persuasive, and so I have now risked once more raising wrath from unexpected quarters. This time, however, I've tried to play it safe by relating adventures and incidents that occurred no later than the middle 1960s. Here and there, I'm afraid, more current events have sneaked in. But in general I've attempted to avoid tramping on more recent vintages. The patina of age on my tales will, I hope, have dimmed any glaring discourtesy, tactlessness or irreverence; in any event, if I have caused offense, in most cases it was unintentional.

The embarrassing question of how a non-writer can even dare attempt a writing project was somewhat resolved when it was pointed out that even Marco Polo's *Description of the World* had been dictated to a scribe—also referred to as a "professional romance writer" (lovely title!)—as they sweated out a prison sentence together in Genoa. Although I don't know a scribe, I have a wife who can type. And while she is by no means a professional romance writer, she does have an incredible memory for trivia (much of which has been incorporated slyly by her somewhere in this book) and a willingness to do almost anything if she doesn't have to talk on the phone. So, if the upstairs lounges of 747s, deserted high school classrooms used as dressing areas for itinerant performers, and dollhouse-sized Japanese hotel rooms complete with the usual furniture plus an upright piano stuffed with a blanket to deaden the sound can be imagined to approximate the confines of a thirteenth-century Genoese jail, then we're in business.

Nevertheless, I'm not sure that my father would have been very pleased with all of this nonsense. As subsequent chapters will reveal, he really preferred that I stick to the straight and narrow. I have a feeling that if he'd known what I was undertaking, he would have looked at me quizzically, raised his eyebrows, cleaned his glasses, drummed his fingers on the table and said something like, "A book? A book? Why do you want to write a book? Better you should learn two more concertos!"

Caveat lector.

CHAPTER TWO

Father, Mother
and Nicholas II

"BUT, GARIKI, you can't go to Novo-Nikolaevsk," my father exclaimed when I read to him that afternoon, so many years ago, the schedule of my first Soviet tour. "It's not possible. It takes five days to get there from Moscow!" He quickly realized his absentmindedness, and laughed. "Can you imagine, it's just fifty years since I last played there, since I left? Now everything is different, even the names of the cities. I know. I know you said 'Novosibirsk.' But I still think of it as it was, as it was in the old days." Taking off his glasses, he pressed his fingers to his eyes for a minute, and sighed, "Ah, those long train trips! You know," and he treated me to a lecherous wink, "the sleeping compartments were for two people and we would be assigned to them without any regard to sex. Those long train trips—if one was traveling alone, of course!—they could be very . . . entertaining."

On the plane to Novosibirsk a few weeks later I saw how

right my father had been. The voyage indeed seemed to take five days. I envied him his "entertaining" train trips as I squirmed in my cramped seat, wedged between two hefty *babushkas*, both snoring mightily as we roared through the night. Impossible to read, impossible to sleep, impossible to talk to anyone. Both my wife Naomi and Marina, the pert Russian girl from the state concert agency who was traveling with us, had deserted me and were sitting alone in other parts of the plane. We had boarded too late to be together. The incident at the telegraph office had almost caused us to miss the flight. How extraordinary, I mused, that in a Moscow airport—even the one servicing Asia—it was impossible to dispatch a cable in Latin characters; and although we were tickled at the thought of what would have happened if we'd sent a reply to Fritz's wire in Cyrillic, I was annoyed at the idea of what lay in store for us when we attempted to phone New York from Siberia. "Mother Russia, what a *noodge* you are!" I remember thinking. Still, unlike those in other places, the pianos were, for the most part, unexpectedly excellent, and in fine condition. And, after all, since the purpose of this journey (as were my other seemingly endless circlings of the globe) was to play the piano, it did seem a little ungracious constantly to be finding fault. But then again, consider the chicken. After we'd been waiting in the hotel dining room for over an hour, it had finally reached us, covered with what resembled pubic fuzz and tasting (for we were ravenous, and tried to eat it) like last year's tennis shoes. "This chicken must have been a good hunter!" With a wry smile, Marina had intoned the standard blessing over tough fowl. We hadn't laughed, which meant that tempers were running thin. So it probably was just as well that we were each sulking alone on this trip. A few hours of silence would calm us. I resolved to think of pleasant, or at least different, things.

Once, in Kyoto, my Buddhist friend Hyman Edelstein (formerly of the Bronx) asked, "Gary, did you ever stop to think of who you were before your father was born?" Without giving me a chance to chew on that one properly, he followed through with another zinger: "What the hell is happening with Xerox, anyway?" This caused an instant change of subject and we never did get back to the original question. It was not the sort of thing I spent much time over, anyway. That night, though, flying over my ancestral homeland with nothing else to do (and probably somewhat moved at the idea of following in my father's half-century-old footsteps), I did ponder for the first time the inexorable chain of circumstances that had culminated in my present discomfort. One thing was certain. Had it not been for the Russian Revolution, no New York pianist named Gary Graffman would ever have been squirming grimly in a darkened jet on his way to Siberia. In fact, he never would have existed—as me—at all. Highly unlikely that my father and mother would ever have met, much less married, even though they had both emerged from within the Pale. The title of one scene of Mussorgsky's *Pictures from an Exhibition*, I thought, expressed the reason most succinctly: They were "Two Jews—Once Rich, the Other, Poor."

But I was being somewhat poetic that night on the plane. In truth, my father was poor only compared to the luxurious surroundings that my mother had enjoyed as a girl. His family considered itself middle class, and his story is not unlike that of many Russian-Jewish musicians who were born around the turn of the century. When one hears tales of Vilna at that time, it seems as if every male Jew was either a tailor or a violinist. The Vilna Graffmans ran true to form. My grandfather was the tailor. He had six children, and the four who survived to adolescence each played an instrument. My father, the eldest, was the violinist. And, as violinists tend to do, he began his studies at an early age. This was very fortunate because his father the tailor died young and Vladimir, my father, soon was responsible for the greater part of his family's income. My father was always very thin and frail (deceptively, as it turned out, for he had a will of iron and lived an incredibly busy life up to and including its last day, which occurred when he was eighty-six), and he was quite short, too. My uncle Joseph, his kid brother (who played the double bass), remembered how Volodya would, as a child violin teacher, give lessons to students almost twice his size, "standing on a table."

Nothing deterred my father Volodya, though, and thanks to the income from his teaching, he was able to continue his own violin studies. Eventually he was accepted as a pupil of the leading pedagogue of the time, Leopold Auer, at the Imperial Conservatory in St. Petersburg. Shortly afterward, his sister Dina was accepted as a piano student, and brother Joseph soon followed with his double bass. Sonia, the youngest, studied piano in Vilna, where she remained with her mother. Although it fell upon Volodya as the eldest to provide the main source of support for his mother and siblings for years to come, he never seemed to feel that he was in any way deprived of his youth, and he always remembered his St. Petersburg days and his life at the conservatory with the greatest of enthusiasm. "Of course I worked," he said, matter-of-factly. "We all worked. Everybody had a job. In summer—every summer—I played in resorts. Every town had an orchestra, and I would be concertmaster, and the whole family would come to spend the summer wherever it was I would be working. And in winter, in St. Petersburg, we would play in cafes, and all our meals were free. Oh, sure, we worked late at night, but you know we never would have gone to sleep early even if we didn't have jobs. And we would go home to Vilna for the holidays, at Christmas, Easter, things like that. Vilna was a beautiful town. It really was nice."

He recounted to me how one day in St. Petersburg he received a letter from Vilna, from neighbors who had a son several years younger than he who also studied the violin. "Jaschinka has been accepted at the conservatory," wrote the boy's father, whom Volodya called "Papa Heifetz." "Would you please look after him when he comes to St. Petersburg? Will you meet him at the station? It will be his first time away from home and he is so young . . . Make sure he wears warm enough clothing." Volodya obliged, particularly as he had always thought a great deal of the little boy's talent. "And he was such a good-looking boy, like an angel, Jascha, he looked

like a little angel," my father recalled. Shortly after Jascha was
enrolled at the conservatory, Volodya brought him to meet
Auer, who taught only the most advanced students. He took
the youngster by the hand and knocked on Auer's classroom
door. When this gruff, impatient pedagogue opened the door
and looked down with obvious annoyance at the two little
twerps, my father meekly said, "This is the young fellow from
my home town, the one I told you about." Auer snapped,
"Now, Volodya, you know I have no room for anyone else in
my class. Just take him downstairs to play for Nalbandian." My
father shrugged and obeyed. After Nalbandian, Auer's assistant,
had heard a few notes of Jascha's playing, *he* shrugged and
took Heifetz by one hand and my father by the other, and the
three of them paraded back to Auer's studio. Nalbandian
banged on the door and when Auer opened it, blurted, "You
better listen to this kid *now!*" When my father told me that
story I asked him how Heifetz had played when he was a little
boy. My father thought for a bit, threw his head back, closed
his eyes, scratched his nose thoughtfully, and finally replied,
"Like Heifetz."

To study with Auer was the highest an aspiring violinist
could aim. All the string players at the conservatory—"even
cellists and double bass players"—would, whenever possible,
stand outside the door of his classroom to listen to, as my uncle
recalled, "how they are playing this or that." But Auer was very
stern, even rude. Prokofiev, a classmate of my father's, described in his memoirs an actual insurrection that took place at
one point, when Auer's unceasing blows, both physical and
emotional, became too painful. "Even standing behind the
door," my uncle recollected, "we could hear him hollering like
hell. At who? At some of the students? No, no, he yelled at everybody." Among those he yelled at, in addition to my father
and Jaschinka, were Mischa Elman, Efrem Zimbalist and another child prodigy, Richard Burgin. My father was fond of
remembering young Richard's excitement when he returned
from a United States tour, which he made while still a student.
Everyone clustered around to hear his tales of the New World.

"And now I know exactly what I want to do for the rest of my life!" Richard announced. He then surprised his audience by elucidating. "I want to be the concertmaster of the Boston Symphony Orchestra." For a long, long time—throughout the Boston Symphony's golden years under Koussevitzky and Munch—he had his wish, and I think he was a truly happy man.

In 1913 Vladimir Graffman graduated from the Imperial Conservatory of St. Petersburg and received the precious diploma proclaiming him *Svobodni Hudojnik*—Free Artist. This was, roughly, the equivalent of an honorary college degree and entitled the bearer to various privileges of citizenship that less educated people were denied, and that had only recently been permitted to professional musicians through the efforts of Anton Rubinstein. He'd already had a great deal of performing experience and now, if he opted for a steady income (which was necessary because he was still virtually the only source of support for his family), many orchestra and teaching posts would be available. The only catch was that some cities were off limits to Jews. St. Petersburg and Moscow, for example, were proscribed unless the Jew was officially a student, a well-thought-of intellectual, a successful merchant or tradesman, or a prostitute, and had an identity card to prove it.

"You know, that was a very funny thing," my father sometimes recalled. "The girls, some of the Jewish girl students at the conservatory, after they graduated, they wanted to stay in St. Petersburg another year or so. Of course, they could have converted, that was very easy; but somehow they didn't want to, some of them, and you know what they did? They got prostitute's cards, and so nobody bothered them."

My father had the choice of nominally becoming a Christian, as so many Jewish artists did in Russia at that time. Once a Jew had been baptized, apparently all past sins were washed away and there was no stigma of any kind. Although my father could never recall any particular occasion when he had been persecuted as a Jew, nor had he ever witnessed a pogrom, his opportunities were somewhat limited, so conversion might have been a practical step to take at that time. Nevertheless, he never made the change.

Naomi was fond of speculating about this and quizzed him endlessly on the subject. "You mean all you'd have to do would be to sign a paper and then you wouldn't be Jewish any more?" "That's right," my father replied. "No restrictions of any kind, you could live anywhere, do anything that any Christian could do?" "Yes," said my father, "it was as simple as that." "And if you didn't," she persisted, "it meant that there would be certain problems . . . ?" "Oh, sure," said my father. "It means, for example, that when I was offered the job of concertmaster of the opera orchestra in Kiev, that was the largest city I could live in at the time. You see, I couldn't play in the Moscow orchestra, no, not as a Jew." "But you weren't in any way religious, you say?" persisted my wife, the Grand Inquisitor. "*Nyet, nyet*, not at all, not even my parents." "Well then, why on earth didn't you? Everybody else did! Even Auer, you said, was baptized . . ." "Look, look," stammered my father, "look, look" (obviously at a loss for words), "no, no, not all of us did, certainly not; not Elman, not Heifetz . . . and me, I don't know, it never really occurred to me to think about it seriously. It wouldn't have been, it wouldn't have been, you know, somehow, *hhhhon*est."

My father's *hhhon*esty was a trait that, like his stubbornness, became intensified with the passing years. He would rarely dissimulate in any way, not even to utter the meaningless little pleasantries that compose so much of everyday conversation. His criticism of students was never destructive, though; he tried to see the best in everything. But his evaluations offered no false hopes. He just said what he thought was right. My friend Piero, who was a faculty colleague of his at the Mannes College of Music in later years, loved to report to me my father's crisp comments which often cut concisely through hours of convoluted discussion at faculty meetings. "Look," he once said of a student whose work was under scrutiny, "the trouble is that he can't play the piano because he doesn't have any technique. *That's* his problem, so why do you talk about philosophy?"

With this clear-eyed view of life came utter practicality. I suppose precocious breadwinning had given him a head start toward accepting things as they were. He was a very positive thinker with the knack of investing genuine enthusiasm into the most tedious activities. And although he was never a rainbow-chaser, I think that he always harbored a secret belief that virtue (i.e., hard work) would be rewarded.

In my father's case it generally was. Shortly after his graduation he accepted a job that combined a good deal of prestige and money with considerable challenge and even exoticism: the directorship of the newly formed Imperial Conservatory in, of all places, Omsk. The idea of going to Siberia of one's free will may seem strange to us, but it was a perfectly normal, if somewhat pioneering, thing to do at that time. Omsk was then the largest city in Siberia and the conservatory was a most respectable one, with a fine faculty and a student body that by no means consisted of grizzly bears. In any event, my father set forth with great high spirits, embarking on one of those marathon train trips, which he found so very . . . entertaining.

He never went back to Vilna, although he continued to send money and, later, food parcels to his family both there and at the conservatory in what was by then called Petrograd (because "Petersburg" sounded too German). "Shortages, shortages. After all, the war was going on, even before the Revolution began," he explained. "And the Revolution didn't start up just like that, one day, bang!—you know. It was a very gradual thing, strikes, nothing working right, things just falling apart . . . like now. But the funny thing was, there were shortages of different things in different places. So we would exchange. Joseph used to send to me in Omsk (yes, the mail was still working) sugar, salt, things like that. And I used to send him sardines."

During that period my father's sister Dina visited him in Omsk. When she returned to Petrograd, where she was still a piano student at the conservatory, she lugged back with her a crate of food that was nearly as big as she was. It was stuffed with several kilos of the best creamery butter, all kinds of candies and a smoked sturgeon on a platter. Nobody who had anything to do with it ever forgot the contents of that coffer, or how much it weighed. I was still hearing about this legendary package in New York thirty years later, from several people who remembered, with many lip-smackings, how welcome a gift it had been.

My father himself went back to Petrograd only once after he moved to Omsk. One might say that his return was a clever bit of unmilitary strategy, for it was to avoid conscription, and it succeeded. His brother Joseph (like Dina, still a student at the Petrograd conservatory), on hearing that Volodya was about to be called into the Army, appealed to the school's director, Alexander Glazunov. Glazunov was known as a nice, easygoing gentleman—someone who could always be counted on for a favor. Joseph's plea went something like this: "Listen, we have only one brother, he's the only one who's making money, he's the only one my mother is living on, he's the only one my sisters are living on, he's the only one that I'm living on, and we have to do something!" Glazunov thought for a while and replied, "Well, we have an opening here for a harp student. So tell Volodya to come back and learn the harp. It won't hurt him." My father re-enrolled at the conservatory forthwith (as students were exempt from army service) and spent the next several months mastering all sorts of fancy arpeggios and glissandos. Soon, however, the Revolution began in earnest in the streets of Petrograd. Bombs exploded; buildings burned; there was shooting everywhere; panic set in; and my father decided he knew enough about the harp. He returned to Omsk, taking his sister Dina with him.

They worked their way back to Siberia playing violin recitals, with Dina acting as Volodya's accompanist. One of the cities in which they played my father never forgot. That was Tobolsk. The Tsar and his family were being kept there at the time, in a rather lenient house arrest in the governor's mansion.

"Everyone in Tobolsk spoke of them with great respect," my

father recalled. "To the last, you know, people were bowing to him. I don't believe any of us really thought about what might happen . . . we imagined, I suppose, that sooner or later they'll have to leave the country. When we were in Tobolsk, they were still pretty free. They were even supposed to come to our concert! In the morning, a lot of people came to look us over, they were not Bolsheviki, they were with the Tsar, and they came to see, you know, if we were . . . okay. And we had a full house that night because everybody who was with him in Tobolsk was at the concert, but at the last minute they didn't come.

"But the next morning, when we drove away, everybody—the whole family—was on the porch of that house, and the Tsarina, she had something wrong with her leg, so she was sitting on the windowsill with her leg propped up on a pillow, and when we passed by, the *izvoshchik*, the driver, took off his cap, and because he had one hand occupied, he put the cap on his arm, like so. I thought, Hah, why should I, a Jew, take off my hat for . . . for . . . for such a . . . and so I didn't. But later, for a long time, I was sorry, because it wasn't nice. And after all, after all," concluded my father pensively, "it *was* the Tsar of all the Russias."

During the years that my father was a student in St. Petersburg, my mother, Nadia Margolin, was suffering in Kiev.

"Ooooooh, how I suffered, how I suffered! How *he* suffered! Unbe*liev*able, how we suffered!" This is the way she recalls those halcyon days—and the young man who came to give her piano lessons. "He, poor fellow, he would come to the house once a week . . . it went on for probably four or five years . . . we always had dogs and he always looked at the dogs, he couldn't look at me, what could he do, poor man? I remember the apartment very well, there were many rooms. It was a big apartment, and when you came in, it was like a foyer, but long, and the telephone was on the wall there, you had to stand to talk (and Grandfather, when he ate, when there was dinner and they called, he always went to the phone, he always answered), and then on the left side was a little reception room and a second room and then a very big drawing room, with yellow seats and the white Bechstein, a grand, certainly. And here he sat and looked at the dogs. I still know the fingering of the scales, though, like this . . . and back . . . *that* I still remember. Yes, I took lessons probably four or five years (how he suffered!) . . . he probably couldn't stand it any more . . . and anyway, we moved." My mother didn't like to play the piano.

But the dacha, the dacha in Kiev, on the island in the Dnieper, where they went in summer, ah, that was different, there was no piano there. There was also no running water and no electric light. "But it was adorable, in spite," explained my mother, who loved to remember the dacha. She often described it to me: exactly where it was located on the island, how vast the grounds, how beautiful the water lilies in the cove, and how they would get to it from the city on their little boat, *Lilliput*, sometimes with my mother at the helm.

Boats figured prominently in the life of my mother's family, the Margolins of Kiev. Her grandfather, born poor, began to work for a steamship company when he was only twelve, and he didn't waste any time. Before too many years had passed he owned the company, becoming responsible for most of the huge steamships that plied the wide Dnieper River with passengers and goods. He was a director of the gas and electric works. He also introduced streetcars—the first in the Russian Empire—to Kiev, and in gratitude was presented by their Belgian manufacturer with his own private streetcar, which my mother recalled as "inside, all red velvet, and even a little icebox, but where could you go? It was on rails, so certainly it was not necessary to have!"

Whatever she may have thought of private streetcars, my mother did not disapprove of the luxury that surrounded her and her sisters, Olga and Luba, when they were girls—especially when they visited their grandparents. My mother remembered her grandfather Margolin fondly. "He liked us girls," she told me on several occasions. "He used to call me *dikarka*, the wild person, because I was afraid of people—I didn't like them. Olga was the show-off, always a good student. Luba was very quiet, did everything she wanted, but without *scandale*. With me, it was always *scandale*" (she grinned mischievously and dropped her voice to a whisper), "and I didn't do what I wanted."

The three sisters lacked nothing in the way of comfort, although, as my mother recollected it, the family lived "simply." They shunned ostentation, and when her mother, for some reason that nobody could ever fathom ("because she was very modest, too"), bought an ermine coat, she was informed in no uncertain terms by Mme. Margolin the elder that "in our family nobody wears ermine." Servants, however, were plentiful. Mother enumerated: "First, and most important, there was Mikhail, the cook, and he had a helper. Then Nikolai, he was the lackey. And there was a second one (I forget his name, but Luba remembers them all, to this day!), and always a woman; and then the French lady, and after her the German lady (Miss May, the English lady, the one I hated, she came later, in Petrograd) . . . and always *nyanya*, the nurse . . . I think that was all."

Even at the dacha, the country house on the island, life was elegant, and very often the *Lilliput* would carry sixteen or twenty guests across the river for lavish dinner parties. These festive occasions were enhanced by the inventiveness of Mikhail, the cook. Mikhail was immortalized for me by my mother. From earliest childhood, I associated "party" with "Mikhail." Whenever she prepared an elaborate dish or we were served anything especially fanciful, my mother remembered Mikhail with a mixture of affection and awe.

"I don't know how he did it!" she would cluck, shaking her head from side to side. "What he made, that Mikhail! The salmon? I'll tell you! I don't know how he cooked it, but it was like nothing else, and so beautiful, you can't imagine! Around it he put all kinds of pretty things, cut cucumbers, radishes, cut asparagus, beets, all colors . . . and he did terrific desserts with *kashtani*, you know, chestnuts. He made from this a paste and he made like big cherries, and he dipped each one in caramel sugar, and it was like a well in the middle, and inside was full of whipped cream . . . and he made all kinds of things from spun sugar—sometimes a little fence: small, small like little threads . . . how he did things like that, I don't know!"

But Mikhail had one failing. He liked to drink. And when he was drunk, he sang. So whenever the Margolins heard operatic arias issuing forth from the servants' quarters, they knew there would be no cooking from Mikhail that day. On such occasions, alternate plans were put into effect. One of the restaurants in town was alerted, and everything for the evening's dinner party would be sent over, in baskets, on the little boat; and Mikhail would be left to sleep it off. Occasional weakness in true genius must be overlooked.

Even though he enjoyed the good life, my great-grandfather David Semyonovich Margolin was by no means a playboy. He was widely known for his social welfare work, and whenever a poor Jew of Kiev needed intercession with the governmental authorities for one reason or another, it was he who was called upon to act as the go-between. His wife Rosalie was constantly engaged in charitable activities, and opened the first child-care center in the area. Between them they occupied a position of eminence and respect in the city of Kiev. They were included by the Tsar himself on his rounds, when he visited the city, coming every now and then to inspect the streetcars, the public utilities and the shipyards. The memory of this honor paid her family never did impress my mother much, however. "Nich-o-las the Second," she once drawled in a pitying voice. "He was such a *stupid* man." Not that she ever met him: I believe that her opinion was formed solely as a result of political events. In truth, I am surprised that she does not entertain warmer feelings toward the last of the Romanovs, as a large diamond ring that he presented to her grandfather is still in the family.

Like many rich men's children, David Margolin's son Arnold —my mother's father—was a Socialist. From early youth, he was interested in jurisprudence, criminology and public affairs. He became a lawyer, and took part in many famous political trials. The most famous of these, known as the Beiliss Case, has achieved the questionable status of providing a catchphrase in the Russian language (*dyelo Beilissa*—Beiliss affair) for "a mess." This mess was not of my grandfather's making. In fact, he gained international distinction at the time (1911–13) as a defending lawyer in the trial, later described by Felix Frankfurter as being "as important in the history of justice as the Dreyfus Affair."

Mendel Beiliss, the defendant, was a Jew who had been accused of the ritual murder of a Christian child. Such an accusation was not unusual in Russia in those days. What was unique about this case, however, was that my grandfather, by pursuing his own investigation (and using his own resources, which is one advantage of having a rich father, even for a Socialist), was able to identify the real murderer (or murderess, as it turned out), expose the machinations of a corrupt prosecution and contribute to the acquittal of the defendant, thus achieving a milestone in Russian law: It was the first time that a Jew defending a Jew had accomplished such a feat in Russia.

My grandfather's private-eye activities on behalf of Mendel Beiliss were, as he knew very well, illegal according to Russian law. As an attorney for the defense, he had no right to try to trap a suspect. So he was disbarred, and the family moved away from Kiev to their Petrograd apartment, where he became increasingly involved in politics.

"But if you were neither a music student nor a prostitute, how could you live in Petrograd?" I asked my mother. "My dear, of course we could live there," she explained. "If a Jew had a high education like Father had . . . or if he was a merchant of the first class, like Grandfather, he could live there. We could go anytime we wanted, anytime at all. But not everybody. The mother of my mother, for example, did not have the right to live there, in Petrograd. And when she came to visit, it was terrible. You had to tip the man who took care of the house, and all that, and Father was always very nervous. But we could live there anytime we wanted. We had the right."

Even so, the Margolins didn't remain in Petrograd for long.

Gradually, but inexorably, the Revolution rumbled to their door. "I'll tell you how it was," said my mother, giving me her pithy synopsis of the Ten Days That Shook the World. "During the war, the soldiers had enough. They didn't want to fight any more, and you felt that something is going to happen, but exactly what, nobody knew. It means, nobody knew what to expect, where to go, what to do. When Lenin came back from Germany, if they—if Kerensky—would have stopped him, probably nothing would happen. We all went back to Kiev because it was Revolution. Father got permission to go through Pskov; I think the Germans were somewhere, it was very difficult, but we got to Kiev, to Grandfather's. We all stayed in Grandfather's apartment, and nobody knew what. We girls, we knew even less. That piano teacher, you remember, the one who suffered when he came to give me lessons? He had a brother who was very much in politics, and they spoke at Grandfather's house that he is in prison, and Luba asked, 'What did he steal?' . . . 'What did he steal?' It means it didn't occur to us to know about political things, even though Father was so involved."

It had become obvious that the climate outside of Russia would be healthier, at least for a time, for the senior Margolins; and my great-grandparents and grandfather went to Germany. Certain that their absence would be only temporary, they left the rest of the family behind in the big apartment on Niko-laevskaya. Apparently, their departure came not a moment too soon. My mother described how "right after they left, the soldiers, the Communists, came to the apartment, and the first thing they did, they shot the pictures of Grandfather . . . they shot all the pictures. Why didn't we all go out to Germany together? I don't know. Maybe it was not possible. Anyway, it wasn't so bad for the women. But Father left because he felt he would be shot right away, and Grandfather.

"Now I'll tell you the most interesting thing," she continued. "When Father and Grandfather left, we had a lot of silver and . . . good things. And there was a special room in that apartment, *kladovka*, storage room. And everything was there, in *kladovka*. Trays like this, big . . . heavy, heavy, all kinds of silver things. And Grandfather said, when he left, 'Never mind. In two weeks we'll be back.' That I'll never forget." My mother shook her head slowly as she repeated, " 'Never mind,' he said. 'In two weeks we'll be back.' "

He was mistaken.

Fifty years later, it was I who represented the family. My parents, smilingly but firmly refusing all invitations to accompany Naomi and me on this tour, reacted as if I'd suggested a trip to the South Pole. "So, you'll tell us all about it," my father had shrugged, indicating no regret that his traveling days were over.

"He would have preferred the train," I thought that night on the flight to Siberia. Imprisoned, with elbows pinioned between my two bulky neighbors, I felt as if I were one of those hairy Soviet chickens trussed for the oven. But the evening's discomfort was only beginning: the next indignity to strike—literally—was the head of the passenger in front of me, suddenly catapulted into my lap (body attached) as said passenger activated the reclining mechanism of his seat. Unable to move in any direction, I was thus free to reflect at length on my parents' exile from their homeland and the years of wandering that had finally ended in New York. "Yes, he certainly would have preferred the train . . . or even a droshky . . ." I remember meditating drowsily as I attained an almost fetal position in my womb of snoring Russians.

CHAPTER THREE

Forward—and Backward— to Manhattan

WHILE THE MARGOLINS of Kiev were protecting their silver in *kladovka* during that fateful spring of 1918, the Graffmans of Vilna—my father and his sister Dina—continued their peregrinations back to Omsk. There, in an area still relatively untouched by the violent upheavals wracking the rest of the country, they settled into a pleasant routine. My father attended to his directorial and professorial duties at the conservatory and traveled to nearby cities giving violin recitals, with Dina as his accompanist. These tours were neatly arranged. An advance man was engaged to precede them to each town on the itinerary. This versatile fellow's duties consisted, simply, of organizing everything. First he made sure that all was in order with the auditorium, piano, programs and so forth—and then he would drum up the publicity. He also handled the ticket business, although my father's suspicious nature caused him always to assume the worst where cash was concerned. "But we

needed someone to do it for us," he would later rationalize,
"even if he did make figgely-miggely at the box office. He
wasn't the first or the last. Anyway, that's how we got to Novo-
Nikolaevsk, and Tyumen, and Ekaterinburg, and places like
that."

It was in Ekaterinburg that summer that the drama of Nich-
o-las the Second, who had given diamonds to my great-grandfather in his steamship on the Dnieper, and had been so rudely
snubbed by my father on the street in Tobolsk, came to its
tragic conclusion. "When we went to play there that July, that
was when we were told that they had just . . . they showed us
that place, the place behind the wall, where they killed the
whole family. They showed us that." Father shook his head
sadly. He was silent for a while, and touched his bald spot, almost as if he were removing a hat, and sighed.

Not long after the summer of 1918, life began to change in
Omsk. Almost every week, it seemed, there was a new government. Gradually—at first imperceptibly—the atmosphere began to cloud. Finally, when the Communists were securely in
power, the bureaucrats took charge of the conservatory. "It was
Tovarich this, *Tovarich* that, from morning to night, so I decided it was time to leave," reported my father matter-of-
factly. As he was friendly with the American consul in Omsk
(there was one, even in that isolated outpost), United States
visas for himself and his sister were issued almost immediately
upon application. But Dina refused to go. Once, when she was
a young girl, a fortune-teller had predicted that she would die
on the ocean. Though she laughed about it in later years, at
that time the prospect of a long sea voyage was too upsetting
to contemplate.

So Volodya decided that they would return to Petrograd.
Shortly after they began their journey, it became apparent how
naïve—indeed, hopeless—a scheme this was. With explosions
and fires surrounding them, bullets whizzing past their ears and
"everything topsy-turvy," there was no doubt that this was precisely the wrong direction in which to flee. They turned eastward once again. "But we didn't run," my father explained

proudly. "We traveled very leisurely, we stopped at nice hotels, there was always an Astor House or a Grand Hotel, and we gave some concerts on the way.

"Money? Of course we had money. I had a suitcase full of Imperial rubles, and I took it with me everywhere, even finally to America. You know, every new little government that came in in those days—after Deniken I don't remember the names—right away they all had their own money. But somehow there was still a feeling that the Tsar—a Tsar—is going to be back, so we were always changing the new money for *Tsarski denghi*, Imperial money." (Even my tycoon great-grandfather Margolin shared this faith in the invincibility of the Imperial ruble. It was, in fact, one of the two currencies in which he had complete trust, the other being the German mark. Both of these indestructible currencies soon collapsed and I was not born a millionaire.)

By the time Volodya and Dina arrived in Harbin, they found many musician friends already installed, having trekked in similar fashion across the Eurasian continent from Petrograd. Harbin, in Manchuria, was the jumping-off place, the way out of Russia. But apparently there was no urgency to press on, and my father soon got the job of concertmaster of the local orchestra. After a while, though (and more out of curiosity than necessity), he and Dina set forth to explore the Orient. They worked their way through Dairen, Mukden and Tientsin, eventually settling in Shanghai, which at the time had a large Russian population—so much so that I don't believe they ever learned to use chopsticks. They found Shanghai an agreeable place and lived there for over a year, going to nearby cities, somewhat the way they had done in Omsk, giving concerts. There were many English people living in that part of the world then, and the concerts were mainly for them. "And that's how we learned English," my father told me. "In China! We never studied, but somehow we got along, because we had to."

Although the audiences in China were largely composed of Britishers, in Japan they were mostly Japanese. My father

remembered that he and Dina were among the very first Westerners to play there ("only after us came Mishel Piastro, and
then the others"), and that they charged three yen for tickets.
After giving several concerts in Tokyo and Yokohama they returned to China, and were soon invited to make a tour to
Hong Kong and "other places like that"(!) But Dina had
heard awful tales about the heat in Southeast Asia—heat so
dreadful that "women shriveled up like prunes." This prospect
dampened her enthusiasm. My father then told her, firmly,
"Well, there's no place left, now. If you won't go to Hong
Kong, we have to go to America." So, finally, they undertook
the dreaded Pacific crossing.

Surprisingly, Dina enjoyed the voyage on the *Sphinx*, a
French ship. It was smoother than expected, and furthermore,
the trip was free, which lessened her fears of shipwreck considerably. My canny father had made a deal, and for a couple of
concerts on board, the Graffmans were treated royally, at the
Sphinx's expense. It was not until the ship put into port in
Honolulu, however, that my father's business acumen reached
its apogee. He was taken on a tour of the island, during which,
as he remembered it, "Somebody tried to sell me some property
near Honolulu. It was a beach near a mountain. But you know,
it was so desolate there. No houses, no people. Who would
want to live in such a place? I thought. It had a funny name,
that beach, something like Vaikookoo or Vaikaka . . . so desolate, that I'll never forget. Of course, I didn't buy."

A similar proposition on the West Coast was similarly
quashed by my father soon after they arrived in Los Angeles.
"There we had many friends," he remembered. "Already a lot
of Russians were there, and musicians. Down there it looked
like Hawaii. Big snow-white flowers everywhere, and again,
beaches, desolate beaches. And again they wanted me to buy.
One day somebody—Mrs. Miltz, I think it was—drove me all
the way in her car to San Diego. She wanted to show me some
property nearby, a beach near San Diego . . . I remember, the
name was La Jolly. She was trying so hard to convince me to

invest in that La Jolly, but I don't know why. Who would want all that desolate, lonely beach?"

After a few months of further avoiding juicy real estate swindles in Southern California, my father and Dina set forth for the East Coast. Shortly after their arrival in New York, however, he accepted the post of concertmaster of the orchestra in Minneapolis, where he and Dina spent the next two years very happily, far away from any desolate beaches.

By the mid-1920s New York had absorbed many Russian émigrés, among them Leopold Auer, who started a school for violinists and invited my father to become his assistant. This was an honor he was delighted to accept, so he moved to New York, where he remained for the rest of his life—over half a century—retaining, nevertheless, his impermeable Russian accent, his bulging suitcaseful of Imperial rubles (just in case) and his matchless sixth sense about real estate. During the depths of the Depression, when, thanks to an abundance of students coupled with his thrifty nature, my father's assets were more liquid than those of many far richer people, he was offered a small building on West Fifty-seventh Street in Manhattan, then known as the Vincent Chalif Studio of the Dance. The asking price was $10,000. My father inspected and then quickly rejected it because it was rundown and "full of cockroaches." He must have been exaggerating. During later years I made frequent visits to that building (when, after changing hands several more times, it eventually became the headquarters of Columbia Artists Management), and it always looked clean enough to me.

During the period of my father's westward odyssey, which he accomplished by progressing eastward, my mother was heading for the same destination via more traditional routes. Much like my father's, her journey also progressed in slow stages.

"Oooooh, Hoek von Holland, Hoek von Holland, oh, my God, how we suffered!" This was how she recalled one of the trips that brought her ever closer to New York. "You can't imagine what it was like on that boat. If we would just try to walk, *choot!* we would fall down. And Father was lying there like nothing, and Mama and I were sick and we asked him next morning, 'Why didn't you help?' and he said, 'If I would help, I would be sick, too!' . . . Oooooh, Hoek von Holland, don't talk to me about that boat trip to London!"

Actually, quite some time elapsed and several cities were visited in depth before the Margolins finally saw the white cliffs of Dover. (Harwich, to be precise.) Nadia and her mother remained in Kiev for well over a year after her father and grandparents had left. They endured an ever more miserable existence, finally realizing that things could only get worse, and when they decided to make the break, they knew it would be for a long time, if not forever. "Yes," said my mother. "When we left, we knew. By then, we knew." They were able to buy false papers and arrange for the services of a man who acted as a people smuggler—a profession flourishing in Russia at that time—to take them out of the country. They left by train ("it was like for animals"), and when it reached the border, appropriate guards were appropriately bribed, and Nadia and her mother continued on, eventually arriving, terrified but safe, in Poland.

After a few days with relatives in Warsaw, where my mother remembers buying a blue coat and a white hat, they were at last reunited with the rest of the family in Berlin. There they lived for a time, but the nomadic existence of Arnold Margolin, then serving the short-lived Ukrainian People's Republic in various diplomatic capacities, meant that a variety of European capitals eventually served as temporary homes.

My grandfather's political activities had completely absorbed him since the earliest days of the Revolution. Affairs—actually, independence—of the Ukraine, the state of which Kiev was the capital, dominated his concerns. He strongly believed in the right of self-determination for all peoples, and had become closely associated with the forces engaged in founding and building a separate Ukrainian democratic state. He was convinced that the territory of each nation belonged to the people who lived thereon, and had no doubt that he, a man of Jewish origin, was nevertheless a bona fide Ukrainian. Actually, he often said, "I have three souls. I am a Russian, a Ukrainian and a Jew," and there is no question that his enthusiastic belief in this triple heritage (although perhaps not a view widely shared by many members of these ethnic groups) was utterly sincere. It was during this period that he learned to speak Ukrainian (quite a bit different from Russian, and before the Revolution not in much general usage among the upper classes of Kiev). As with everything he undertook, he did it with consummate success, his command of the language being described by a contemporary Ukrainian intellectual as "better than Mazepa['s]" (Isaak Mazepa was premier of the newborn state), "who spoke it with a distinct Byelorussian accent." Although the Ukrainian Republic existed as an independent country only from 1918 to 1920, during those years my grandfather held a series of responsible positions. He was Deputy Foreign Minister; a member of the Ukrainian Delegation to the Peace Conference (signing many documents for the League of Nations in behalf of the Ukraine); and, finally, Chief of the Ukrainian Mission in London.

Soon after the demise of the Ukrainian People's Republic, my grandparents emigrated to the United States, living, for most of the time I was around, in a city that thereafter became irrevocably known to me as VashingTON. From his base there, my grandfather Arnold remained active for the rest of his life (which ended abruptly in 1956, when he was seventy-nine and, absentmindedly crossing a street, was hit by a car), as a lecturer, writer, jurist and adviser on public affairs, particularly United States foreign policy as it applied to Eastern Europe.

I remember him as a rather short, rotund man with wonderfully twinkling eyes, who loved to play the violin, which he predictably did remarkably well (especially considering that at the time I knew him he did not own one and played only when he came to visit us, borrowing my father's instrument for an evening of chamber music). He was very jolly and full of good stories and it was always hard for me to think of him as a serious political philosopher. But when I was still very young we sometimes took long walks together, and he would discuss with me most thoroughly various political questions, first in simple terms, and later, as I grew older, in more sophisticated ways. Current events, or occasionally a chance meeting, would spark these talks. Once, on West End Avenue, he introduced me to a distinguished-looking gentleman, who embraced him warmly. After we walked on, Grandfather said, "Do you realize that the man we just met was the only leader of Russia ever to be elected in a free election?" He then told me all about Viktor Chernov, and how he had become president of the Constituent Assembly at the beginning of the Revolution only to be quickly overthrown by Lenin. This story led to a minute dissection of the various governments that had existed between the downfall of the Tsar and the establishment of the Soviet Union, and we were, as usual, late for lunch.

Grandfather's stubbornness in maintaining what he felt were the proper principles resulted in some inconvenience to his family during the Second World War. Never one to change his course according to which way the political wind was blowing, he was among the few who reacted with only restrained enthusiasm toward the Soviets at a time when it was considered highly inappropriate for Americans to find fault with their dauntless comrades. While naturally delighted at the turning of the tide of war after Stalingrad, Grandfather didn't see how winning that battle could have miraculously enlightened the hated Soviet government, and he continued to speak and write against Stalin, Vishinsky *et al.* as in previous decades.

This caused our Soviet allies in V*ashing*TON to inform our State Department that Arnold Margolin, the Russian Ukrainian Jew, was obviously a Nazi agent, thus unleashing on all of us many unannounced visits by clean-cut, pleasant young men with short hair and button-down shirts who introduced themselves as FBI agents and pressed my parents for details about Grandfather's comings and goings.

Matters were further complicated by our acquaintance with a lady named Ghermina Rabinovich. She was a friend of my mother's sister Olga and her husband Genia, and occasionally visited our home, where I would see her. As she was lame in both legs and walked with difficulty with the aid of two canes, she could not easily pass unnoticed. Nevertheless, she mysteriously disappeared, and we heard nothing about her for quite some time, until one day we read in the paper, under a blazing headline, SOVIET SPY RING EXPOSED IN CANADA, WOMAN ESCAPES TO RUSSIA, that a number of spies had been arrested but that the leader, one Ghermina Rabinovich, had managed to slip away. (How she could have accomplished this when she could barely walk eluded us.) We were further surprised to note that the address listed for her was "in care of" my aunt Olga and uncle Genia.

Like a dog chasing its tail, the FBI now had the rather unusual task of investigating us for being involved with both a Nazi spy and a Soviet spy (cozily drinking tea together, I liked to imagine) in our bunker on West Ninety-seventh Street.

But of course all of this occurred many years after the time of which I have been writing—the time when my Margolin grandparents first came to America—to New York—in 1922. The New World's first rebuff of my grandfather's shining idealism came soon after their arrival, when he found that Harlem was not yet quite ready for his advanced sociological outlook. Hunting for an apartment near Columbia University, where he was studying to obtain an American law degree, he'd answered an ad for a reasonably priced flat in a lovely building on Lenox Avenue only to be told by the owner, "Sorry, but colored people live here." "Oh, that doesn't matter to me!" my ecumenical grandfather smiled ingratiatingly. "Maybe not, but it does to *us!*" snapped the owner, slamming the door in his face.

Thus it was that when my mother, after a couple of years of high living in swinging Berlin, finally (and reluctantly) joined her parents in the United States, she found them in "a terrible apartment" on Claremont Avenue, in quite different circumstances from the ones they had known in the old days in Kiev.

"They had a very difficult time at first in New York, Mama and Papa," my mother recalled. "Papa did translations, things like that; Mama" (she of the impetuously purchased ermine) "did embroidery. And I lived with them in that terrible apartment until I got married.

"How did I meet Volodya? It was through the Kahns, you remember them," she reminded me. "They were friends of my parents. And Mrs. Kahn told Mama once, 'Come on, I'll introduce Nadia to someone.' So she invited us to dinner, and she also invited—I don't know, I think he was a lawyer, the man she wanted me to meet. He didn't look at me. Then Volodya called—he was teaching Kahn's son—and so they asked him over, too. And after we left, Father said to me, 'The other one, the lawyer, you won't see him; but this one, mmmmm, you'll find out—he'll be around!' And that was Volodya. Father was very glad it was a musician, a violinist. That he was very glad of."

It could never have happened in Kiev. We figured that even if my father had taken the job of concertmaster of the Kiev Opera Orchestra, and even if he had thus been invited for a musical evening at the home of my opera-loving, violin-playing grandfather, undoubtedly my mother Nadia (whose clearest memories of the operas she attended in Kiev involve her falling asleep—"and how I suffered!") would have arranged to be Not at Home. New York is indeed a melting pot.

And so it was that instead of Vilna, Kiev, Petrograd, Berlin, Omsk, London, Harbin, Shanghai or Waikiki, I made my entrance into this world on Manhattan's West Side, where I have lived, more or less, ever since.

"We lived near Riverside Drive then," said my mother one night, as we sat around the dining table drinking tall glasses of steaming tea and playing our ritual game of "Do You Remember When?" "Your father was teaching all the time, day and night. Oh, he had pupils! We didn't go away for one day. It was when we lived on Ninety-fifth Street—now it's terrible, but it was nice then. Between Broadway and West End on the left side, and on the ground floor, because Volodya felt there would be less complaints about his teaching, and all that.

"And that's the way Emmanueli came. He heard music out-

side and he walked in and asked whether Papa would teach
him, because he was Puerto Rican. At that time, you understand. He asked if Volodya would be willing to teach a Puerto
Rican. Can you imagine? And then, later, for years he gave
haircuts to both, to both of you. He's probably dead by now."

"No," I said to my mother. "I saw him when I was in Puerto
Rico."

"When?" She sounded very surprised.

"About a year ago."

"Are you sure? Emmanueli?"

"Yes, he came to my concert and said he was playing the violin, and teaching."

My mother paused, looked very pleased, and then continued
with her historical tales.

"Auer . . . you know, it was a concert of his pupils once,
Volodya took me there, I think it was Aeolian Hall, and all of
a sudden, Volodya pushes me—he pushes me nearly out of my
chair! I fell asleep during the concert! The pupils of Auer! . . .
I found a letter just now, very nice, how he writes to Volodya:
'I send you a pupil, listen to him, take him, and if he is good,
in a few months I'll hear him, if he can pay.' That letter I
saved . . . *'if he can pay!'* "

As unfailingly happens with children of musicians, there was
a good deal of speculation, from the time of my infancy, as to
my possible talents. Certainly I was exposed to music. My father taught at home throughout the day, with hardly a break,
and he played many evenings as well. My mother compared my
reactions to all of this with those of our Pekingese, Cin-Cin.
Cin-Cin was fascinated by one particular composition, a violin
arrangement of the "Habanera" from *Carmen*. My father used
to walk around when he played, and whenever he swung into
the "Habanera," Cin-Cin would arise from her pillow or feed-
ing bowl and dog his footsteps, pushing at his shoe with her
paw, and howling. She reacted to that one piece only; and, as
my mother explained to Naomi, "We never knew if she loved
it or hated it. Personally, I think she couldn't stand it. *I*
couldn't!" I, on the other hand, was observed to giggle delight-

edly (surely acceptable behavior for a tot of less than a year), which led to endless discussions by the grown-ups as to whether this was because I liked what I heard or, simply, because I enjoyed the silly spectacle of that man walking around with that funny noisemaker and that yapping dog at his ankles. It was not until I was almost three and took to bursting into the music room where my father was giving a lesson, screaming, "*Nyet, nyet!* No! No! NO!" whenever a student played an audible blooper, that they definitively decided I *did* have some interest in music, after all.

Our trip to Europe clinched it. Just before my third birthday, my mother took me to visit relatives in Germany, and on the ship one afternoon, my mother reminded me, "You *completely* disappeared! I looked all over. And finally I found you in a room on another deck, so far away I couldn't believe you got there all by yourself. But you did." To Naomi: "And in that room, what do you think? My dear, it was the whole Boston Symphony Orchestra sitting there, playing cards. And he, Gary, was on someone's lap, saying, 'That's a spade, that's a club . . .' How did he know to find the Boston Symphony just like that, not quite three?"

"I remember," I said, proud of my unerring good taste, "and I also remember the storm we had later on that crossing . . ."

"Oooooh, it was terrible!" my mother groaned. "Not many people were in the dining room, but *we* were . . ."

"As usual," interjected my wife. "He wouldn't miss a meal, even when he was three."

". . . He just sat like that, hugging himself, pale." My mother turned to me and whispered, "Coward!" She continued, "He kept saying, '*Parahod shataietsa.* The boat is shaking.' But not loud, you know, in case someone might hear. '*Parahod shataietsa.*'" My baby Russian, reported by authentic parental sources, was tinged with an Armenian accent, totally illogical since we have no Armenians in the family. I have no idea where I got it from. "And, my dear, his grammar! His grammar is *impossible*." My mother shrugged hopelessly. "He just has no *ear*."

Shortly after our return on the shaking boat, my father decided the time had come to develop my *ear*—and fingers, and general musicality—and began to give me violin lessons. It had never occurred to him that this might not be an appropriate instrument for me, and he was extremely disappointed when he discovered, after a few months, that I didn't particularly take to it. Thinking that perhaps the father-teaching-son situation might be causing the problem, he took me to one of his colleagues, who was known for his way with young people. I am told that after scratching through a few scales for this gentleman (I don't remember any of it), he said to my father, sadly, "Why didn't you bring him to me a year ago? He is already three! Now it's too late!"

After my father recovered from that shock, he decided, in his usual stubborn way, that just the opposite must be true: I was too *young* to play the violin. After all, I could barely hold the damned thing. So he decided to continue my musical training on an easier instrument (which is how violinists generally regard the piano) until my hands and arms became agile enough to cope with the fiddle.

That is how the piano came into my life. And with it came a sweet lady, Mrs. Morris, who, when she was not trying to convert us (she was a Christian Scientist), proved to be a most thoughtful and sympathetic teacher. Under her excellent guidance, I made rapid progress.

"He started with Mrs. Morris in the spring," my mother reminisced. "And in the summer, when we were . . . you know where the car turned over and you said, 'What happened to my lollipop?' while everybody else had broken bones—Mrs. Schwarzbram's relatives, and they had a summer home, and we stayed there, and across the road there was a barn with a piano, and when Gary practiced—so tiny at that big piano—there was a crowd often listening how he practiced, already then . . ."

"A cow?" asked my wife.

"A crrrrrowd," corrected my mother. "Even then. And when we came home in the fall, Mrs. Morris gave Gary lessons almost every day, and Volodya sat with him when he practiced, that was always. No, there was no problem with the practicing. Because you understand, so: he knew that he has to eat; he knew that he has to go to school; he knew that he has to practice. And Gary went first to kindergarten and then they took him at Columbia Grammar School, where he could have all his classes early in the day and then come home to practice. When Volodya told Mrs. Morris that he will try to see if Curtis Institute will accept Gary—that was three years later—she had absolutely nothing against it, against his playing for Vengerova. Only when he left, then. She was very unhappy, very angry. You know, she only came finally to his concerts many years after; many, many years after. But she felt terrible. That was when you were just seven . . . So, tell me, you really saw Emmanueli in Puerto Rico?"

"Really." I recalled with pleasure the soft-spoken, smiling gentleman who for so many years during my childhood studied violin with my father and gave us both haircuts after his lesson.

"How did he look?"

"Older."

Emmanueli is only one of the unending parade of violinists I meet in the course of my travels who remember my father as a teacher or a colleague. Orchestras abound with them, and when I first started to tour, there was hardly one where the cry, "Regards to Dad!" was not a standard refrain from the first desks. Later, I was more frequently hailed by familiar-looking players who reminded me of their lessons on Ninety-seventh Street and never failed to tell me what a brat I was. So it has never been at all unusual for me, when I sit down to play a concerto, to sense, right behind my back, the presence of someone who knew my father very well. During my early days, this person was more often a former schoolmate from St. Petersburg than a former student from Ninety-seventh Street, and I sometimes felt it was all a conspiracy to keep me from getting away with anything. Alexander Hilsberg breathed down my neck at my Philadelphia Orchestra debut, and although I never again sat on the lap of a Boston Symphony player, I did take comfort for many years in the joyful serenity of Richard Burgin's presence behind me in the concertmaster's chair there. In Detroit was Josef Gingold, and after he went to Cleveland, Mischa Mischakoff; Harold Dicterow still beams at me in Los Angeles; and always there are Fishbergs—Fishbergs everywhere, from coast to coast.

But it was only on that first tour to the Soviet Union that I realized how lasting an impression my reticent father had made. Fifty years had gone by, and still they came backstage, intrigued by my name on the concert posters, to ask if I was, by any chance, related to their old friend Volodya. It was in St. Petersburg-Petrograd-Leningrad that I felt the tug most poignantly.

The glorious old auditorium must have looked exactly the same when he was a student. The brilliant crystal chandeliers had been buried during the nine-hundred-day siege in the last war and escaped any harm, and the building was kept in perfect repair. The white paint dazzled, the gilt glittered, and backstage in the artists' room the elaborate Russian Empire furnishings were carefully encased in Soviet plastic. There, after my performance, I was greeted by a stream of well-wishers who seemed to regard me as a long-lost relative.

They came, armed with documents of one kind or another to show me, to prove to me how at one time the threads of our lives had been intertwined. How they managed to preserve those clippings, photos, letters, pamphlets and programs over the years and through the wars, I can't imagine. Unbe*lie*vable, as my mother would say. At first my visitors were shy and diffident and then, when they discovered that we could communicate directly in Russian (even with my Armenian accent, bad grammar and—endlessly amusing to them—pre-Revolutionary embellishments), they became voluble. I was suddenly surrounded by an entourage of adoptive uncles and aunts.

"So you *are* Vladimir's son," a grizzled old man said. "I thought you might be, but why is your name spelled with two *ff*'s? . . . Anyway, look at this photo I brought you." A yellowed snapshot is thrust into my hand. On it I see a rowboat in a lake, two young boys and two pretty girls. "You see that one," the man points. "That's me. And that one" (unmistakably), "that's your father." And the girls? "Ah," he smiles. "Those were the days! . . . Be sure to tell your papa Goldwasser sends greetings."

A wrinkled lady stood behind him and observed our interchange with growing excitement. When her turn came, she presented me with a tattered newspaper. Not a clipping, the whole thing. It was a Vilna paper, and the date was sometime in December 1912. I stared at it, unbelieving. The mere fact that it still existed was a miracle. I saw ads for shoes, underwear, stoves, concerts. The lady pointed to a column with my father's name (one *f* in Graffman) in the headline. "You see, your father gave a recital in Vilna then, and I was his accompanist." Of course, that was before Dina's time—she hadn't even begun at the conservatory. It was the year before my father had graduated. No food parcels yet, no thought of the grim years to come. My father must have gone home to his beautiful Vilna for the holidays and, as usual, he had wasted no time. As I studied the newspaper, fascinated, the lady became emboldened. She didn't want to go, and obviously had something on her mind. Finally, she took a deep breath and said, all at once, "I studied here in St. Petersburg at the conservatory then, too. I had a wonderful teacher. She was very young, hardly older than I, but very, very strict. And such a wonderful teacher she was! But then the war came, and then the upheaval, and she went away—to America, they said, although we never heard from her again. But I never forgot her, she was such a wonderful teacher. Her name was Isabelle Vengerova. Tell me, maybe, did you ever hear of her in America?"

CHAPTER FOUR

Explosions on West End Avenue

ISABELLE VENGEROVA—Madame Isabelle Vengerova—was an imposing figure. Although not very tall, she was extremely wide, and she sailed around her studio like an overstuffed battleship in search of the enemy, cannon loaded and ready to fire. Or so it seemed to those of us who were her piano students. She inspired fear and trembling among the most stouthearted (especially, for some reason, the females). I was less intimidated than most, perhaps because I had known her from the time I was conscious of knowing anybody, and also because I was never really intimidated by anybody. To me she was a battleship, but a rather motherly one.

When I reached the age of seven, my father felt that the time had come to broaden my musical horizons. He had known Isabelle Vengerova from his student years in St. Petersburg when she was a young faculty member at the conservatory, and his sister Dina had been one of her pupils there. It was at Vengerova's doorstep, in fact, that Dina had shyly placed the bulky parcel of smoked sturgeon, creamery butter and candies that my father had packed for her to take back from Omsk during the early days of the Revolution. Dina never forgot her embarrassed delight at being thanked publicly for the parcel in class next morning, and Vengerova apparently never forgot its contents, to which she alluded more than once during my memory —usually at Eastertime, when my mother presented her with the traditional Russian *paskha*, or cheesecake. (Any doubts about the condition of the traveling sturgeon and butter after a few days on the Trans-Siberian Railway were quickly squelched by my father, who loved to point out that there was never anything new under the sun. "Frozen foods!" he would snort. "That's no modern invention! You know, in Siberia, peasants made barrels of borscht, with meat, vegetables—a whole meal it was. They put the barrels outside. The borscht froze. On droshky trips they would drag the barrel along and at dinnertime they would chop off a chunk of borscht and heat it over the fire. *Nu*, what's so special about frozen foods?")

Like my mother, Vengerova came from a prominent family in Kiev, and my mother's father, my *Ded* (grandpa) Arnold, remembered her as an occasional dancing partner at the balls they had attended together. In New York, two decades later, she and my parents became part of an ever growing community of Russian émigrés. They all knew each other and what everyone was up to, and gossiped on the phone for hours. Vengerova visited us every now and then; my father sometimes played chamber music with her; and so, as I said, I don't remember ever *not* knowing her, although in my earliest recollections she seems to have been a soft, fluffy pillow. That is why it was not at all overwhelming for me when my father took me to her apartment to play for her.

Vengerova taught at the Curtis Institute in Philadelphia, and suggested to my parents that they take me there to play at the annual auditions for prospective students. She explained that she would be but one member of the jury that decided on admissions, and that the results would depend not only on how

I played but somewhat on luck: upon how many places might
be open for new piano students, and upon who else might be
auditioning. Also, and most important, although Curtis students were generally very young (". . . It is never too soon for
a big talent to have a great teacher. Then I have fewer bad
habits to undo!"), she admitted that accepting a child of my
tender years might be stretching things a bit. "But why not?"
she mused. "*Chem chort nye shutit?* What have you got to
lose?"

The Curtis Institute, just about three years older than I, was
already regarded as a distinguished—perhaps unique—academy
of music. Based on the same principles as the Imperial Conservatory of St. Petersburg, it was a school for young musicians
who were hoping to become solo artists—a school for virtuosi.
Its faculty consisted of the acknowledged leaders in their fields,
many of whom had received their *Svobodni Hudojnik* diplomas
in St. Petersburg; and its director was no less a personage than
Josef Hofmann. Unlike its Imperial counterpart, however,
Curtis was run completely on a scholarship basis. It had been
endowed by Mary Curtis Bok, of the Curtis Publishing Company family, and there was no tuition fee of any kind for anyone who was accepted as a student. It was a small school, and
Mrs. Bok took a familial interest in all the students, freely giving away instruments, winter coats and anything else that
might be necessary or helpful for the students' well-being. In
later years, Mrs. Bok (by then Mrs. Efrem Zimbalist) helped
pay for two of my Town Hall recitals, and was apparently quite
shocked when, after the second one (the box office receipts
having been better than expected and the loss therefore less), I
took a hint from my father's strict accounting methods and
sent her a check for $318.25.

But before I played for the jury at Curtis, my father, never
one to count unhatched chicks, took me to play for some other
prominent musicians. Like someone with a mysterious and un-
diagnosed ailment, he felt he needed several opinions. I remember José Iturbi's studio, with swords mounted on the walls
adjacent to the piano. As soon as I finished playing, Iturbi

started to pace around the room nervously, exclaiming over and over, "Kill his teacher! *Kill his teacher!*" That, plus the swords, made me quite uneasy.

Next, Leopold Godowsky. I hope he recovered from that visit. Having just turned seven, I was very conscious of my advanced age. When he spied me he cried, "Oh, what a cute little boy! How old are you?" I, in short pants, was about to reply, "Seven," when my mother said, "Six," thinking, no doubt, that there was nothing wrong in postponing my birthday by a few days. I bellowed out, *"Seven!"* at which point she admitted I'd just had a birthday. "And what will you play for me, little man?" he asked in the same cloying manner. I advised him that I had no intention whatsoever of playing for him that afternoon. My parents, upset, began to coax and cajole me, whereupon Godowsky said, "Oh, don't worry. I know how to handle children." He was seated on a long couch, and he picked me up, lifted me quite high, and plumped me down on his lap. I assume he intended to discuss repertoire with me, which I did not allow him to do, as with great force (even for a six-year-old), I kicked him in the stomach. He fell backward on the couch. I then announced that I was ready to play, and did so.

Moriz Rosenthal was another of my victims. I don't remember much about that encounter except that he received us in his pajamas.

I do remember clearly, though, the train trip to Philadelphia and my glee in reading for the first time the sign that still greets the traveler passing through New Jersey's capital city: "Trenton Makes, The World Takes." Finally we arrived at the elegant old building on Rittenhouse Square that houses the Curtis Institute. We sat for a long time in the vast, paneled drawing room, my father and I among what seemed like hundreds of parents and children awaiting the call into the audition room. I wasn't in the least nervous. Nowadays, the very idea of playing for such an august group of musicians—especially after a train trip, with no opportunity even to warm up—appalls me, but at that time I was a dragon slayer and nothing bothered me.

When my turn came and I entered the studio, I saw about half a dozen people, Vengerova and Hofmann (whom I recognized from photos) among them. I don't remember who the others were, or what and how I played. But I do believe that what impressed Hofmann more than anything else about me was that I spoke to him in Russian, using the familiar form of address. I didn't know any other.

Soon after that day a letter arrived to my parents saying that I had been accepted as a Curtis student. It also warned that my father was not to ask for financial aid over and above the free tuition, which must have embarrassed him no end, as that is the last thing he ever would have done, even if he had needed it. This was during the depths of the Depression, however, and it must have been awfully difficult to keep all the needy students in winter coats. I imagine that Mrs. Bok's earlier generosity had begun to be expected as a matter of course by some students and their parents, and probably the protective clause was necessary to avoid a deluge of appeals. Curtis Publishing Company stock, like everything else at that time, had plummeted, and I know that there was at least one year during that period when the faculty agreed to teach without recompense.

Now that I had been accepted by Curtis, a new problem arose. Studying there implied, of course, living in Philadelphia. It would be impractical to commute, but it was unthinkable for us to move from New York, as my father had an established teaching schedule. And I was far too young to live by myself. The school administrators were very flexible in such matters, however, and the obstacle was overcome simply by moving the mountain to Mohammed. It was agreed that once a week I would walk from Ninety-seventh Street between Broadway and Amsterdam Avenue, where I lived, to Ninety-third Street between Broadway and West End Avenue, where Vengerova lived, for my lesson. (As it turned out, I had lessons more than once a week, but the extras were unofficial.) So it was my teacher who did the commuting, for although she lived in New York, she spent a couple of days each week in Philadelphia.

It was when I first started visiting Vengerova on a professional basis that I cast aside childish things. My nickname for her, *Tyotya Belochka* (Auntie Bella), was soon abandoned, not because she desired it but because I heard everyone else calling her "Madame." So "Madame" she became to me. But unlike most of the other students (who, it is true, were older), I was accompanied to my lessons by my father, who listened earnestly to everything Vengerova had to say and made sure I didn't forget any of it when practicing at home.

Madame's home and studio was a sprawling, comfortable apartment on the eleventh floor of one of those typical big-family buildings that line West End Avenue. She seemed to teach all the time. In addition to her weekly excursions to Philadelphia, she was on the faculty of the Mannes School and the Henry Street Settlement, and she had private students as well. So we always had to wait, usually for about half an hour, and there was always somebody waiting when we left. The length of our waits depended to a certain extent on what time of day it was. The later the lesson, the longer the wait, as Madame started the day off on schedule but, like a doctor, gradually fell behind. It seems to me, when I look back on it now, that people were not as intensely concerned with keeping strict schedules—the "time is money" philosophy—as they are today. When Madame gave a lesson it lasted until she was finished. No clock watching. And I, waiting in the foyer, sometimes in the company not only of my father but of the current Vengerova cat, would read—I remember that *Dombey and Son* filled my waiting time during the course of one season—while my ears were frequently assailed by extramusical sounds emanating from the studio. Shouts, screams, threats, curses and stampings were the norm, and on special occasions even the crashing of furniture could be detected. Every now and then came a calm in the storm, when the voice of Vengerova would assume a plaintive "Oh, what's the use?" tone. This, of course, was the worst that could happen.

In later years I frequently heard my colleagues describe the clammy-handed terror that gripped them as soon as they set foot in the elevator leading to the torture chamber (and how Grace, the sympathetic elevator operator, tried to make their Last Ride as cheerful as possible), but I was never particularly bothered by the Vengerovian storms that raged during my lessons. They were just a fact of life. After violent, dramatic scenes during which she sometimes picked up a chair and slammed it down on the floor to emphasize her displeasure, she would announce to my parents that there was no hope for me in any field of endeavor whatsoever. I think that what bothered her most was my imperturbability. "He does not listen, he will not listen. Whatever I tell him, however I tell him . . . *kak sgoosi voda!* Like water off a goose's back!" she would scream into the phone to my mother so penetratingly that her voice was as clear as if it were originating in our own apartment.

What did she want of me, anyway, that caused such tantrums, such passions to erupt? She was after only what she herself had been taught by Leschetitzky and Essipova: I suppose one would call it "the Russian school of playing." She was interested primarily in sound—she had an obsession with beautiful sound and legato. To achieve this, she was quite dogmatic in her teaching about hand positions (which I never really followed) and extremely slow practicing, hands separately, with accents every so many notes (which I do, to some extent). But I never could or would do the things with my wrists that she espoused so flamingly, and this drove her wild until, eventually —maybe about nine years later—she just gave up. Although from one point of view she thought very highly of me as a talent, she was always disappointed that I didn't use her "method" to achieve the ends we both desired. Later, when I was in my late teens and started to play fairly regularly in New York, she told her younger students that—as I had found my own way, technically speaking—she would not recommend that they emulate the manner in which I was getting the keys down on the piano. "Absolutely do not watch Gary at the concert!"

she would warn, as if doing so would turn the observers into pillars of salt. "You might get into ir-re-vers-i-bly bad habits!"

Vengerova was really only interested in the piano and how to coax the largest range of beautiful, subtle, dazzling, dramatic, velvety and singing sonorities from that intractable black beast (although, in truth, one of *her* two beasts was brown). She would prefer that I spend another hour on whatever Schumann piece I might be working on at the moment rather than play chamber music or sight-read through a symphony or an opera, although she never stated it so baldly. But that's the feeling I had. She was also ambivalent about the time that I was spending on schoolwork (my father was adamant that my general education not be neglected), although she never suggested that I do less. But I think she'd have been just as happy, or happier, if I had been uninterested in academic work and spent all my waking hours at the piano.

But I liked school, and I was a generally good student, usually placing second or third in my class; and I was really almost as interested in science and other subjects as in music. I also indulged in all the sports that a boy of my age normally did. There was never any of that "oh, you can't do that because of your hands" talk from my parents, and when I was twelve I broke the fifth finger of my right hand playing basketball. But as the conductor Thomas Scherman was later to say about me during a poker game, I could fall into a latrine and come up with a rose: the finger broke in such a way that when it healed I had a slightly bigger reach at the keyboard than before the accident. (In truth, hand size is of practically no importance in playing the piano. Hofmann had an abnormally small hand and Rachmaninoff a huge one.)

Unlike so many parents of musically gifted children, my father was anxious—even overanxious—for me to lead as normal a life as possible. Nonetheless, he unfailingly sat through all my lessons and then sat with me while I practiced at home to make sure that I didn't stray too far from the tenets that had been laid down by Madame during that session. Now that I think back on it, this must have been a Herculean task, if only considering the time it involved. Sitting with me three or four hours each day as well as spending at least six hours daily with his violin pupils must have set his head spinning with music at night. He undoubtedly became more intimately acquainted with piano repertoire than any other violinist before or since.

Vengerova, of course, suggested the repertoire that I should learn, but it was a kind of flexible suggestion, as my father also had ideas of his own. (A number of years later, his independence backfired somewhat. Summertimes, when Vengerova fled the city for two months of peace in the Adirondacks, she would tell my father what new things I should work on while she was away. One year she said, "I think it is time for Rachmaninoff concerto!" My father obligingly went out and got the famous Number Two, which I obligingly learned. When Vengerova returned, she was somewhat taken aback. "I had expected Number One!" she exclaimed. No harm done, but I only wish that, since my father misunderstood her instructions, he had come home with Number Three. Probably the only time I could have learned that magnificent knucklebreaker would have been when I was still too young to know fear.)

Some of my father's piano pedagogy was unorthodox but extremely practical. Even before Vengerova days he decided that the purely technical exercises of Czerny and Hanon, which were a staple of every aspiring pianist's diet, could never be productive or useful in themselves. Instead, he would have me spend perhaps the first half hour of my daily practice playing very slowly, hands separately, a much too difficult piece for me at that time to play in tempo. These pieces (Chopin études, for example) served as my Czerny and Hanon and the result was that after several years of practicing them just for exercise purposes to solve the technical problems that each one posed, I suddenly knew a considerable number of them. My father continued to sit with me during the bulk of my practicing until I was ten or eleven, so I undoubtedly did learn more quickly than if I had been left to my own devices. Also, during my early years with Vengerova, one of her assistants occasionally made a house call just to confirm that I hadn't drifted off course between my semiweekly lessons with Madame.

Vengerova's constant watch over me was only natural, thanks to *her* training. I once read that her teacher, Leschetitzky, sometimes walked beneath his pupils' windows after dinner at night, listening to discover if they were obeying his precepts. One anecdote relates that on occasion he even went upstairs to their rooms and surprised them. Once a girl pupil (could it have been the young Isabelle?) emerged from her room to find the master calmly parked in front of her door, cigar in hand. "I have been here two hours," he told her, "and you will never play those triplets unless you take them more slowly."

My lessons at Vengerova's never took just the hour allotted. They were usually extended in direct proportion to how close I was to a performance. There were very few of these for me, as my father only wanted me to play in public enough to have a goal to work for—maybe three or four times a year. He felt, and I agree, that one practices in a different way if one knows that at some point in the ever nearing future one has to walk out before an audience and do one's best. At the same time, he did not want me to do anything that would interfere with my normal development, very much wanting me to enjoy childhood. He knew that just because I happened to play extremely well for an eight-year-old, it was by no means ordained that I would therefore grow up to be a concert pianist. Possibly my life would not even be in music. So he was concerned about my general education and wanted to be sure that when I finished school I would have options. It was for this reason that, when I was offered at around the age of ten the possibility of performing in a movie for Paramount Pictures requiring my (and therefore one of my parents') presence in Hollywood for a month in the midst of the school term, he rejected it.

Even though my father was dead set against turning me into a child performer, daily practicing came first: I practiced every morning from 7:20 to 8:20 before school (in addition to the other two or three hours afterward). Whether or not I wanted to do this was never a consideration. My parents brought me up in a loving but strict, European, manner. I was not consulted in such matters. One went to school; one ate what was set before one; one practiced. It was as simple as that. And if I transgressed? Well, the incident of the *Hindenburg* haunted me for several years.

The arrivals and departures of the German passenger zeppelin that wafted over New York in the 1930s on its journeys between Frankfurt and Lakehurst, New Jersey, naturally attracted a great deal of attention. It seemed as if all our neighborhood windows flew open around the time it was expected overhead. On one such day, in 1937, my father felt that I had interrupted my practicing to such an extent that I couldn't possibly be concentrating, for I kept running from the living room, where the piano was, to my bedroom window, which had an unobstructed view to the east, all the way to Queens, where the *Hindenburg* would first appear. After about my twentieth trip, my father told me that enough was enough, blurting out, "Oh, I hope that damned thing explodes!" Two hours later, over Lakehurst, it did, and my feeling about my father's omnipotence reached a wide-eyed zenith.

At twelve, I played my annual New York recital in a "grown-up" auditorium—Town Hall—for the first time. What I remember most vividly about that occasion was the drama that swirled about our heads (or to be more accurate, knees) at home for several weeks before the event. It concerned my concert attire. I assumed I would wear long pants. My mother assumed the pants would be short. Since my mother was never involved in my musical life, my father obligingly kept out of this domestic imbroglio and let my mother and me slug it out. Eventually I was taken to Saks, where a compromise, in the form of elegant-looking knickers, was effected. Knickers were at that time a most acceptable form of dress for boys, although possibly not at a concert. Be that as it may, with silk stockings and garters that left marks around my legs for several days afterward, I made my Town Hall recital debut. One of my aunts later said that I looked like a midget Cossack.

The piano lessons that increased in length as a concert equinox approached increased in intensity as well. Vengerova became even harsher, more sarcastic, more bitter about inevitable failure. Although she must have adjusted her musical approach to individual students, I doubt that she altered her psychological procedures. She just did what came naturally, and that was to scold. Even I felt an occasional twinge of dread. One had to have nerves of steel (which one needs anyway to perform in public) to survive her mounting concern as the date of an important concert drew near.

I use "important," of course, in the context of what was important for a particular student at that particular stage of his development. One concert important for us all was a performance for which I joined my colleagues in Philadelphia—the annual student recital at Curtis. Student recital, indeed! Think of a situation in which a nine- or ten-year-old (or a seventeen- or eighteen-year-old, for that matter) walks onstage to play his half program and sees in the audience, besides his own teacher and fellow students, the likes of Josef Hofmann, Fritz Reiner, Gregor Piatigorsky, William Primrose, Rudolf Serkin, Efrem Zimbalist and Marcel Tabuteau. But such were the listeners in attendance at those concerts in Casimir Hall, and they gave us all their undivided and wholehearted attention. (Many years later, when Rudolf Serkin was director, I was among the alumni invited to play at Curtis in honor of its fiftieth anniversary. We agreed on a date just a couple of days after my New York recital. "That's wonderful!" Serkin beamed. "Your Carnegie Hall recital will be a perfect tryout for Curtis!" And he wasn't kidding.)

Preparatory lessons for such an occasion culminated during the week before the event in several marathon evening sessions of several hours, during which it became increasingly clear to Vengerova that the student was about to disgrace himself, her, his family, the Curtis Institute, music in general and (during the Second World War) all of the Allies. "Ach," she would sigh, in a calmer moment, "I must have been mistaken. Yes, it could only be that I was mistaken . . . in a weak moment

. . ." In a weak moment, what? "To think that such an imbecile as sits before me now," her voice became stronger, healthier, "could have had even a glimmer of talent, technique" (*crescendo*), "taste, perception or" (*fortissimo*) "ANYTHING NECESSARY TO PLAY THE PIANO, or for that matter" (here her voice dropped, *subito piano*, to a whisper), "live."

Vengerova, nevertheless, looked after her own, and I am told that if anyone dared speak ill of me in her presence, the mother tiger would claw him to shreds with her sarcasm. But to me and to most of her other students she rarely had a kind word. I believe that her ferocious shouts and furniture-throwings were pretty much standard procedure. This I deduced not only from what I heard while waiting for my lesson or from what I observed in later years while accompanying colleagues in concertos during their lessons, but mainly from the behavior of Vengerova's cat. This cat (or, rather, these cats, as there was a succession of them over the years), which was generally somewhere in the room while the lessons took place, was never in any way ruffled by anything that occurred. The most cataclysmic pandemonium elicited from the animal only the slightest movement of its head as it proceeded tranquilly with the intricacies of its toilette.

My stubbornness was the main cause of the frequent violence Vengerova directed toward me. Although her most stinging vituperation was mainly reserved for such purely technical matters as hand positions, wrist action, general relaxation of the arm and so forth, memorable battles raged over musical interpretation as well. Considering my obstinate insistence on doing things *my* way, it was a foregone conclusion that once a point was made of *her* preference, I would naturally escalate resistance to what she wanted. I guess I came by this naturally, as my mother constantly berated my father for his stubbornness, and everyone always recalled *Ded* Arnold's intransigence in political matters.

So when Beethoven, in the D minor Sonata, writes that the pedal should be held over several harmonies, I pushed the

pedal practically to the floor like a drag racer and took fiendish
delight in magnifying the resulting dissonances to create an
effect quite beyond anything Beethoven ever could have had in
mind. In a case such as this pedal indication, the musical philosophy embraced by Vengerova—and, for that matter, all Rus-
sian-trained musicians including my father—would be to go to
the other extreme and to minimize the discordant quality—to
smooth over any rough edges, so to speak. With one swoop of
the pedal, then, I managed to create not only discord at the
keyboard but seismic disturbances in the Vengerova and
Graffman households.

It was at times of crisis like this, throughout the ten years
that I officially studied with Vengerova at Curtis and for several years afterward, that the telephone enjoyed its finest hour.
Vengerova used this instrument to as great an effect as her
piano, although the sounds that emerged from the receiver
were mostly *forte agitato*. She called not only my parents but
apparently everyone in the Russian circle—even those who
were not among her intimates—to bemoan her failure to save
me from a lifetime of dissolution. "*Chto budet snim?* What
will become of him?" she would wail, darkly hinting, in a
strange combination of Russian, English and French (to make
sure that everything she said was clearly understood), that any
hope of salvation had passed, and that the devil himself already
had me in his clutches.

But I, too, reveled in a good *forte agitato* now and then. In
fact, this dynamic marking was the cause of the unforgettable
Carnaval brouhaha which took place when I was about sixteen,
playing the piece at that year's Curtis recital. In the Schumann
Carnaval it was traditional (in the Russian school of piano
playing) to play the section entitled "Chopin" rather quietly
the first time and even more softly the second time. Schumann's markings, however, indicate that this section is to be
played the first time *forte agitato* with many dynamic changes,
thus rendering it in complete contrast with the quietly played
repetition. Well, I really tore into that *forte agitato*, so that
there could be no doubt that I knew exactly what I was doing.

The rest of my performance was, as far as I remember, normal and uneventful. But when Vengerova descended on me backstage afterward, she was trembling with fury. The flowers on her little hat shook as if a hurricane were about to strike. The silk that encased her rotund body rustled ominously. Even the glass eyes of the fox face on her fur scarf flashed fire. *Her* eyes narrowed to slits and she hissed only two words: "*Chto sluchilos?* What happened?" It was as if she would never be allowed back in Philadelphia after that *forte agitato* I had committed. For several weeks afterward, she was alternately furious, hurt, trying to be understanding, not able to be understanding, regarding me as thoroughly untrustworthy, a scoundrel, a viper in her bosom, possibly criminally insane. Finally, though, she did admit that during my performance, when the shock of that scandalous moment had passed, Zimbalist had leaned over toward her and whispered, "Is it really written like that in the music?" She confessed that she had then explained to him, "Yes, but nobody . . ." with exasperation, to me: "As you well know, Gary . . . nobody . . . *ni kto* . . . *ni kagda* . . . *personne jamais* . . . IT JUST ISN'T DONE!"

CHAPTER FIVE

A Hornet in Carnegie Hall

THE COMMANDMENTS of Madame Vengerova (the ones I deigned to accept, that is) were only a few of the influences that broadened my horizons, musical and otherwise, during the thirties. For I was lucky to grow up in New York City when I did. The United States—especially that narrow strip of East Coast between Philadelphia and Boston—was fast becoming the intellectual center of the world. Many of the leading creative artists, thinkers, scientists, scholars and performers of Europe had already come to our shores by the early 1930s, and many more arrived during the next few years. The Russian Revolution and Hitler were largely responsible for the flowering of the arts and sciences in America.

Very specifically, for a young musician growing up at that time, a glorious panoply of performers was in residence, and their concerts were available to anyone with even a limited budget. Among pianists, Hofmann, Rachmaninoff, Rubinstein,

Horowitz, Serkin and Schnabel toured constantly, as did other instrumentalists such as Heifetz, Elman, Szigeti, Busch, Milstein, Kreisler, Piatigorsky and Landowska. Conductors like Toscanini, Koussevitzky, Reiner, Monteux, Walter, Stokowski and Ormandy spent close to twelve months a year in the United States, often exclusively with their own orchestras, honing them to the kind of responsiveness that can result only from uninterrupted authority. Composers such as Schoenberg, Stravinsky, Bartók and Hindemith had also settled in this country. Few, if any, of these would have made their permanent homes here had it not been for the upheavals in their countries. But their emigrating to the United States meant that for the first time in the history of Western music, for better or for worse, a student could be—and, willy-nilly, would be —exposed to a variety of artistic and philosophical influences from the giants in their fields, interacting on each other, with most interesting results.

I wish I could say that I spent all my free time attending the historic musical performances that were taking place just a short subway ride from my home. Until my middle adolescence, however, it was much more fun to be a Hornet. We Hornets were a street gang. This was not at all sinister at the time. Street gangs then consisted simply of neighborhood kids of similar age meeting after school to play stickball (a kind of baseball game which I believe is indigenous to the New York City streets in which the rules are adjusted to fit the players) and maybe crash a party now and then. We wore purple satin windbreakers and occasionally broke a window during our stickball games, but that was about the extent of our mischief.

Some of our activities were even benign. During the war, we assisted Uncle Sam as junior air raid wardens. I was still too young to qualify, so I lied about my age, adding two years to my fourteen. Although I felt nervous about this for several months, nobody ever checked, and I was soon assigned the regulation helmet, gas mask, armband and whistle. Whenever the sirens screeched (which they did frequently for tests), I would tear down seven flights of stairs—one was not to use the elevator during air raids—with all my official paraphernalia draped about me, ordering passersby off the streets.

For about four years I thrived on hanging out with the Hornets most afternoons. I suppose it compensated somewhat for my rather gracious living during the rest of the day. Columbia Grammar School, which I attended on scholarship for twelve years, was by no means a snobbish place, but a goodly number of rich kids were my schoolmates, and it was not at all unusual for an upperclassman to receive a Cadillac from his parents for his seventeenth birthday. I am amazed and grateful that my street pals never held that existence against me. To be sure, they knew about my other lives, but as soon as I was enveloped by my magic cloak of gleaming purple with the name HOR-NETS emblazoned in gold across the back, I became one of the gang.

Gradually, though, I began to spend more time with another gang, in some ways rougher and tougher than the Hornets. They were my fellow piano students, and instead of stickball we played our current repertoire for each other. The rules of this game involved criticism with no holds barred. (It should be mentioned here that pianists, perhaps more than any other strain of musicians, tend to be good colleagues. Maybe we have to stick together to fend off the innumerable outside evils which beset us, like rotten pianos—of which, more later—but whatever it is, young pianists, especially, travel in packs—or did when I was growing up—and my pack saw each other or spoke on the phone at great length practically daily.) So we met often for marathon playing sessions at which we requested and received the uninhibited comments of our peers. And here is where we felt the interaction of the different influences that had taken root in America during the previous three decades.

For not all these friends—and one learns a great deal from friends—were being brought up, as I was, in the Russian tradition of piano playing. While the education Vengerova and my father were giving me came direct from St. Petersburg, some of my friends were receiving the same kind of training that they would have had if they'd grown up in Berlin or Vienna. These were, mainly, the students of Schnabel and Serkin. And this is what I mean by the infinite possibilities that were available to us in New York during that particular era. This variety of musical philosophy (and purely piano-playing pedagogy) that abounded on the West Side of Manhattan at that time meant that when we played for each other we were thinking harder, trying harder to convince each other that the approach each of us was learning toward a particular piece, or toward the instrument in general, was without doubt the only right one.

Many evenings we met at my apartment and played far into the night. When our solo repertoire was exhausted, we read four-hand music of all description, including those now archaic delights, transcriptions of symphonies. Recordings were already rendering these piano arrangements obsolete as a form of musical enlightenment, but, still, not everything was as handy as it is today. Bruckner and Mahler, for example, with whose works we became acquainted in this manner, were rarely performed in concert halls then, and very few of their compositions were available on discs.

What there was, though, we heard. Gilman Collier, a classmate of mine at Columbia Grammar School, had the largest record collection imaginable, and one of those gigantic Capehart phonographs with all the latest gizmos to play them on. This miraculous machine enabled us to listen to an entire symphony without moving, quite a feat in the days of 78-rpm records. After the first side was finished, the Capehart—wonder of wonders!—proceeded, with many diabolical whirrings and clickings, to flip the record over. Then, after a few thumps and hisses, the needle would gently lower itself and the second side commenced. When that side was completed, a snakelike slithering sound was heard, indicating that the next disc was being slid into place, and the entire operation began anew. Of course, we got up anyway to watch the performance, so delicate and precise was it; and also to be nearby in case (as rarely but occasionally happened) friend Capehart threatened to maul or reject the foreign objects so tenderly placed in its clutches.

In my apartment there was only an ordinary phonograph.

But then again I was the only one in our set to have two pianos, which enlarged the scope of our performances to almost endless permutations. Also, my mother kept our strength up by plying us with hams, herrings, piroshki and her specialty, something she called *salade vinaigrette*, which involved beets, and which she had learned to make from Mikhail in the summer house in Kiev. So we played, listened, ate and discussed for hours on end, touching all subjects but hovering mainly around Music and the Interpretation Thereof.

Some nights, not content with the conclusions we had reached by the time the *vinaigrette* was demolished, we would pile into the subway and emerge in Greenwich Village, establishing ourselves at an informal nightclub called the Salle de Champagne, which had a good piano. There, over a bottle of bubbly provided by the indulgent management, we would continue our performances and discussions, giving not only ourselves but innocent paying customers insights into the various interpretive possibilities of Brahms's *Variations and Fugue on a Theme by Handel.* We had our lighter moments, too. Whenever a waitress worth impressing appeared on the scene, I'd launch into either *La Campanella* or Rachmaninoff's *Elegy*, depending upon which piece I guessed would ensnare that particular maiden in our web. It was always one or the other—never both—and the ploy rarely failed. It was in this manner, and under my expert tutelage, that Jay Harrison, a slightly older schoolmate from Columbia Grammar who later became music editor of the New York *Herald Tribune*, refined his discriminative powers. I had discovered that all females could be divided into two categories: those who fell for the pyrotechnics of Paganini-Liszt, and those who swooned over the lush and bittersweet harmonies of Rachmaninoff. Jay quickly learned to spot the significant traits, and together we prided ourselves at being almost infallible in discerning, just by the looks of the girl, which type she was and how the evening would end. In general, blondes preferred *La Campanella.*

It was around this time that the Green Editions came into our lives. So called because of their pale green covers rimmed with darker green edging, they were reprints of early editions of important eighteenth- and nineteenth-century piano music and were in a number of ways quite different from the editions of the same pieces that other Vengerova pupils and I had been studying. A plague of green locusts on her living-room rug could not have upset Vengerova more. She, like most pedagogues of the Russian persuasion, assigned her students rather heavily edited music. By this I mean editions prepared by certain famous nineteenth-century pianists who had made revisions or corrections that they deemed appropriate. These changes—of phrasing, dynamics, pedaling and sometimes even notes—were usually not gleaned from any particularly scholarly studies but were merely what had been fashionable or traditional when these pianists were performing.

And as Vengerova had made eminently clear from her explosion at the time of my *Carnaval* performance at Curtis, it was traditional in the Russian school to continue these customs, right or wrong. Even today, Hans von Bülow's edition of the Beethoven sonatas, for example, is used in the Soviet Union. In my opinion, this is a disaster. Although it is certainly interesting to know his thoughts about these sonatas, there is no way, when using his edition, of discerning which are Beethoven's own markings and which are von Bülow's ideas of what they should be.

Vengerova was more enlightened in this matter than some of her colleagues. Although she had learned her Beethoven from the von Bülow edition, she recommended for her students' use the scholarly yet wittily incisive Artur Schnabel edition. And here is an example of what a great musician can do to shed light on a murky swamp of misinformation. Schnabel examined the extant manuscripts, studied early editions and had his edition printed in such a way that one can see at a glance what is the original Beethoven and what are Schnabel's suggestions.

There did exist (although mostly out of print and comparatively expensive when found) volumes of the complete works of the major composers that had been compiled at various times during the nineteenth century and were sometimes called

Urtext or "unedited." Others were edited, but more discreetly than usual. Although some of these still contained mistakes and in many cases would today not be considered really authentic, they were much closer to what the composer wrote than the heavily emended editions that were so popular with the Russian school. But it was not until the Kalmus green-covered reprints, with that hallmark of purity, "URTEXT," prominently displayed on the front, started to appear in the serious New York music stores during the early 1940s that the quest for accuracy among the new generation of pianists began to pick up momentum.

Jacob Lateiner, our gang's resident researcher, became the first Vengerova student to pounce on these Green Editions. He brought them to his lessons and the ensuing dramas involved not hand positions or practicing methods, as Vengerova's battles with me largely did, but rather what Jacob had discovered between those green covers versus what he had previously learned from editions approved by the Russian school. And of course, as any red-blooded teenager would do, he exaggerated and amplified these differences. I was present at a spectacular moment in Tanglewood in 1947 when Jacob, at a rehearsal with the Boston Symphony for what was probably his first major engagement, explained certain things about the second movement of the "Emperor" Concerto to Koussevitzky. (Most of the editions of the "Emperor" in use at that time indicated that this movement was to be played four beats to the bar. A few of them, however, marked the tempo *alla breve* [two beats, rather than four], which could make it considerably faster. Jacob's painstaking research as to which of these markings was truly Beethoven's extended as far as Vermont, where a visit to Rudolf Serkin produced proof, in the form of a photograph of the manuscript, that *alla breve* was indeed what Beethoven wanted. And *alla breve*, therefore, was what he got from Jacob.) Koussevitzky, although startled, took it all in stride—he was a kind man—and accompanied his headstrong, nineteen-year-old soloist in some rather extravagantly untraditional tempi.

Jacob, of Polish descent, was born and reared in Havana. He came to Curtis and Vengerova when he was twelve, and his family settled in Philadelphia for the duration. We were just about the same age and became friends. Soon, when I paid my semiannual-or-so visit to my music school, I was invited to stay at the Lateiners', where Jacob's father (whom his violinist brother Isidor referred to as a "barber Pole") sometimes, in addition to hospitality, offered me a haircut.

Jacob was also a scholar and a connoisseur. He looked and acted every inch the part. In his mid-teens he read Spinoza, collected incunabula and the works of German Expressionists, and imbibed unblended Scotch and rare cognacs. Slightly stooped, with horn-rimmed glasses that gave him an owlish expression, he maintained his serious demeanor while constructing the most inventive and elaborate practical jokes. His voice, even under extreme circumstances, remained at scarcely more than a hushed undertaker's whisper. His brow was high and his complexion bookworm-pale. He seemed most relaxed when surrounded by mountains of learned tomes—preferably first editions. (His first wife, the dancer Marian Horosko, achieved immortality one summer at a beach party—when Jacob sat serenely under an umbrella, reading, while his sun-bronzed companions mindlessly splashed the afternoon away—by likening his pallor to that of "a mushroom growing in the basement of a synagogue.") Jacob was definitely an indoor person.

Jacob employed his investigative bent for research into all fields, including studies of what were then considered "exotic" restaurants. In addition to playing our repertoire for each other, he and I would, more than any of our other friends, explore these bastions of ethnicity. We were undoubtedly among the first wave to venture into those hole-in-the-wall Chinese restaurants that would serve Westerners tree ears, sea slugs, white fungus and tiger-lily stems. It is probably because of people like Jacob (or, more accurately, simply Jacob) that Calvin Trillin, who correctly believes that one memorable meal should instantly be followed by another, wrote in a recent book, "concert pianists . . . are as a group undoubtedly the most devout searchers-out of quality restaurants."

We followed Jacob into more than just restaurants, and quite soon practically all of our crowd started to rely on the green Kalmus *Urtext* editions. I must say that Vengerova did resign herself to our passionate erudition; although occasionally when Jacob, after having rooted through a facsimile manuscript (the original undoubtedly found in the basement of a synagogue) stumbled upon a hitherto unnoticed phrase mark that we all agreed was of Copernican significance, Vengerova would mildly suggest that perhaps notable performances of that music had been given prior to his revelation.

Not content with exaggerating the musical differences between the way Vengerova expected me to play and what I absorbed from these new editions and from continuous dialogues with fellow students, I also studied diligently what my friends in the Serkin and Schnabel camps had already perfected, adopting (as almost all students of great artists do) the external mannerisms of the teacher, as if these are the secrets of what makes the playing of the teacher so inspired.

I found the secondhand Serkin mannerisms particularly congenial, as they consisted of exactly the opposite of how I had been taught to behave at the piano. While I was barely permitted to move, Serkin students indulged in thrillingly angular arm-flailing, exciting foot-stamping and even occasional humming—although their humming never reached the Olympian heights of the Schnabel students, who practically sang a duet along with their Schubert sonatas.

Vengerova, much as she admired and appreciated Serkin and Schnabel as artists, was constantly vigilant for any infiltration of these corrupting influences on my playing and stage deportment, and as usual, she did not hesitate to express her feelings. She regarded my contortions at the piano with a jaundiced eye, inquiring sardonically, "Do you really believe that the excitement of a Serkin performance and the absolute conviction that he manages to transmit to his listeners are caused solely by his physical gyrations and the stamping of his left foot? So? Are you, perhaps, planning next to imitate what we all agree is a beautiful Schnabel performance by playing the same wrong notes?" Inscribed on the inside front cover of my copy of the Chopin E minor Concerto, which I was learning at around that time, is the following exhortation in my teacher's bold, firm handwriting:

"Watch your left foot you beating time
"Your left arm you ~~throw~~ kicking it up
"Your posture is too erratic"

Vengerova was extremely articulate in several languages including English, so her regression to this garbled syntax can only mean that she must have been very annoyed indeed.

Of course what Vengerova really objected to was not what Serkin or Schnabel did themselves, but the inescapable fact that their students would imitate them and that I, in effect, was imitating the imitators. It was about then that I became an avid concertgoer, thus learning my imitations from the originals. I must have gone to four or five concerts a week, at least, during my late teens. My devotion soon became noticeable to the regulars. Henry Levinger, a critic on a musical magazine of the day, once heralded my breathless, almost tardy arrival for a performance by booming out, "Ah, ladies and gentlemen, at last! No concert can possibly take place unless Gary is with us, so now we can begin."

The auditoriums at which concerts took place almost nightly were Carnegie Hall and Town Hall. Although anyone could rent Carnegie Hall to put on a recital, it just wasn't done quite as casually as it is now. One had, somehow, to be an accepted major artist to play in Carnegie—or so it seemed, anyway. It was as if there were a taboo on it otherwise. Everyone but the very top performers, even including some very great artists who preferred a smaller hall for musical reasons or felt they couldn't fill the 2,760 seats of Carnegie, played in Town Hall.

Few concerts those years were sold out, and even some of the best-known artists had "student coupons" printed for their recitals. These little cards were strewn about the city with great abandon and could be found not only in music schools but in music and record shops and in restaurants frequented by concertgoers. With a student coupon and twenty-five or fifty cents, one could buy a four-dollar ticket, which was about the top price for even the most important events.

Exceptions were the orchestral performances. In addition, of course, to the New York Philharmonic, the Boston Symphony and the Philadelphia Orchestra made regular appearances at Carnegie Hall, and I was at most of them. On such occasions, as well as for the few recitals for which no discount tickets were available, my standard procedure for admittance to Carnegie Hall was to present myself at the Dress Circle entrance, where I palmed fifty cents to a ticket-taker named Harold and then slid into any available seat with his blessing. Harold's courtesy was extended to as many friends as I cared to bring along, and for several years the meeting place for our gang would be in front of Carnegie Hall at 8:20 (concerts began at 8:30, or even 8:45, then). When we were all assembled, I herded my dozen or so friends upstairs, multiplied noses by fifty cents and handed the sum to a beaming Harold.

When one wanted to be closer to the stage than the Dress Circle, there were other (admittedly less elegant) ways of getting into Carnegie Hall. For example, by memorizing the sequence of labyrinthine corridors and winding stairways of the adjoining rabbit warren known as the Carnegie Hall Studios, one could enter as if about to attend a ballet class and, after making certain abrupt turns, backtracking, walking up one staircase and down another, one could suddenly open a series of unmarked doors and find oneself in the little corridor leading to the first-tier boxes, innocence personified.

Getting into Town Hall was a different story. There was no one to bribe and there were no corridors to conquer. But, with few exceptions, student tickets were available for all performances. For debut recitals and even for somewhat well-known artists at the early stages of their careers, Town Hall was the place to play. Even William Kapell, who was already beginning to have popular success in the 1940s, played most of his New York recitals in Town Hall. And there were a few of the greatest artists like Myra Hess and Wanda Landowska who chose to play in Town Hall because they felt more at home there. It was a lovely and intimate place, with sparkling chandeliers and a medieval-like tapestry which, for something like thirty dollars extra, would be unfurled as a backdrop on the stage. Town Hall also had splendid acoustics, although nobody talked about such things then; good sound was taken for granted in concert halls until the fatal opening of Phiharmonic Hall in 1962.

One famous and perennial chamber music series that took place in Town Hall was the New Friends of Music. You could tell when you were at one of those concerts just by observing the audience: Generally middle-aged and then some, they looked terribly serious, spoke German and carried scores. They turned up at other chamber music concerts and at performances by Central European artists, mostly—although hardly ever at virtuoso recitals and slam-bang orchestra concerts—and they were known as the Old Friends of Schnabel.

One of my young Schnabelian companions was a fellow named Jack. For him, there was simply no other pianist. All the rest were equally despicable, except those who were still worse because they also played trash: Prokofiev, Rachmaninoff, Tchaikovsky and others of that ilk. Jack later became a stockbroker. He made a killing almost immediately and promptly retired, a millionaire, I was told, at the age of thirty. Most of my other friends were not so lucky, as they became musicians.

Although I never got any market tips from Jack, he performed a service far more valuable by introducing me to a boy named Piero Weiss. Newly arrived in New York from Trieste via Switzerland and England, Piero had just started to study with Vengerova, so we had much to discuss and soon became fast friends. Piero's family was very close to Toscanini, and Piero worshiped him. Occasionally the Toscaninis visited the Weisses (they lived near each other, in Riverdale), and I was invited to join the party. Piero's musicological knowledge was far greater than mine, and covered much more than just piano literature. He also spoke Italian, of course. So when Toscanini was present, Piero could converse with him on an almost human level. This was astonishing to all of us, because Toscanini held a position of eminence at the time which I don't think is equaled by any conductor today. The object of our reverence was a very tiny man, but to us he couldn't have been more impressive if he were eleven feet tall.

On one of these afternoons at the Weisses', Piero and Toscanini fell into a discussion of *Parsifal*. "There is a misprint in the score that everyone always plays," Toscanini complained in his cracked and quavering voice. "Have you got the score? I'll show you what it is." Piero instantly obliged. Toscanini opened the score and peered nearsightedly at it until he found the offending spot. He took the pencil Piero proffered and corrected the mistake. He also happened to be chewing on something and talking as he made the change. Not surprisingly, a small particle of whatever he was eating was propelled from his mouth to the score, where it settled on the open page. With incredible sleight of hand, Piero snapped the book shut (practically catching Toscanini's nose in it) in order to preserve forever not only the autograph but, like a rare species of wild flower, the speck of partly chewed hors d'oeuvre as well.

Some months later, Piero told me, the Toscaninis were visiting the Weisses again when the subject of *Parsifal* came up. "You know, there's a misprint in the score that everybody always plays," Toscanini complained to Piero in his cracked and quavering voice. "Have you got the score? I'll show you where it is." Piero excused himself and came back a few minutes later, empty-handed. "I can't imagine what happened to it, Maestro," he apologized, "but I just can't seem to find it anywhere." Piero was always a gentleman.

Once the Weisses were invited to a New Year's Eve party at the Toscaninis', and Piero was told that he could bring his friend (me) along. It was quite a departure from the evenings of playing, discussing music and listening to Toscanini records that I was used to spending with *my* gang. Here, some of the guests appeared in costume for a kind of skit. Samuel Chotzinoff was Siegmund, I remember, desperately trying to yank his sword free from wherever it had been stuck; and Nathan Milstein, dressed as a gypsy with long dangling earrings, wandered through the crowd playing his violin, to which had been affixed a tin cup. It was an altogether awe-inspiring experience, although I think we were a little shocked to find the creatures who breathed the rarefied air atop Mount Parnassus cavorting in such mortal fashion.

But by far the most lasting effect of my slight brush with Toscanini was that, thanks to the Weisses' friendship, I was invited to attend, with Piero, the famous concerts and—even more importantly—rehearsals with the NBC Symphony, then in its heyday. This was extremely lucky because although the concerts were free, tickets were almost impossible to obtain, as NBC's Studio 8-H, where they took place, didn't seat many people. And entry to the rehearsals was truly an achievement, for NBC employed a bouncer to remove those unfortunates who somehow managed to sneak in and whose credentials didn't pass muster. The tight security at rehearsals was understandable, for Toscanini's temper made Vengerova's chair-throwing sessions seem like tea parties. The legends about his tirades and baton-breakings are not exaggerated; and, in addition to expanding my musical understanding, I emerged from those rehearsals with a lifetime supply of shockingly foul Italian obscenities, for which Piero had obligingly provided simultaneous translation.

We went to these rehearsals a couple of times a month over a period of several years. Toscanini was certainly the major conductorial influence on me then, as I assume he was on many musicians and music lovers of my generation in the United States. I imagine that his strict adherence to the composers' instructions, in most cases without any feeling of pedantry (in fact, quite the opposite: a feeling of great excitement, since he was the most exciting of all the great conductors), had an extremely salutary influence on all of us who came in contact with him, no matter how peripherally.

Heifetz was also a major influence on me. His perfection seemed nothing short of magic, and I felt—as I still do—that there is no pianist who has such unearthly control over his in-strument as that incredible violinist. He never smiled, he never moved (Vengerova would have been happy if I'd imitated *his* stage deportment), and I don't think I ever heard him make one slip of any kind. He always knew just what he wanted to do, and it always came out. The most remarkable thing about all of this, for me, was that nothing ever sounded planned or overworked. The phrases that he would spin out so voluptu-ously (but with such fantastic varieties of sound!), the dare-devil feats that he would toss off so lightly (and with such per-fect intonation!) had such vitality and spontaneity that a blasé teenager like myself came away with goose pimples.

But by far the greatest number of concerts I attended during those years involved pianists. Pianists in recital, pianists with orchestra, pianists playing sonatas and chamber music, pianists playing with other pianists, sometimes even pianists accompa-nying singers. There was no shortage of pianists. (There never is.) But what is surprising was how many truly great pianists were performing regularly then.

Hofmann was the first of the giants I heard, and that was a few years before the time of which I'm writing, at the famous Jubilee Concert that he gave at the Metropolitan Opera House in 1937. Even though I was only nine, I remember it vividly. Perhaps the fact that I'd recently played for him at Curtis (and, having *tutoyéd* him, our resulting intimacy) had some-thing to do with it. Nevertheless, the remarkable sound he effortlessly charmed out of the instrument, with never a hint of harshness, is with me still.

I heard Rachmaninoff a few times at Carnegie Hall. He died when I was fourteen, so the last time was probably shortly be-fore that; but I was old enough to appreciate the extraordinary rhythmic propulsion that underscored his performances and the utter clarity of his playing, with those infinite nuances and gradations of sound that meant the difference between life and death to Vengerova.

I also heard others of that era, but it was Rachmaninoff and Hofmann who exerted some influence on me. I really mean "some," because the overwhelming piano influence that I felt was unquestionably from Horowitz, Rubinstein, Serkin and Schnabel. I attended almost every performance they gave in New York during those years.

These were the artists who made me lose myself completely in the music. Their playing was very, very different one from the other, and yet I would be so convinced by the way each of them played—actually, carried along by his thoughts—that it seemed, when listening to any one of them, that there was no other possible way of performing that work at that moment. This, of course, is what artistry is all about. Each pianist in his own particular way utilized the little black spots that the composer put on the paper as more than simply a point of departure. For, as freely as he may have played, he was really trying to re-create through himself what he passionately believed the composer's wishes to be.

I began to realize that the performer of a Beethoven sonata had a relation to the composer similar to that of an actor to Shakespeare, and although a great artist must have something unique to offer and must play his music or role with such authority, devotion and abandon that the audience will be utterly convinced, it must be within the boundaries of the composer's or playwright's instructions. Shakespeare used words and Beethoven, notes. But Shakespeare actually gave fewer instructions as to how to read one of his sentences, let alone paragraphs, than Beethoven did within a single phrase of his music, not to mention an entire section of a work. For example: in bars 4, 5 and 6 of the last movement of his A-flat Sonata, Opus 110, Beethoven gives no less than eighteen admonitions pertaining to mood and attitude, tempo changes, dynamic changes and quality of sound. In addition, there are phrasing instructions and even (in one area of this section) fingering (in order to achieve a particular effect). Neither the damper (right) nor shift (left) pedal is neglected in these orders. The former must be employed during two long sections, while the latter (already in use from the beginning of the movement) must be raised in the middle of bar 5, only to be depressed again shortly afterward. And to make things more difficult, the performer, rather than appearing to be confined in a straitjacket by these injunctions, must, while respecting all of the above, seem to be improvising freely under some divine inspiration. Yet I came to understand that, miraculous as it may have seemed, there were as many different great performances of these three bars as there were great performers.

The gradations of tone that a player strove for in a phrase; the pedaling that he used; the space between individual notes; the breathing, or lack of it, between phrases; all of these slight shadings that great artists do instinctively became, for me, much more successful when done with subtlety. Now, what was subtle for one listener might have seemed overdone for another or not even have been noticed by a third. That was where taste came in. Within certain boundaries, there was certainly no right or wrong. But when I listened to a simple Chopin waltz played by Horowitz or Rubinstein (each of whom played it quite differently) or a Schubert melody played by Serkin or Schnabel (also quite differently one from the other), there was a kind of natural unity and beauty that—most importantly—never sounded contrived. (This ideal, as I have found with the advancing years, changes somewhat from generation to generation. Perhaps, as with skirt lengths, fashion reigns, and where at one time an exposed ankle would cause raised eyebrows, now not even frontal nudity surprises.)

These were some of the things I began to perceive in my almost nightly forays on the concert halls of Manhattan; but regrettably, it was still the external manner of my heroes' playing that the blotting paper of my psyche most thoroughly absorbed. Vengerova never failed to notice how an evening with the real thing spurred my mimicry onward and upward. She was fond of calling me back down to earth, when I played for her while under the spell of one of these paragons, with what was for her a gentle nip: "It is becoming increasingly unnecessary for me to leave the house, now that you are so considerate to display for me with such per-fec-tion all the idiosyncrasies we encountered at Carnegie Hall last night. Only a trained chimpanzee could do better." Her ever present concern about the bad habits I could pick up extended even to her favorite pianist, Horowitz. Waving her hands like claws in front of my face, she would cry, "Keep the fingers curved, curved, always coooooorved, like this! Yes, yes, I *know* he gets a beautiful sound by hitting the keys with flat fingers, but *he* can do it, and you *can't*."

Vengerova's bark was by far the most dangerous thing about her, and in spite of our spats, she gave me an A+ in piano playing on my report card when I graduated from Curtis in 1946. (I mention this here for the record because my report cards have been downhill ever since.) I continued to play for her on a more informal basis until her death ten years later, and although we still had some tiffs, she seemed to holler less. Either she mellowed or she figured it was more sensible to save her breath for the next generation, since I was already lost.

Madame Vengerova was sick for a long time before she died, but she never lost interest in piano playing, pianists, nonpianists, musical events and the world in general. Her bedroom, rather than her studio, became the command center. Naomi and I and, of course, other friends and students would visit, sometimes playing, always gossiping. The last pieces I played for her were the three Brahms Intermezzi, Opus 117. Afterward, I remember going to sit with her by her bed. The phone at her side rang almost incessantly. At first she appeared almost too weak to pick it up, but if the conversation proved interesting, she gathered strength. One caller seemed to be seeking advice, for Vengerova patiently embarked upon a lengthy analysis of certain problems inherent in performing the Chopin A-flat major Ballade. The discussion progressed in a most detailed fashion.

". . . Yes, yes, my dear . . . I understand your problem, naturally. But, you see, one cannot be arbitrary . . . it depends to a great extent how far you depress the pedal and when you release it . . . also the acoustics, the volume of sound you are getting out of the piano . . . many other imponderables . . ." She seemed most amused by some of the questions that were

being put to her, and occasionally looked over at us and rolled
her eyes up to the ceiling in mock exasperation. "I know, I
know," she eventually concluded. "But that may really turn out
to be the best way, after all. Try it, then, and see . . . and let
me know . . . Certainly, my dear, not at all, not at all. Let me
know what happens."

She finally hung up, glanced at us and, with the tiniest glimmer of malice, sighed, "Ach, that little Rosina"—her colleague
Rosina Lhévinne, three years her junior, being then about
seventy-five—"that Rosina, she is *soch* a child!" Then, closing
her eyes, with a sweet smile on her face, she fell asleep, and we
tiptoed out.

I guess it was mostly Eugene Istomin who convinced me,
around the time I finished Curtis, that the wisest course was to
become hypercritical of oneself. As with Vengerova, I can't
remember a time when I didn't know Eugene. His parents, like
mine, were among the Russian émigré group in New York, and
they visited back and forth a couple of times a year when we
were both very young, sometimes dragging us along. For we
were by no means friends: our age difference was far too great a
chasm to bridge. We would circle each other warily and engage
in stilted, uncomfortable conversation: for an eight-year-old
Eugene to be forced to pass the time of day productively or
even pleasantly with a five-year-old Gary was too much to expect. Then he and his family moved to Philadelphia during the
years he was studying at Curtis with Serkin, but even when
they returned to New York after his graduation—I think he
must have been around seventeen—I was still too young to be
anything but an admirer from afar. And admire him I did. He
was starting to give important concerts; he played chamber
music with Adolf Busch; he won the Leventritt award; he
played with the New York Philharmonic. I went to his concerts
and absorbed everything I could (more, of course, than Vengerova wished). In my eyes, Eugene was already an established
artist, and when he finally deigned to recognize me on an adult
level, when I was about seventeen, I hung onto his every word.
"Why?" he would ask, when I played a passage for him in a

certain way. "What made you do it like that? Don't just *play*. Think!" He made me analyze the way I was playing a great deal more than I had been doing; as a result, I started to practice with increased intensity. Eugene was intolerant of any sloppiness, and I did have a habit of getting carried away by the passion of the moment, sometimes pressing down only a vague approximation of the correct notes in my search for the Big Line.

Eugene's watching over me was not unlike the nurturing *he* had received from William Kapell. Willy set an impeccable musical example for all of us. He practiced more than anyone else, and not for any lack of technique. He wanted to arrive at conclusions about why every nuance, every phrase, every pedal was the way he would finally play it, and not a different way. He was undoubtedly the most important, as well as the most successful, pianist of his generation, and I occasionally find myself even now, so many years after the air crash that removed him so prematurely from the field of battle, wondering, when I hear someone play a particular piece, how Willy would have done it.

Willy was a very close friend of Eugene's, but only a much-admired acquaintance of mine. He, after all, was *six* years older, and that was too much for anything but an occasional pat on the head or (more often) a slap on the wrist for lazy thinking, careless playing. He phoned me occasionally to give advice and encouragement and then, a few years later, a Dutch uncle lecture that I never forgot. That was in 1950. Carnegie Hall was no longer sacrosanct to the élite, and I had just given my second recital there. The next morning I received a summons from Willy.

"I want to talk to you," he announced portentously.

I went to his house. He didn't waste words. He had been at the recital and informed me, "You played like a pig." He then proceeded to tell me why, leaving no grace note unturned. In general, he diagnosed, the problem was that I was getting lazy, and in fact he had heard from Eugene that I hadn't been practicing as seriously as I should.

"You have to decide what road you are going to take," he said. "It's not that you can't have great success if you continue to play like a pig—in fact, some very successful performers *do* play like pigs" (he named a dozen) "—or not have success if you play like an artist. But you have to decide what you're going to do with your life." He went on to say that he was simply informing me as to what I had to decide, since I was already twenty-two, and not getting any younger. He continued, firmly, "By the age of twenty-five, a first-class artist is already first-class, or he never will be." He then added, very seriously, "Before my fee became one thousand dollars, I felt that even if I didn't play my best there was enough for the audience to get its money's worth. But now, now that I'm getting one thousand dollars" (which was a hefty sum for a concert in those days), "there is *no* excuse. I really have to do everything in the best possible way."

Willy certainly practiced what he preached. Years after his death, I heard a tape that had been made from a performance on what must have been a lousy piano in a small town in Australia—one of the last concerts he gave—and the playing was of a quality that could just as well have been in Carnegie Hall. Very few artists give so much of themselves under all situations, and he was one of the most uncompromising.

Among the many things that my friend and mentor Eugene taught me was fear. Although I must admit that a good number of years elapsed before this lesson sank in, God knows he certainly worked hard at indoctrinating me. He kept warning me that I should prepare myself for "the awful moment when you walk out on stage and sit down at the piano and start to play—when it's too late to go back." What awful moment? I thought it was fun. (Ah, that three years' difference in our age meant a great deal then—although I do believe that Eugene always took things more seriously than I.)

One of the inoculations Dr. Istomin prescribed to lessen the horror of that "awful moment" and the awful moments to follow was a procedure I came to call "devirginization." This took place when we played a new piece for our merciless colleagues, who knew the problems as well as the score. We didn't let each other get away with anything. And although it was customary for the listening colleagues to cry "Bravo!" whenever one of these performances came to its rip-roaring conclusion, the victim could sense from the tone of voice, the expression on the face, the very vibrations that emanated from his audience how many "buts . . ." would follow, and how serious they would be. I can't remember, though, that we ever gave each other criticism that wasn't constructive. We were always very careful not to say merely that something seemed wrong, but to try to verbalize or demonstrate how we thought it could be improved, no matter how harsh the judgment was.

Most important of all was the ritual of the gradual "devirginization" of a new concerto. Sometimes (very rarely, it is true) I feel sympathy for conductors, because they have no way of practicing privately. When they're conducting a piece for the first time they have to make their mistakes in front of the hundred or so pairs of beady eyes of their orchestra players, who know all and forgive nothing. For a soloist, playing a concerto for the first time at rehearsal is a similar experience. Unlike a solo piece, it requires not only fine playing, but meshing with the orchestra. It is especially unpleasant to have to do this nowadays with a new concerto at an orchestra rehearsal, because financial considerations have turned many of them into scarcely more than run-throughs. Incidentally, a soloist must never admit to the conductor (as I found out to my sorrow some years later) that he is playing a concerto for the first time, even when he is eighteen years old. The conductor will be sure to find more fault with his soloist's interpretation than he would if he thought the fellow had just played the concerto (exactly the same way) six times with the London Symphony. Some conductors, as I was to discover, felt insulted that a concerto was being "tried out" on them. Others, more secure, would growl something like, "Well, at least you're lucky to have *me* to make sure nothing goes wrong." (One of the advantages of reaching middle age is that I can now use this same line with young conductors.)

So, how does one go about deflowering a new concerto? For this you need two pianos, a colleague to play through the orchestral part on the second instrument and, preferably, one or more additional colleagues to serve as audience, teacher, critic and Greek chorus, with scores in hands and "show me" expressions on faces. To a certain extent we had all done this when working on concertos at our lessons. But no matter how much a teacher might bellow, there was something far more final about playing for the ultradiscriminating ears of one's peers. Also, of course, we were now getting to the point where we were actually performing, or hoping to perform, these pieces in public, so there was more immediacy and urgency to our efforts.

For these sessions we would generally meet in my living room, with its two pianos. The player of the orchestral part really didn't have to give a polished performance. What was important was that he'd give all the cues at the right time, keep the rhythm and, in general, try to give a reasonable approximation of what sounds the soloist could expect to hear from the orchestra, and when. An experienced colleague like Eugene could also make things harder (and later, in real life, easier) by anticipating in his accompaniment some of the unexpected little things that often occur in certain places—little changes of tempo, for example, which are not marked, but which frequently seem to happen; and teaching little signals the soloist must be prepared to convey to the conductor at certain points with a subtle accent, a nod of the head or even a raised eyebrow. (Eugene was very good on eyebrows.) "Be prepared!" was the message coming from him at the accompanying piano.

My father, who almost always sat in on these sessions, also adopted this motto with regard to my future. As a musician, he was well aware of the pitfalls that awaited a soloist in orchestral accompaniments—and he also knew that I might not be lucky enough to find myself in a position to require orchestral accompaniments. My progress and early success were no guarantee that I would be able to make a living as a "concert pianist." I am often sadly amused when approached, usually backstage after a concert, by a college student who tells me that he's studying to be a concert pianist. One can study to be a musician and one can study to be a pianist, but being a concert pianist depends upon somebody's asking you to give concerts, which, unfortunately, is usually not the case.

So it was always understood in my family that I was expected to earn a college diploma as well as my Curtis credentials. This was unusual for a young musician at that time. A great many—perhaps the majority—of the best-known artists devoted only a minuscule part of their time and thoughts to any subjects outside of music or even outside of their specific instrument. Nowadays the outlook is quite different and a general education for a musically gifted youngster is considered far more important than it was when I was growing up. Very few of my pianist friends went to a normal school. Some had tutors, some read a great deal and others, later in life, did take academic courses. Nevertheless, this was by no means the path chosen by the parents or advisers of the majority. But in my house it was considered prudent to wear suspenders with a belt; and so, in the fall of 1946, armed with a scholarship and boundless enthusiasm, I set forth on my bicycle for Columbia University. In this case, however, with the best of intentions (the kind they say the road to hell is paved with), my father's careful planning came to naught, and I never did graduate from college. Rachmaninoff and S. Hurok took care of that.

CHAPTER SIX

"Mr. Hurok,
You're Fired!"

IN 1946 a musical competition was conceived in homage to Rachmaninoff, who had died three years earlier. It was to be the most exciting, glamorous, well-organized, musically valid— in short, the classiest—competition ever devised. Designed to honor various facets of Rachmaninoff's gifts, the contest, scheduled to take place annually, was to be held one year for pianists, the next for composers, and the third for conductors.

The first competition was announced for pianists. But not just any pianists: before the supplicants were permitted to perform for the national jury in New York, regional competitions, or mini-contests, were to be held, and a subjury was to scour the country searching for candidates who could meet the rigorous standards. The final eliminations were to take place first in Town Hall, where the contestants' solo repertoire would be explored in depth, and then the event would move uptown to the holy of holies, Carnegie Hall itself, where these chosen ones would be heard in concertos, accompanied by the NBC Orchestra and Fritz Reiner. The panel of judges was star-studded, including even Horowitz. The prize consisted of money, an RCA recording contract and performances with practically every orchestra in the United States on a triumphal tour to be managed by not one but both of the leading concert bureaus, harmoniously and altruistically collaborating to further this artistic goal.

Of course I entered the competition.

The regional competitions took place in two stages. After participating in the initial play-off in Philadelphia, I was among those invited to return for more two days later. I was not at all surprised. But when I played the second time and it was announced that I was the winner for that region, I really thought that I had misheard. My father was even more puzzled. When I phoned to tell him the news, he was convinced that I was joking.

"Now tell me what *really* happened," he insisted.

The Philadelphia competition was the first of these several regional ones to be held throughout the country. However, as each subsequent competition took place my position became more enhanced because—to everyone's surprise and to the consternation of the Rachmaninoff Foundation—there were no other winners. I reigned alone and, at eighteen, suddenly found myself quite a celebrity in the musical community. The press paid what was for that time an inordinate amount of attention to the progress of this competition, and as each regional area failed to find a winner, more and more was written about me. I basked in the adulation of friends and blossomed when my inane comments on all subjects were accepted and quoted with solemn appreciation. Finally, I was offered a contract by Hurok, then in his heyday, and tasted glory.

The contract guaranteed me ten concerts at an extremely low fee, but the mere idea of having my name added to an artists' roster which included Marian Anderson and Arthur Rubinstein was enough to make me insufferable. As things turned out, few of the promised concerts materialized, and al-

though the Hurok office did pay me the guaranteed income, at
that stage of my life it would have been far better to have
gained the experience of playing concerts, even for no money.

Then came endless discussions with my parents, Vengerova
and the Hurok people over a decision which we had to make:
since I had been the only winner of the Rachmaninoff regional
competition, and since the Rachmaninoff Foundation didn't
want to have a final play-off with only me competing against
myself to see if I could also be the Grand National winner,
they decided to have another year of regional competitions. If I
agreed, I could then compete with these winners at the Grand
Finals, which would take place a year later than originally
planned. I was invited but not obligated to do this, and since I
had no career to speak of, I decided to accept the challenge.

Meanwhile, as my prize for winning the regional portion of
the competition, I was supposed to play with the regional orchestra. In this case, the regional orchestra was that of Philadelphia. The conductor of the regional orchestra, one Eugene
Ormandy, felt that he would first wish to hear this regional
winner before committing himself, which, of course, was his
prerogative. A date was set for an audition. I appeared at the
Academy of Music at the appointed hour, and there was Maestro Ormandy as well as his concertmaster, at that time Alexander Hilsberg. Since there was no second piano onstage, nor
had I been told to bring an accompanist, I asked, "Do you
want to hear some solo repertoire?"

"No," replied Ormandy. "I'd rather hear a concerto."

So I told him what was in my fingers, and since the concert
that I was being considered for was an all-Rachmaninoff one,
he asked for the Rachmaninoff Second. I don't remember what
part I played first, but without a second piano it would not
have been productive to start at the beginning of this piece as,
after the first eight bars, the soloist is merely accompanying the
theme, which is played by the orchestra. I do remember asking
him, though, if he wanted me to skip around and play some of
the themes in order to give an idea of how I played the con-

certo, and I do recall that I played many sections of it. Finally I stopped, and he said, "And now, please, the cadenza."

Well, there is no cadenza in the Rachmaninoff Second, and Ormandy, perhaps better than any other conductor, knows this very well, so I assume he was either trying to be funny or to see what I would do. I just couldn't bring myself to say, "But Mr. Ormandy, there is no cadenza," so I muttered something about playing more solo passages, which I did. Ormandy stopped me.

"Very nice," said he. "Now play me the cadenza."

Sweat poured down my brow as I searched for an as-yet-unplayed solo passage, and I desperately played still another section. During this, I could hear whispering in the auditorium, and I imagine it was Hilsberg telling Ormandy to go easy on me, and maybe to ask for something else, which he did, because I remember playing something from the Prokofiev Third.

I never found out if Ormandy was teasing or testing to see how I would react, and to this day I don't know if it was a Hungarian's idea of a musical joke or a musician's idea of a Hungarian joke.

In any case, when this ordeal was over, Ormandy told me that I would play with him a couple of months later, the Rachmaninoff Second, on the regular subscription series, which meant two performances. In those days, by the way, it was far more unusual for an unknown youngster to play with a major orchestra than it is now, and in the light of what happened, it is just as well that I didn't have a chance to get into trouble with more orchestras and conductors than I did with the Philadelphians and Ormandy.

This was to be the first time in my life that I would play with a truly professional orchestra. The event began with a piano rehearsal with Ormandy. At a piano rehearsal the soloist usually plays the entire solo part of the concerto through and the conductor either listens or, if he is a pianist, plays the orchestral part through on a second piano. Then the conductor discusses with the soloist any questions he may have about whether the soloist really intends to do some of the things he did. Naturally, as the soloist gets older and the conductor, therefore, gets younger, there is less of this questioning as, in general, the conductor is expected to be receptive to the soloist's ideas, within reason. (Years later, when I played with Monteux for the first time—the same Rachmaninoff, as a matter of fact—I was puzzled because no piano rehearsal had been scheduled. After we were introduced, I asked Monteux if he didn't want to hear me play the piece before the orchestral rehearsal. He smiled and asked, "Do you do anything strange?" I replied, "Not in my opinion," and that was our piano rehearsal.)

The piano rehearsal in Philadelphia was followed by two rehearsals with the orchestra. Ormandy is one of the greatest accompanists imaginable and, together with his orchestra, had always been very close to this particular concerto. In addition, I was well prepared and had had these substantial workouts with him. Nevertheless, I felt somewhat uncomfortable as the time for the first performance approached. Only later did I realize that my innocence of the perils of playing with orchestra was aggravated by my almost total lack of chamber music experience. I had absolutely no concept of the give-and-take essential in chamber music which should exist as well with an orchestra, even when playing the so-called virtuoso repertoire. I had played most of the standard violin sonatas many times with my father, but these were readings and did not involve serious thought. To make matters worse, I knew nothing about the protocol of deportment at rehearsals, as this subject was not taught along with octaves and double thirds. I thought that if I heard something not quite to my liking, I could just stop playing and say, "A little faster, please, Mr. Ormandy." This was the equivalent of farting in a cathedral, although, contrary to popular belief, the former sin bears consequences immeasurably more severe and of longer duration. (There are, of course, subtle ways of achieving the desired changes by the orchestra, but at that time of my life subtlety in human relations, unlike stubbornness, was not one of my strong points.)

Ormandy, however, got back at me and had the last word. When, after the first performance, I asked him if he could let me trill a little longer at the spot in the slow movement before the recapitulation when the winds make their entrance so that I could make a longer diminuendo, he said something to the effect that he would keep it in mind. At the second perform-ance, after I had trilled for what I thought was just about the right amount of time, I looked up at him, expecting him to be ready to bring the orchestra in. But he was gazing raptly off into the distance somewhere over my head. This meant that I had to make a crescendo and then yet another diminuendo. By that time my hand felt as if it was about to fall off. Ormandy then smilingly brought the orchestra in to my rescue.

A year after I'd signed with Hurok I received a letter renew-ing the management contract for another year at a slightly higher fee, but minus the guarantee. Twenty-four hours later, Gary Graffman, aged nineteen, sent Sol Hurok, aged fifty-nine, a registered letter, as follows:

January 29, 1948

Dear Mr. Hurok:

Since you have not complied with the terms of our Agreement dated July 3, 1947 in regard to renewing the Agreement under terms stated in the same Agreement, I am unable to accept your contract for the season 1948–49.

The next day, Marks Levine, one of Hurok's associates, phoned my father three times to ask if he knew what I had done; whether I was under the influence of strong drink or evil spirits; or whether I had simply taken leave of my senses. From what I remember, my father defended me somewhat.

"Marks," he said, "you must know by now how unbelievably stubborn Gary can be, and when he gets into one of these moods, there is absolutely no way to reason with him." Also, my father agreed that I did have a point: If the Hurok manage-ment didn't get me concerts when they had to pay me anyway, why would they get me more concerts when they *didn't* have to pay me anyway?

But this obvious situation was only part of the reason for my refusal to sign the new contract. A few months earlier, just after it had been decided that I would indeed play again at the

Rachmaninoff competition, Marks Levine had charmingly advised me, "If you don't win this contest, my boy, you're a dead duck." It gave me great pleasure, now, to have the power of upsetting him, as it gave me great pleasure, shortly thereafter, to be able to announce to my friends that I had told Hurok to go to hell. Unfortunately, nobody believed me.

During the next couple of months three more regional winners were selected, as well as one Honorable Mention winner who was permitted to advance to the Grand Finals. So at last there were five of us scheduled to compete in New York that April.

The first part of the finals took place in Town Hall before a large audience. I played many solo works and felt that I did about as well as I could. The orchestra finals followed, in Carnegie Hall, with Reiner and the NBC Orchestra. There I played the Rachmaninoff Second Concerto perhaps as badly as I have ever played it, which is saying something.

The winner was a fellow Curtis graduate, a Serkin pupil, Seymour Lipkin. I received what was called "the Special Award," which was a polite way of saying second prize. It was concocted on the spur of the moment, as no second prize had been planned, and included the gift of a Carnegie Hall recital at the end of the year, to be presented by the Rachmaninoff Foundation.

Although I was disappointed that I didn't win first prize in a competition where I had been so close, I felt even then that the way I had butchered the concerto entitled me to no prize whatsoever. A few years later I realized how totally unprepared I would have been to handle such a prize—particularly all those orchestral concerts—at that stage of my life.

The main reason for the difference in my playing on those two days of the finals (besides the inescapable fact that any musician can play better one day than another) was that when I went onstage at Town Hall to play the solo repertoire I was doing what was normal for me. Playing the "Waldstein" Sonata for my father, Vengerova, friends and anybody who would listen scores of times had given me enough poise and

confidence to withstand the tensions of a public recital performance. But, as the Philadelphia Orchestra concerts experience had indicated, playing a concerto is quite different, and
involves not only a collaboration but also at least an elementary knowledge of what the problems of the conductor are in
relation to the soloist. Running through the concerto on two
pianos with a colleague doing the orchestral part was not at all
the same, especially because I pretty much ignored my accompanist, who, knowing what I was aiming for, would obligingly
try to fit in with my idiosyncrasies.

Reiner, for his part, had to rehearse with five inexperienced
youngsters in a very short time, so our rehearsal was not really
worthy of its name. My stubbornness thrived in a situation
such as this. I thought that not enough time or effort had been
lavished on the work and therefore tended, angrily, to exagger-
ate what was not right. Normal nervousness exacerbated the
situation, of course: never within living memory (and probably never since) had a musical competition drawn such an illustrious audience. The very idea of stepping out on the Carnegie
Hall stage to face this gala, expectant and musically knowledgeable crowd would have made me uncomfortable under the
best of circumstances.

Therein lay, I think, the fatal flaw in the idea of the Rachmaninoff competition. Since the only performers eligible to
enter it were those with virtually no professional experience, it
was unlikely that any victors would be able to sustain the excellence of performance expected. The first prize had been designed to involve them in the kind of grueling schedule, both
in quantity and quality of appearances, that even a veteran
would find taxing.

In any event, Seymour played the concerts that were his due,
I played the Carnegie Hall recital that the Foundation sponsored, and the Rachmaninoff competition folded its tent and
was never heard from again.

The Leventritt Competition, on the other hand, maintained
a discreet profile. Although the award brought with it the

highest possible prestige, the Leventritt family at that time seemed almost to go out of its way to avoid publicity for the contest it sponsored. Founded in 1939 to honor the memory of Edgar M. Leventritt, a music-loving lawyer, this competition was distinctive during those days in at least two ways. To begin with, there was no cash prize. This, however, did not diminish its lure, for the orchestras with which the winner would play were temptation enough. Although the list was not as vast as that promised by the Rachmaninoff, it included such plums as Cleveland, Chicago and the New York Philharmonic-Symphony. The Leventritt's second distinction was a "fail-safe" device: if its jury didn't feel that any of the contestants, no matter how gifted, were mature enough to cope with the problems of playing with these orchestras or, as they put it, ready to embark on a full-scale career, it was not committed to give any prize at all. Conversely, on the rare occasions that more than one contestant exhibited those qualities the judges deemed worthy, they were free to award more than one prize. There was, however, no such thing as a second or third prize. The Leventritt award was either given, or it was not given. The contestants were not supposed to be battling it out against each other to see who among them was "best," but, rather, against a standard of excellence and ripeness determined by the discriminating board of judges, themselves musicians of unimpeachable standards—Rudolf Serkin and, until their deaths, George Szell and William Steinberg almost always figuring prominently among them. For this reason, the mere fact that a Leventritt Competition took place didn't necessarily mean that the result would be another Leventritt award winner.

By 1949 Eugene Istomin had already been a winner, as had Sigi (now Alexis) Weissenberg, whom I had recently met and whose playing I admired. I was at liberty, having fired Hurok, although his WASP counterpart Arthur Judson intimated that he would probably offer me a contract in the near future.

"But," said Judson, "when one divorces, one should wait a little while before getting remarried."

Meanwhile, I had few concerts and very little to lose by entering the Leventritt.

That summer I diligently prepared the required repertoire—three concertos and a great deal of solo music—for the contest, which was to take place in early fall. My friend Leon Fleisher did yeoman service by paying house calls to my family apartment several times a week to play the orchestral part of the concertos on our second piano. (As mentioned earlier, I was the only one of our set lucky enough to have two pianos at the time. There was the one that the Curtis Institute had sold my father for a token sum when I graduated, and there was also a piano always on loan from the Steinway company, which in those days coddled almost all the artists who played its pianos, whether they were at the top of the heap or, as was I, still completely submerged.) Leon's playing was extremely beautiful, with the most natural phrasing. He was also a marvelous sight reader and chamber music player. One of Schnabel's students, Leon was almost exactly my age, and already enjoyed some professional success: Monteux had engaged him to play with the Philharmonic when he was sixteen or so and thus he, too, was in that small group of youngsters who had the privilege of appearing with a few of our most distinguished orchestral institutions.

For relaxation, we played a lot of four-hand music. Then Leon would graciously listen—as did everyone else I could buttonhole—to the solo works I was preparing. Although he occasionally offered suggestions (which, after all, was the point of his listening), he didn't do so nearly as readily as Eugene, for whom I also played. Part of this was probably Leon's reticent personality, but also I suppose the three-year age difference between Eugene and me, which seemed so great then, had a good deal to do with Eugene's unstinting criticism. In any case, practically every evening Leon faithfully appeared, seated himself at the second piano, and we would attack Prokofiev, Brahms and Rachmaninoff.

Summer in New York in the years before air conditioning

meant that there was a good deal of sweat over and above the
normal amount engendered by playing concertos. The windows
were always flung wide to catch any breeze that might dry our
dripping faces. As a result, other open windows caught more
than stray sounds that emanated from my parents' living room.
I am amazed that nobody called the police. (Unbeknownst to
us, though, the Druzinskys, a family of musicians whose apartment was just across the court from ours and who were acquaintances of my parents and thus knew what was going on,
were following our progress avidly—how could they help it?—
although they had no idea who my colleague was. The following year, when Eugene and I were spending a few days in Marseilles, we met Dorothy Druzinsky, who was bicycling from
North Africa to Paris. We suggested that she look up our
friend Leon, who was living there at the time. She took our advice, married him and subsequently found out that it was he
who had contributed mightily to keeping her awake during
that long hot summer of 1949.)

The opening sessions of the Leventritt took place in a little
auditorium of what was then the Steinway Building, appropriately called Steinway Hall. (At that time the Steinway
Building housed not only the offices of the piano company but
nearly all of the music business offices of New York, including
Columbia Artists Management and the New York Philharmonic-Symphony. The address was 113 West Fifty-seventh
Street. When the Steinways sold the building several years later
to the Manhattan Life Insurance Company, its number was
changed to 111 forthwith.)

The Steinway Building's 13 was not unlucky for me that fall,
though. When my turn came to play, I started, as was customary, with the piece of my choice. (In the Leventritt, as in some
other competitions, the contestant is permitted to begin with a
work of his own selection. Thereafter, he does what he is told.)
My choice was no less than the Brahms Concerto No. 1 (with
the Fleisher Philharmonic at the second piano). The judges let
me play the first movement all the way through. That was it.
When I called in at the designated time to see if I'd passed the

first round, I was told that I'd play at the finals in Carnegie Hall.

"But there is something I have to explain to you that may seem rather odd," I was told by the Leventritt spokeswoman. "There will be no semifinals." Pause. "And you're going to be the only finalist."

"I see," I said, not seeing at all.

"You must understand, though, that your chances of winning are no better or no worse just because nobody else is in the finals."

"I understand," I said, not understanding, really.

"Remember, you're not competing against anyone in this contest." (There was that invisible, evanescent standard again.) "You must be prepared to play any of the repertoire that the judges may request, and for as long as they want to listen," she continued. "It may be for an hour or even longer, if they wish. Then, when they've heard enough, they will decide either to give you the prize or not to give you the prize. Is that perfectly clear?"

I nodded at the phone and hung up, feeling perfectly confused.

At Carnegie Hall the next day there were, besides the judges, a few hundred curious listeners. (As I recall, Mrs. Leventritt at that time never actively invited an audience to the finals, but she never kept any interested people away, either.) Again I was allowed to start with the music of my choice, so I continued through the second and third movements of the Brahms concerto. Nothing was going to deter me from playing the whole damned piece! Then I was asked to play the Beethoven Opus 109 Sonata. This was followed, in rapid succession, by about half of the Schumann *Carnaval*; a Bach prelude and fugue; some Debussy; the Paganini-Liszt *La Campanella*; one or two other short pieces; and a movement each of the Rachmaninoff Second and Prokofiev Third concertos. Leon's performance of the orchestral parts was extraordinary, and I later heard that one of the judges proposed giving *him* the prize.

I don't remember what I did when I was finally told,

"Enough!" I may have mingled with my friends in the audience or just brooded in a corner, but I recall that after a certain amount of time had elapsed—maybe a year or two, it seemed—the judges shuffled out onstage looking sheepish and somebody eventually mumbled something about my having won. It was all so vague and offhand that it could even be that there was no announcement at all, and that somebody who saw me hanging around told me to go up on stage. Anyway, the sheepish-looking judges congratulated me, one by one, and one of them said to me, "Actually, we had decided to give you the prize as soon as you finished the Brahms, but we were enjoying ourselves, so we just let you go on and on." I don't know how true this was, or whether he was just making conversation, but there's no doubt that I gave them an earful that afternoon.

George Szell then discussed what I would play with him in Cleveland a few months later (it turned out to be the Beethoven Third), Steinberg asked for Chopin in Buffalo, and Arthur Judson advised me that the correct amount of time had now elapsed since my divorce from Hurok, and he would add me to his list. Where Hurok's roster had been graced by the name of Rubinstein, Judson's was then headed by that of Heifetz. In addition, he handled just about all the conductors worth playing with as well as the New York Philharmonic-Symphony. Legend has it that this conflict of interest made it natural for Judson artists to appear most frequently with those conductors and that orchestra. If this was in fact the case, I never became one of those so favored; it later seemed to me, indeed, that he bent over backward to make sure that I didn't have many of the sought-after engagements. But at the moment of winning the Leventritt award, all of this was far in the future. Meanwhile, a gloriously plumed phoenix had arisen from the dead duck's ashes and it was impossible for me to imagine that there would ever be any further hurdles to overcome.

Competitions have proliferated in what seems like geometric progression since the times I've been describing. Nowadays, they appear to be almost as numerous as the army of young hopefuls who enter them. They have even spawned a mutant breed of performer, the "professional" contestant—what my friend Claude Frank calls the "contest whore"—who pops up at every competition from Dallas to Dubrovnik until he either wins one or is disqualified by age. A great deal has been written about the evils of competitions: that they are cruel; or that they are the only route a young artist can take to make his mark in this cruel world; or that a performer who does well in them is chosen simply because his lack of individuality avoids upsetting the cruel board of judges, often composed principally of pedagogues. ("Cruel" seems to be the common adjective in all these points of views.)

Like all generalities, these statements are sometimes true and sometimes not.

Most competitions are of questionable quality. As is the case with most human endeavors, some are innocuous and some, in my opinion, are downright deplorable. Whenever I hear of a new one, or one that I don't know very much about, the two things that interest me most are how freewheeling the rules are and how free-spirited the judges are. A competition is only as good as its jury and the flexibility with which its rules can be bent to fit the needs of the contestants.

By "flexibility," I mean that the competition should be geared to help individual contestants achieve their best, rather than to demand that they conform to stringent regulations. A good example is that of repertoire requirements. The imposed material is sometimes spelled out so specifically that no leeway is possible. All contestants *must* be prepared to play, say, the Chopin G minor Ballade. Why on earth should this be necessary? If the judges want to hear a big Chopin piece, it shouldn't make any difference which one it is. Aside from the obvious unfairness of one contestant's having played that ballade since he was ten and another one's having to learn it especially for the occasion (although the latter may have played the other three ballades since *she* was ten), it must also be horribly boring for the jury. Naturally, each contestant's abilities to play different kinds of repertoire should be explored in depth. But it seems to me that this can best be done through requirements that are broad, rather than specific.

The repertoire requirement for the Leventritt, for instance, was certainly as all-encompassing as that for any other major competition, even though there were almost no specific requirements. The only exception was that at least one of the three concertos offered by the applicant be by Mozart, Beethoven or Brahms. The required solo repertoire embraced in time about one and one half recital programs and had to include some large, major works. Which works they were was up to the contestant. Applications were checked by some of the judges, and those applicants who submitted insufficient material were asked for more. If, on the other hand, too much was offered, *that* applicant was advised to concentrate more on less, and was asked what he would like to remove. The idea was to find the best from each, without imposing an arbitrary list of compositions which, like roulette, would indiscriminately favor some contestants over others. After all, a major competition looks for a potential world-class artist, and whether he develops in the direction of a Horowitz or a Schnabel is not at all the point.

Rule-bending should also be observed, I believe, in the case of an extremely gifted person who displays a particular affinity for certain music even though it may be at the expense of something else. When teenaged Van Cliburn played Beethoven at the Leventritt, the judges were not as impressed as when he played Chopin, Liszt, Rachmaninoff and Tchaikovsky, which thrilled them beyond words. Yet if they had been using a point system, as many competitions do, his lower marks for Beethoven would have dragged down his "average," just like a grammar school report card. How silly! Yet this is the way winners of some important competitions are chosen. Surely, it is far more impressive to hear an extremely gifted young artist reach the heights in just one segment of the repertoire (provided, of course, that at no time does he sink beneath a certain level) than it is to hear a competent performer play the entire gamut of styles quite well. If all great artists were judged by what they play least well, nobody would be very good.

A competition in which the jury is obliged to select a winner
—or worse yet, first, second, third etc. prizewinners—is also
pointless, in my opinion. Suppose there is nobody outstanding
that year? Does that mean that the prize has to go to the least
worst? And in that case, since he doesn't measure up to the
abilities of the contest's previous winners, does that not lower
the caliber of the whole event? On the other hand, suppose
two extraordinarily talented contestants appear during the
same year. Why should it be necessary to choose one over the
other, if they're both worthy of winning?

I think that on the whole the Leventritt family, who sponsored and ran their competition, did a good job over the years
of helping individual contestants to achieve their best by not
asking them dogmatically to hew to a set of preordained rules.
But looking for someone who was "ready" for a career rather
than for someone simply better than the others meant that
maybe one out of every three Leventritt contests produced no
winner. Conversely, when Kyung-Wha Chung and Pinchas
Zukerman turned up at the same competition—a vintage year
for violinists!—the judges were able to award two equal prizes.

The Leventritt jury, and, to a slightly lesser extent, the jury
of the Tchaikovsky and Queen Elisabeth competitions, have
been as good a panel as one could hope for. When I say
"slightly lesser extent" for the other two, I mean very
specifically that in order to give the most international appearance possible, the organizers of these competitions always invite some of the judges simply to have more countries represented, even if they are in no way on a musical par with their
colleagues at these events. But in spite of this there is always at
least a nucleus of first-class musicians, and the proof is in the
excellent record of successful winners for these three competitions.

In fairness to other competitions, it must be said that the
most desirable judges are the most difficult to obtain. Although
some of the world's most prominent musicians may be willing
to give up a week every year or so for one particular competition, it is unlikely that they would consider sacrificing concert

or holiday time for more than that. This problem, incidentally, has created a species related to the "professional" contestant: a group of similarly single-minded judges, who appear on the jury of practically every competition, sharpened pencils and score-cards in hand.

At this point the informed reader may either smile or grimace, wondering if my appreciation for the Leventritt jury's ability stems entirely from my many years of membership in it. Modesty does not prevent me from praising its qualities, however. I was one of at least a dozen on an extremely outspoken panel. In spite of differences in our musical point of view, our decisions were either unanimous or very close. Arguments occurred mainly at the preliminary stages and mostly about who should be advanced to the second round. Those who were seriously considered as potential winners were hardly mentioned in the earlier rounds as their superiority was obvious.

Although competitions in all fields have existed since before the beginning of civilization, a new and humane school of thought is growing among music benefactors who have decided to reward excellence without forcing a young artist to endure the traditional agonies. "Competitions single out a certain type of performer, leaving the less aggressive artist to wither away, unheard and unloved," they reason. "By their very nature, they are unfair and cruel."

But so, unfortunately, is the life that an aspiring performing artist is seeking. One way or another, he will be competing as long as he is performing, whether he likes it or not. I am by no means suggesting that all young pianists must, or even should, enter competitions. But I do think that the neophyte's reaction to the atmosphere of such situations is a pretty good indicator of how suited he is emotionally for the kind of activity in which he hopes to spend his life. Far better that he should crumble under the tension of a competition, where he may be remembered as talented but not seasoned enough to appear in public, than during an orchestral performance with a conductor who will remember never to have anything to do with him again.

Entering a competition is only one way for a young artist to begin a career, and winning it does not guarantee instant Nirvana. For every winner of a major competition who is now in the mainstream of the concert circuit, there are at least another three who are not. Many noted performers have never won competitions or even entered them. (Among pianists, these include such artists as Horowitz, Serkin *père et fils*, Glenn Gould and Byron Janis.) But although winning a competition is certainly not the only way to advance a career, some of the other ways are not all that different. A performer by definition has to perform. And so if he doesn't begin by playing at a competition, then it is usually by auditioning for a conductor, which, of course, is a competition of another sort. Sometimes he tries to circumvent this step by scraping together some money and putting on a recital in New York or London. This, sadly, is usually a terrible waste. An unknown performer will rarely attract much of an audience, and good reviews, while pleasant to receive, usually don't mean very much to a conductor. I sometimes imagine what a conductor must think when a manager sends him a marvelous review about a young artist written by the same critic who savaged that conductor the week before. I can only hope that his feelings about the critic's judgment will not be vented on the innocent young artist (who the next time might be fortunate enough to be clobbered, and thus win the conductor's respect).

One of the first concerts I played after winning the Leventritt was in Buffalo with William Steinberg, and ever since then any slick brochure with dazzling reviews has reminded me of our conversation the afternoon I arrived. He asked if I would wait in his office a few minutes while he looked through the mail on his desk. I noticed a pile of envelopes with logos of the big concert managements. Steinberg carefully slit open each envelope, took out a brochure, shook it to see if there was anything else inside, and then threw it away without even a glance. When he saw my astonishment, he explained, "Oh, I have to open everything. After all, there might be a letter which concerns something that needs an answer. But as far as these leaflets are concerned, why should I look at them? Do you really think that there's any performer anywhere who doesn't have a dossier of rave reviews? And do you really think a manager is going to send a bad review?"

Ultimately, then, in the latter half of the twentieth century, a career for a soloist is only as good as the interest conductors have in him. Once I heard a simply terrible performance by someone I thought utterly without talent or even technique. He was playing with a famous orchestra. After the concert, I had supper with the conductor, and of course this disaster was mentioned. "You know," said the conductor, "Mr. _____ has played with us twice." I was amazed.

"Yes, twice," my friend continued. "Tonight. The first and last time."

CHAPTER SEVEN

Life Among the OYAPs

WHILE I WAS still under the Hurok management, I met through a friend a rather mysterious family who dwelt in splendid fashion on a sumptuous estate not far from the city. It was always interesting to visit them. They were very involved in politics; or rather, were very involved in being with very famous people who were very involved in politics. Actually, they did not limit their associations to any particular field. They liked to collect people from all walks of life with well-known names. Arthur Judson was one of them. So I met him socially a number of times at their home. Hurok, I think, did not feel inclined to play with this family, as he was never present at their parties. In addition, my hostess continually advised me to precipitate a falling-out with him. She seemed to want me to leave Hurok and, of course, to go with Judson.

I suspect, although I do not know, that they borrowed a certain amount of money from Judson before unaccountably vanishing a few years later. My suspicions, as well as my disenchantment with the family, dated from the afternoon Mme. X took me for coffee to a very elegant salon on Fifth Avenue, paid for two coffees and two pastries with a hundred-dollar bill (far more impressive then than now, alas!) and invited me to invest $1,000 in a business venture which would pay me back $1,100 a month later.

I didn't take her up on this financial speculation, but I did join the Judson Division of Columbia Artists Management, as she had so often suggested. And every three or four years, until he died a quarter of a century later, Mr. Judson would remind me of our mutual friends with a question that went something like, "Oh, say, by the way, Graffman" (I don't think he ever addressed any of his artists by either first name or title), "do you ever hear from those people—that lady—you know who I mean?" Although I never wished him any ill, it always amused me to think that someone as astute as Arthur Judson might possibly have been conned.

Mr. Judson (as I addressed him) was, after all, one of the founders of the Columbia Broadcasting System, not to mention the mega-management of which he was then honorary president. A.J. (as he was known to his closer associates) was gruff and pragmatic. He didn't mince words and he didn't waste much time on the kids. He was more involved, understandably, with Heifetz, conductors, his New York Philharmonic and the Grand Scheme of Things.

Nevertheless, there was a goodly group of my contemporaries on the Judson artist list. He seemed to specialize in pianists, and they came in all shapes, sizes and fees. Those of us who had yet to prove our commercial worth, however, rarely came into his presence during the normal course of events, except for an audience—something like a medical checkup—once a year or so. We were known as the OYAPs (Outstanding Young American Pianists), and our business affairs were attended to by several of his associates, who handled our bookings, if not our careers. Of course there were exceptions, but in general, I don't think that any of us was especially promoted by our management. While they may have liked some of us perfectly well, the motto seemed to be Wait and See If It Sinks or Swims. In the long run, this very likely was the most practical way of doing business with such unknown quantities. Nevertheless, I think it fair to say that a passionate lack of commitment characterized the way Mr. Judson treated most of the younger artists under his management.

Or at least the OYAPs. For A.J. loved to introduce foreign performers. Most of them seemed to be French lady pianists of a certain age, not to mention a certain inability to cope with the keyboard. Although they were generally as unknown in their own countries as they were in ours, they came cheap (remember what the franc was worth in the early fifties), and there's no denying that novelty is the spice of the concert business. Most conductors would accept—at least for the first and last time—any soloist their mentor, A.J., decreed appropriate. So there was a constant stream of these babes, usually with the sexy-sounding first names one might find in a different sort of establishment. They looked, unfortunately, not at all like their names, and descended each year, a plague of spinsters, to take all our dates away from us. Occasionally, however, one of them fell ill, giving one of us our Big Chance.

"Gary!" a voice on the phone, practically strangled with excitement, would shout. "Mme. _____ has twisted her thumb in Montreal—I've got you the concert—it's the Beethoven Fourth with Klemperer—you leave in ten minutes—the tickets will be waiting at Grand Central, Window 31—good luck!"

"Good luck or else," the voice should have said. For one of the things that never really seemed to be understood by most of our managers was that it is not in the best interest of a young and inexperienced artist to send him off to play a work for which he may have had only sketchy preparation as his debut with a major orchestra and conductor. The conductor, decent human being though he might occasionally be, is not interested in excuses. He is interested, rather, in a first-class performance, and he'll always remember a bad one. (It's amazing how conductors can forget fine performances, considering how

impeccable their memories are for the less good ones.) But the
"lucky" kid is in a real quandary, or at least that was the way it
was for most of us. For if he asks, "Do you really think it is
wise for me to do this? You know I've never played the Beethoven Fourth in public," or, "I haven't played the Fourth for a
year, and haven't touched it since then, as I'm not scheduled to
play it this season," the caller would rarely offer a negative, or
thoughtful, opinion. Either the voice on the other end of the
phone heartily cried some words of encouragement like, "Of
course you can do it! You play the piano, don't you?" or it
remained ominously silent. And we could be sure that if we
turned down the sugarplum that was dangling before us (and
who would want to, anyway?), there would always be that un-
said, "Well, you *had* your chance . . ." waiting to be uttered
on the day we asked for more business to be thrown our way.

Fortunately, Les Girls and their occasionally masculine coun-
terparts rarely returned more than a couple of times. But after
they'd done the American concert circuit once or twice, new
and fairly interchangeable models inevitably appeared to take
their places. So it was, indeed, pretty much a case of Sink or
Swim for most of us OYAPs, even though *we* were the envy of
less fortunate colleagues whose names didn't appear, like ours,
scattered among the greats on the lustrous lists of the major
concert managements, somewhat like the egg-and-onion gar-
nish on a plate of caviar.

In the early 1950s, Columbia Artists Management was composed of five divisions. Each division was almost like a separate
concert agency. (I believe they had all been so at one time and
eventually banded together like covered wagons on the prairie
to ward off enemy attacks.) Although they shared the same
offices and services, it is an understatement to say that there
was a good deal of rivalry between the divisions. At the time of
which I write, the Judson Division—then called Judson,
O'Neill and Judd—reigned supreme. I guess it had the largest
number of distinguished artists, if not the largest number of
artists, for whom it was responsible. Mr. Judson was already
over seventy, but a more vigorous gentleman would have been

hard to find at any age. Two of his colleagues, with whom I dealt on a more daily basis, were of similar age and vitality, although both were female.

Ruth O'Neill, who had started her career in the music business as Mr. Judson's secretary many years before when he was manager of the Philadelphia Orchestra, had risen to eminence at Columbia Artists, and was not only his right-hand lady but the treasurer of the corporation. It was she who doled out our advances when fallow periods, such as summertime, came upon us. (There weren't many summer festivals in those days, and whatever few there were didn't often invite us.) Miss O'Neill never failed to accompany the check with a little lecture on the virtues of frugality, especially in our risky business; and she was genuinely upset if she caught us in any frivolous spending, like going to the movies. The late critic Cecil Smith once wrote that she had "a brain like a cash register," and Willy Kapell was fond of saying, "Nickels roll out of her eyeballs."

But we were impatient. Willy, still in his twenties, had already made the big time, although his friends well remembered how, at the conclusion of his first season of touring for Columbia not long before, he received his final accounting with the observation, "Good. Now I can go and buy myself half a suit at Finchley's." So every now and then we would, without too much hope, beard Ruth O'Neill in her lair to try to convince her that for the following season our services were worthy of a higher fee. She would purse her lips and stare at the supplicant like a schoolteacher who's just been told by a favorite pupil that a term paper would be delivered late, and reply, in the sweetest, auntiest-like voice, "Dear, how *old* are you?" It was hard to carry much clout when the answer was "Nineteen." This scenario was played out for a number of years. "How *old* are you?" became an OYAP battle cry. We mimicked her whenever one of us complained that he wasn't making fast enough progress in his pursuit of the pearl of fame and fortune (if not wisdom). After Eugene had gone through this routine for about eight years, he fantasized the possibility of one day hobbling in to the treasurer's den, bald and gray-bearded, to

ask the annual question. "Eugene, how *old* are you?" the ancient crone behind the desk would quaver. "Ninety-three,"
Eugene would wheeze in reply. The thought became too much
for him to bear, and he betook himself to the Hurok Management.

As Ruth O'Neill was always anxious to assure us of our eternal childhood—"Why are you rushing things so? There's
plenty of time!"—Willy Kapell adopted the *ars longa, vita
brevis* attitude, and in certain instances acted as a most aggressive spokesman for younger colleagues in whose gifts he had
faith. He was sometimes accused of being a bad colleague,
mainly by those who felt the sting of his implacable honesty,
but he was actually exactly the opposite. If he believed in
someone, he would tell every conductor he played with (meaning just about all of them) about his protégé, hounding the
conductor mercilessly until the younger artist was engaged.
(He would also never hesitate to scream at conductors for
knuckling under to management pressure and engaging somebody—like one of the French ladies—he felt was without
talent.) Once he overdid his enthusiasm with Ormandy, who
allegedly scolded him, "Listen, if you mention the name of
_____ to me once again, *you'll* never play with me any
more!" That shut Willy up for at least twenty-four hours, but
in the end, he did manage to work things out for his buddy,
opening the door to a lasting musical relationship.

The other lady in the Judson office was Ada Cooper. Her
title was Booking Director, and she was a legendary sales-
woman. She was younger than A.J. and Ruth O'Neill, I believe
—probably only in her sixties at the time. But in the twenty-
five years I knew her I don't believe she changed at all. She was
small, dark and rather birdlike in looks, with a voice that was a
cross between a croak and a shriek. She also retained a bit of
the brogue of her native Belfast and had a minor speech im-
pediment which made her r's sound like w's. I doubt that anyone who ever heard it could forget that extraordinary sound.
(Many years later, I am told, when Sir Clifford Curzon arrived
in New York for his biennial United States tour, he was set-

tling himself in his hotel suite when the phone rang. He picked it up. "CWIIIIFFFOOOOD?" a voice cried. "Ada! How are you?" replied Sir Clifford. "HOW DID YOU WECOGNIZE MY VOICE?" shrieked Ada.)

Ada had total recall, and could recite who played what where and for how much with an accuracy that was nothing short of stunning. Clients, upon entering her office, were like mosquitoes caught in a giant spider web. Or perhaps it was more like walking on quicksand. The more they struggled, the deeper they were sucked in. Ada had a weakness, though: As soon as she sensed a kill, she started to lower the fee that she had originally proposed. I guess the point was to make the artist in question totally irresistible. (This, of course, was at a time when most of her clients suffered from what is now pityingly referred to as "Depression Era mentality," and did not think, as many concert presenters do today, that the more outrageously high a sum they pay for an artist's services the better a performance they'll get.) However, by the time Ada locked up any dates for me—whose asking fee in 1951 was a ripe $400—there really wasn't much left over for the frivolities that Ruth O'Neill was so anxious for us to avoid.

The fourth member of the management team with whom I was involved was William Judd, who I suppose was being groomed to take over for A.J. eventually. He was young, Bostonian and a gentleman. He was also a second-generation concert manager, as his father, the distinguished silver-haired George E. Judd, was then manager of the august Boston Symphony Orchestra. Bill's younger brother, George Jr., handled the press affairs of this management division, and eventually rose to the post of manager of the New York Philharmonic before his untimely death in 1961 at the age of thirty-six.

Although Bill arranged the bookings, guided the careers and listened to the complaints of a large group of artists in this division, the responsibility for my affairs fell nominally in the bailiwick of Ruth O'Neill and Ada Cooper. Nevertheless, I felt the most rapport with Bill. He seemed the only one more interested in the long-range building of a career than in the fast buck. He was as much of an idealist as it was possible for a businessman to be (or perhaps it was the other way around), and considering him a friend as well as a manager, I adopted him. We also developed a close, if rather odd, relationship around 1953, when my wife became his secretary. Naomi had come to work for Columbia Artists the previous year, before we were married, following a stint at the magazine *Musical America*. She loved her job at Columbia and adored her boss. But I know that her feeling of guilt at being in a position where she might be suspected of using some influence to help my career in any way caused her to attempt precisely the opposite. As a result, she never took my part in any arguments I had with my managers, a nasty habit she maintains to this day. But we both became good friends with Bill, and had many memorable, if somewhat liquid, evenings together.

Having a wife at Columbia Artists did, however, offer one benefit aside from the obvious one of her small income's supplementing my small income. This was the luscious gossip to which she was privy, and which she brought home like bones to a dog. We would gnaw these scraps with great gusto at the dinner table, as installments of earth-shattering events unfolded. One such drama occurred during the first American tour of what was then called the Philharmonia Orchestra of London. Herbert von Karajan was to conduct, and these concerts were to mark his American debut. Many concertgoers were disturbed by his scheduled appearances because of his unsavory wartime reputation, but in spite of this, the two New York concerts that had been set were sold out almost as soon as announced. Karajan and/or his advisers thus decided that an extra concert was in order, and they so informed Ruth O'Neill. Her cash-register brain did some quick calculations, and she suggested that they leave well enough alone. But her advice was ignored and she was instructed to book Carnegie Hall for the extra concert. In this instance, Ruth O'Neill's prudence was not overcautious. It seemed that everyone who wanted to hear Karajan and the Philharmonia had already bought tickets for the other concerts. There was no activity at the box office, and as the

concert date drew ever closer, many meetings took place in the
offices of Columbia to dream up a lure for the public.

Up to that time, no Soviet artist had played in the United
States since the war, and although David Oistrakh had already
been scheduled for his debut recital in New York, that was to
take place later in the season. So the thought occurred to management that perhaps Oistrakh could advance this debut, and
introduce himself to the New York public as soloist with
Karajan. As interest in Soviet artists was semihysterical then, an
Oistrakh appearance would assure a sellout. While negotiations
to obtain his services were going on, news of this possibility
somehow leaked, although no official announcement was ever
made. Nevertheless, business began to pick up at the Carnegie
Hall box office, even though the program announced for the
concert in question had no violin concerto listed.

Then, by some mysterious means, word filtered over to the
Soviet agency in charge of the musical negotiations reminding
them of whom, exactly, Oistrakh would be aiding by playing
this concert. The next thing anyone knew, it had been decided
that he would not, after all, be making his debut with Karajan
and the Philharmonia. That Sunday there appeared a curious
item in the music section of the New York *Times* to the effect
that in spite of the fact that there had never been an announcement that Oistrakh *was* going to play at that concert,
this was an announcement that he was *not* going to play.

The next morning, Naomi reported, a near riot occurred at
the Columbia office. As every concert- and theatergoer knows,
POSITIVELY NO EXCHANGES OR REFUNDS are available for purchased tickets. Technically, therefore, nobody was responsible
to make a refund to anyone who had bought a ticket to a concert on the basis of a rumor that a certain artist might appear.
But so many irate customers besieged the Carnegie Hall box
office that Monday that they were eventually shooed along to
the Columbia offices across the street, where, I believe, arrangements for refunds were made in order to avoid bloodshed.

When the smoke cleared, the unfortunate presenters of this
concert were once again confronted with the looming specter

of an empty auditorium. Orders went forth to the Columbia
employees to "dress it up." This meant they were to give away
as discreetly as possible as many tickets as possible. Naomi was
given the Dress Circle to dispose of. Since the chances of filling
that vast space with bodies—particularly at the last minute—
seemed dismal, she conceived the plan of at least dressing the
Dress Circle artistically, in some sort of design, perhaps, somewhat reminiscent of the way cheering sections at football
games are often deployed. What, after all, could be a more cordial greeting for Karajan as he faced whatever audience there
was for his initial bow than a healthy, old-fashioned Anglo-
Saxon expression spelled out in people? (After all, it *was* an
English orchestra.) Sadly, this dream of glory never materialized because, as Naomi explained, "I never could find enough
audience to spell out more than the first letter!"

During those years I had a modest number of concerts each
season, usually highlighted by a few major engagements. Although a goodly number of these did come about because of
someone else's illness, an increasing portion, comfortingly, had
my name on the contract from the beginning. I had already
played with some of the big orchestras as a competition winner,
and gradually I began to play with others. Some of these dates
were the result of requests from conductors, but most were gar-
nered through the wily persistence of Ada Cooper and her co-
horts, one of them being a nice young blond fellow who had
just joined the staff, name of Schuyler Chapin.

When I look back, I am amazed at how well we lived then.
We had a small apartment carved out of part of the parlor
floor of a walk-up in the West Eighties, and it seems as if we
had parties every week, often using first-growth Bordeaux of
1947 and 1949 vintages as our ordinary table wines. During the
summer of 1954 we rented a very small bungalow on Long Island. We didn't have a car, and Naomi was the weekend com-
muter. She came out by train every Friday evening, stopping at
the market near the station to pick up provisions, which she
carried (neither of us can remember how) the mile and a half
to our cottage. She left Sunday night, again on foot, for the

train station. During the weekdays I was alone, and although I
occasionally went to sea in a rowboat with a portable radio to
listen to the McCarthy hearings, mainly I practiced an enormous amount. I learned a great deal of repertoire including, I
remember, the Beethoven Opus 110 Sonata and the Tchaikovsky B-flat minor Concerto.

Another work I learned then was the MacDowell D minor
Concerto, which I was scheduled to play in a special bicen-
tennial concert that Columbia University was putting on in
Carnegie Hall that fall. The program was made up of music by
composers who were, in one way or another, associated with
Columbia University. They had engaged the New York Philharmonic and Stokowski to conduct.

I had never played with Stokowski, and at that time he was
not admired tremendously by my colleagues or me. We would
never buy his recordings of anything if there was a Toscanini,
Walter, Koussevitzky or Rodzinski version available. Nowadays, when I listen to the old Stokowski records my only conclusion is that I was crazy.

Nevertheless, come November, I was to play MacDowell
with Stokowski and the New York Philharmonic at Carnegie
Hall. It has always been particularly difficult for me, as I guess
it is for practically every performer, to play a work for the first
time. No matter how diligently one has practiced, one feels insecure, to say the least. This feeling is at least doubled if the
first performance is in a big city. I didn't have the opportunity
to give the MacDowell any out-of-town tryouts, so in my usual
pedantic fashion I diligently practiced and repracticed it, playing it over and over with friends accompanying on the second
piano.

So I came to the first rehearsal well prepared, but it did seem
to me that the sounds emanating from the orchestra had not
much relation to what I had been expecting. Also, we were not
together most of the time, and Stokowski wasn't stopping the
orchestra at all. I stopped a few times, but things didn't really
improve with repetition. When the rehearsal stumbled to its
conclusion I was extremely depressed and angry. I spoke to

some of the orchestra members I knew. They were uncon-
cerned, assuring me, "Don't worry. This is normal for a work
Stoky doesn't know." I didn't understand why that meant I
shouldn't worry, but then one of them explained, "The thing is
that he learns incredibly fast. So he figures, why should he
study on his own time when he can do it on the Philharmonic's? Wait until tomorrow." I remained unconvinced when
Stokowski walked over to me and said, "This is a new piece for
me, young man. Is there anything you want to go over or discuss before the dress rehearsal?" I replied, "A great deal." He
said, "Then come to my dressing room and we will go over the
score." I did, and while Bill Judd bought Naomi an appropriate
number of martinis—she claims seven—in the Russian Tea
Room next door, we went over every page, practically phrase by
phrase. I had the feeling that after a few minutes of listening
to my passionate comments Stokowski began to look at me
with amusement, but I didn't care; I was mad, and I told him
everything about the music that was on my mind.

At the dress rehearsal the following day, not only was
Stokowski completely accurate and well-studied but he somehow commanded from the orchestra the kind of sound that he
was so famous for producing. It was as if he and they had been
playing the piece for years. The performance was similar. (I
subsequently received a kind of thank-you letter from Mrs.
MacDowell, slightly different from what one would expect a
composer's widow to write: After the obligatory compliments
about the success of the performance, she commented, "Musically I've always felt the concerto was not too good, but it *is*
very effective, nevertheless.") I do remember particularly how
gorgeous the sound of the orchestra was. So Stokowski had, in
fact, learned on the Philharmonic's time. Although it worked
for him, this is not a method I recommend for young conductors.

It is sad that in his later years Stokowski was never accorded
the kind of veneration that his abilities and especially his
unique sense of sonority deserved. How wonderful it would be
if, at that time, when he was still at the peak of his powers and

when recording techniques had already been developed to such remarkable heights, he had been given the possibility to record all his sonic extravaganzas with really great orchestras. Still, it is undeniable that the pre-LP, pre-hi-fi, pre-stereo discs that he made with the Philadelphia Orchestra (the very ones I so pompously maligned as a teenager) compare amazingly well with the electronic miracles currently flooding the market. Too bad there weren't more of them. By the way, I remember seeing Stokowski, several years later, standing rather forlornly by the entrance to Philharmonic Hall after the concert that had opened that auditorium to the public for the first time. He stood there, a wattled old man, shaking his fluffy white mane and muttering, "If only they had asked me!" No comment necessary.

A few weeks after the Columbia University concert I played again with the New York Philharmonic, this time on their regular series, with Szell conducting. My admiration for Szell was as great as my distrust of Stokowski had been, and the concerto I was to play—the Prokofiev Third—was much more solidly in my repertoire than the MacDowell, so I approached these concerts with far less trepidation. A lesson that booby traps lurk everywhere awaited me.

During the Sunday afternoon performance—the one that was broadcast, live—at the very beginning of the concerto, where the tempo changes from *andante* to *allegro*, and before the piano has even made its first entrance, Szell gave his usual impeccable beat. But for some inexplicable reason, some sections of the orchestra played their parts exactly twice as fast as they should have, and twice as fast as the rest of the orchestra. Though the music still fit the beat, disaster loomed ever closer. The time was approaching for my first entrance, but I really didn't know at which point I should jump in. I could see the back of Szell's head turning red and I felt like someone who had been tied to the railroad tracks as a train whistle is heard in the distance. The train whistle, in this case, was the flute flourish just before the piano's scheduled entrance, and John Wummer, the motorman—or rather, the first flutist—desperately caught my eye and then played, "Wheeeep!" But it didn't seem to me like the right time to come in yet, so I didn't. He played "Wheeeep!" a second time. Silence from the keyboard. Then, after the third "Wheeeep," I finally took the plunge. Almost immediately everything righted itself. Szell made some magic passes in the air and led the orchestra safely across the Red Sea.

After the performance, as we left the stage together, Szell glowered at me and snapped, "What happened?" although he knew, of course, that for once his soloist was innocent, since I could have done nothing wrong before I was even expected to play. I don't think he meant to blame me, but was honestly seeking information. Neither of us could ever figure out what actually *did* happen, and I sometimes wonder whether, if I had made my entrance against my instincts at either the first or second "Wheeeep," anything different would have occurred. In any case, the incident gave Szell the opportunity to make a few trenchant observations on the reason, and the only reason, why things got together again: Unlike some of his young colleagues, he had had the old-fashioned training of working in opera houses before doing anything else. "After dealing with tenors," he explained, "the New York Philharmonic is child's play." I am sure he was right, as he was in almost everything.

Later, when I was given a transcription of this broadcast, I could hardly bring myself to put the record on. I very rarely listen to tapes or records of performances I have given, but in this case curiosity drove me to play it to see what actually did take place. After hearing it, I was still not sure. Those few measures came and went so quickly I could hardly make out what was going on, which seemed very odd since, while it was happening, it seemed to take at least three or four hours.

Szell, incidentally, felt the same way about Philharmonic Hall when it first opened as Stokowski did, although, unlike the latter, his association with it was more intimate, as he conducted there during the inaugural week. He instantly condemned it as a "Scheisshalle"; described the acoustic clouds that had lights in their centers as "pregnant frogs with illuminated belly buttons"; and prescribed that the only sensible way to improve it would be to "tear the whole place down and start all over again." In effect, that is what eventually was done, proving once again Szell's omniscience.

And so my years as an OYAP under the benevolent if somewhat absentminded guidance of Arthur Judson and his crew continued. Thanks largely to Ada Cooper's tenacity and Bill Judd's imagination my position steadily improved. Bill bagged an RCA recording contract for me—no small feat either then or now—and I began to record with some big orchestras. This happy turn of events brought me into contact with one of the nicest conductors I've ever met: Charles Munch, then the music director of the Boston Symphony. We had a cordial relationship, extending over many years, that consisted mainly of large smiles. I must have played with him dozens of times, but I can't remember that we ever engaged in any form of conversation. This was at least partially due to the fact that we didn't admit to sharing a common language. I would never have dreamed of using my schoolboy French in his presence, and he would never confess—until he left the Boston Symphony and returned, safe at last, to Paris—that he had excellent command of English. During his years in Boston, he hid this accomplishment very successfully behind a smoke screen named Leonard Burkat, who, under the title of Music Administrator (a post which Erich Leinsdorf later described as "*de facto* music director"), nobly served as Munch's interpreter and kept the world—or at least the non-French-speaking world—at bay.

Anyway, Munch was very different from most conductors. I always had the impression that he would go out of his way to avoid making trouble. And so, when our mutual recording company judged it appropriate for me to give the world my interpretation of the Brahms D minor Concerto in collaboration with him and his orchestra, he graciously agreed.

Prior to making the recording, we gave a long string of performances in Boston and—as the Boston Symphony management designated such cities as New York, Philadelphia and Washington—"the provinces." Although I had prepared assiduously and played the best I knew how, there was one particular passage in the first movement that always gave me trouble as far as hitting the right notes were concerned. It involved big jumps in the right hand, and try as I might, I would always hit some clinkers in the same place each time. No matter that this thorny passage has stung many pianists who pass its brambly way; the fact that it had been muffed by others didn't make me any happier. But Munch never seemed in any way perturbed; actually, he appeared not to notice. The night before our Carnegie Hall performance, however, when we were playing in New Haven, Eugene came along to check things out. He was a great friend of Munch's (his French is first-class), and after the concert was closeted for a rather long time in Munch's dressing room. He then returned to my dressing room, choking with laughter.

"I have a message for you," he announced. Taking the score, Eugene pointed to my trouble spot and chortled, "He asked . . . he said to me, 'Tell your friend—would you be so kind, my dear?—tell your friend that he seems, perhaps, to have misread a few notes here.'"

A couple of years later, Munch treated me with even greater tenderness. I'd had a hell of a time getting from Seattle to Boston because of blizzards everywhere. Having missed the last connecting flight in Chicago, the only thing to do was to fly to New York and then creep up on Boston via the Midnight Owl, a sleeper train on which I did not sleep, arriving just in time for the morning rehearsal. This time we were playing the Chopin E minor Concerto, and I remember being entranced as I listened to the orchestra play the entire opening *tutti* (which at that time was frequently truncated with an enormous cut). My entrancement may actually have taken the form of a doze, because at a certain point I realized, as if in a dream, that it was time for me to begin to play. I did so; but instead of playing the opening chords I started sixteen bars later, with the *espressivo* theme. The sounds I made on my favorite piano, sent up from New York for the concerts, were so lovely that it took a while before I noticed that the orchestral accompaniment didn't match at all. The orchestra seemed to be playing something completely different, which of course it was. This continued for a few more measures, and things began to sound queerer and queerer. I kept doggedly on. Eventually, I became conscious that Munch had stopped conducting, left the podium, come up behind me, put his arms around me, shaken me gently and pleadingly asked, "*Qu'est-ce que tu as, mon vieux?*" (We were friends by then.) Much raucous laughter followed, and at the beginning of each performance of that series, I remember seeing the face of Joseph de Pasquale, then the first violist in Boston, peek around from the rear of the piano, where the violists were seated, to satisfy himself that I was awake. (Years later, after he had moved to the Philadelphia Orchestra, he continued to do it there.)

Another kindly conductor of that era was Josef Krips. During the same season that I played the Brahms D minor with Munch and his orchestra in various cities and at several periods during the year, I also played it with Krips in Montreal and a few times in and around Los Angeles as well. Munch favored fast tempos and more or less gave me my head when I chose to race through the last movement. Krips, on the other hand, had a Viennese outlook and kept slowing me down. (He also liked to make sure that the orchestra didn't overpower the soloist and had a habit of crying out at rehearsal, "Disappear! Vanish! *Evaporate!*" while bending his knees and curling himself up, becoming shorter and shorter and shorter until I feared that *he* would evaporate, in a puff of smoke, at the very least.) Over the course of that winter I'd alternate between a fast Brahms with Munch and a slow one with Krips until I began to feel like a Ping-Pong ball. Left to my own devices, I liked to play it fast, but eventually I became convinced of the validity of the slower tempo and by the springtime when I returned to Boston to record the piece, the last movement was considerably different from what it had been in November. (In later years I played it even slower.) Munch accepted this amiably, with no comment; most agreeable, as always.

Although in some ways Krips was less detached from the real

world than Munch, he was more mystical, and he always asked to be alone for a few minutes before each performance, during which he would pray. I think I found out eventually to whom some of his prayers may have been addressed. It came about when we were discussing repertoire for a future season. I suggested a Beethoven concerto. Krips agreed, but wanted to be sure I realized that, as far as he was concerned, Beethoven was not the be-all and end-all of music.

"Beethoven reaches the heavens, that is true," he assured me. "But," he continued, with a divine light in his eye, "it is Mozart . . . Mozart . . . who lives there."

As I began to learn a bit about the foibles of great conductors, I also learned that great orchestras have distinctive personalities, too. It was well known that among them the New York Philharmonic required the most delicate handling. After all, Toscanini had been its music director. Who could hope to match him? Thus the orchestra seemed to greet each new conductor with all sorts of little tests, not only of talent, but of will. (This testing perpetuated itself through generations, and years later, players who weren't even born when Toscanini resigned from the Philharmonic-Symphony—as it was then called—still required proof that a conductor was worthy of them.) A guest conductor walked a tightrope over a yawning—and I use that word advisedly—chasm: no net, and one hundred turtlenecked alligators smiling up at him. Once I was playing with a young guest conductor, and I knew he would go to the top when I heard, at the first rehearsal, the following exchange:

Conductor, to clarinetist: "Could you please play that a little louder?"

(Passage is repeated and clarinetist still can't be heard.)

Conductor, to clarinetist: "A little louder please—I still can't hear you."

Clarinetist, to conductor (snippily—are you telling me my business?): "I'm playing as loud as I can."

(A moment's silence. Will this start a scene? One false move and the conductor will disappear forever within the smiling alligator jaws. Pause. Finally:)

Conductor to orchestra (kindly): "Well then, I guess we'll all have to play a little softer."

At the concert, needless to say, the clarinetist's solo soared gloriously above all else.

Ceremonial observances, I soon gathered, were necessary warm-ups to successful performances. Szell chomped on chocolate or raisins for quick energy; Ormandy swallowed salt tablets; Krips prayed; with the Philharmonic, ritual wolf-fights occurred upon a guest conductor's invasion of their turf. Gradually I devised my personal set of sacraments. The first of these, passed along by my father, who had been in a position to notice absentminded soloists when he was concertmaster in Minneapolis, was to double-check that I was buttoned (or, later, zipped) just before starting to walk out onstage. (Even Heifetz, my father told me, had overlooked this once.) The second ritual, yet more crucial (as I discovered as soon as I began to appear at open-air summer festivals), was to wash the piano keys.

Changes of temperature and humidity, especially out of doors, cause a film of moisture to condense on the keyboard. This, plus my own sweat from the earlier rehearsal, plus that of the tuner who comes to work on the instrument afterward, often causes the keyboard to attain the consistency of mucilaginous cod-liver oil. The problem first came to my attention at an outdoor concert in Milwaukee when, with youthful *panache*, I majestically descended on the low E-flat in the opening cadenza of the "Emperor" Concerto. Although my aim was impeccable, the E-flat (due to circumstances beyond my control) was rapidly followed by an unintended E-natural and then a momentary absence of any sound at all as my finger slipped off the piano entirely. The remedy was to arrive early and wash each key carefully with witch hazel, alcohol or just plain water. (Beginning the "Emperor" more carefully also helped.) Although stagehands often offer to do this cleaning chore for me when they see me approach the piano in my white concert jacket bearing a handful of wet and dry towels—or in a pinch, sometimes even streamers of toilet paper—I must do it myself in order to feel really safe. Even the best plans can be foiled, though. Once, a stagehand who had been instructed to polish the piano—not by me, certainly!—did so. He polished all of it, including the keyboard. This was discovered about fifteen minutes before concert time when I approached the piano, which was still offstage, and smelled synthetic lemon. Furniture polish on plastic keys is about the best formula to cause a pianist to give up his profession. I scrubbed the keys with everything in sight, but although the rags and paper towels became permeated with the furniture polish, there didn't seem to be one iota less on the keys. Finally, somebody got the bright idea of dusting them with rosin—in powdered form, like talcum. By the time I walked out to play, this stuff had combined with the residue of furniture polish, and the keys felt like melting asphalt mixed with used bubble gum, and the only thing I can say about my performance that evening was that I was stuck with it.

In spite of occasional disasters caused by anything from lemon-scented pianos to fouled-up transportation schedules (although in one memorable instance the latter redounded to my benefit when I was able to substitute in Columbia, Missouri, for a colleague who missed the date, having been misrouted to Columbia, South Carolina), I was soon playing enough concerts to support a full-time wife, and Naomi, with a certain amount of ambivalence, retired from the office battlefront. But we were not completely deprived of gossip, thanks to our lasting friendships among some of her former colleagues. As we were on the road most of the time, though, and much of it abroad, only the most vital reports reached our ears. Artists and employees came and left. Ada Cooper retired, was given a testimonial dinner, a gold watch and a mink stole, and was back at her desk the next morning. When she was finally made to understand that "retirement" meant "home," Schuyler Chapin became the new booking director of the Judson artists division. In 1959, Schuyler, who had four very hungry sons, asked Ruth

O'Neill for a minimal raise. I think it was something like five dollars a week. She must have rolled her blue eyes at him and said, "Schuyler, how *old* are you?" because he promptly left for bigger and better things, starting as Director of Artists and Repertoire for Columbia Masterworks Records.

By 1963, Arthur Judson had reached practically a generation beyond normal retirement age. But he resisted all invitations to step down that were first subtly and then less delicately extended to him by other members of the Board at CAMI, as Columbia Artists was by then known. When, finally, he and Ruth O'Neill were voted out, or actually forced by the Board to retire, they did not, as people in their eighties are commonly expected to do, plop down on rocking chairs in some sunny clime. Nor did Ruth hole up somewhere, as she had frequently threatened, to write her memoirs, which were to be entitled *Bitches and Bastards I Have Known*. No. Instead, they rented a small office a few buildings east of the CAMI headquarters on Fifty-seventh Street, where they speedily set up what was in effect a government-in-exile.

At first this geriatric kingdom followed a benign course. Old friends and well-wishers were the only visitors, dropping in to pay homage to the deposed sovereigns. However, these sovereigns had other plans. One day Frederick Steinway, then affiliated with his family's piano company next door, stopped by to pay his respects, and found himself seduced.

"I only intended to say 'hello,' " Fritz (as he is most often called) reported. "But before I knew what was happening, they offered me a job." He accepted.

Next to succumb was Harry Beall, who had worked at CAMI as a sales representative—his efforts in my behalf contributing mightily to Naomi's early retirement—and then as Bill Judd's assistant. He had left a couple of years later to become press representative of the Boston Symphony. In town with the orchestra one day, Harry made a courtesy call on his former associates, and before *he* bid farewell to the octogenarians he had mentally moved his family back to New York.

So the two young men joined forces with the two retirees

and formed a new management. Initially, however, they were zookeepers without a menagerie.

Although I was still under contract to CAMI, I had begun to be frustrated by its ever inflating size and sprawling impersonality. After Ada and Schuyler and Harry had moved on—and now even Ruth and A.J., who at least offered the comfort of familiarity—only Bill Judd was left, of the original troupe, to tilt on my behalf at the corporate windmills.

In any case, having been the first person to notice that the new management's title of Judson, O'Neill, Beall and Steinway was an unintentional acronym for JOBS, I became intrigued by this combination of the old and the new, even though the most trenchant conversations I'd had with Mr. Judson during the past few years consisted mostly of his harrumphing, "Oh, by the way, Graffman, do you ever hear from those people—err, that lady—mmmm—you know who I mean?"

CHAPTER EIGHT

Measles
Across America,
or
Smile When You Bow

AMONG THE JOYS and horrors of being an OYAP were the recitals we gave under the auspices of an organization known, cozily, as "Community." Its official title was Community Concert Service (or, sometimes, Community Concerts, Inc.) and it was a subsidiary of Columbia Artists Management, as its counterpart, Civic Concert Service, was affiliated with the other giant management, then known as National Concerts and Artists Corporation, and which included the Hurok list. The purpose of these subsidiaries was to bestow a blessing called the Organized Audience Plan upon the cities, towns, villages and hamlets across North America whose music associations didn't feel up to tackling the financial risk or intellectual chore of engaging artists independently. Via the Organized Audience Plan, everything was neatly arranged for them by Big Brother.

Community's Big Brother, at the time of which I write, was a folksy gentleman with a flat, Midwestern accent and the unfortunate habit of greeting us with the cheery cry of "Hiya, feller!" usually accompanied by a hearty thump on the back or a friendly punch on the shoulder. His name was Ward French, and he had been involved with this organized-audience concept since its introduction in the twenties, so he knew just what was necessary. He assumed that the audience Out There was composed of musical illiterates and ensured their remaining ever thus by convincing them that they were getting culture while providing them with what he thought they *really* wanted. And what Brother Ward decreed they wanted was mostly ensembles like the quintet of nubile harpists who wore bouffant white gowns and assumed beatific smiles in spite of the evil thoughts running through their heads (I know this because most were Curtis graduates) as they plucked ardently away at a five-harp arrangement of *The Swan*. The Angelaires, as this gang of five was called, could then be followed at the next concert by a dose of medicine known as Rudolf Serkin, as long as the following event—the Men of Song, or, even better, the Revelers—then arrived on the scene to dispel any lingering taste of unsweetened Beethoven. To be sure, Community was in business to make money and not to educate the masses, but I guess what riled us fellers so much was the sanctimonious attitude that pervaded the pandering.

The system was honed to razor sharpness. Each year, the music clubs affiliated with Community or Civic were visited by their duly appointed sales representatives (or organization directors, as they were discreetly described), sent from New York or one of the other centrally located offices, to plan the next season's concert series. These series, by the way, were exactly that. Subscribers bought, for an extremely reasonable sum, seats for the entire package of four or more concerts, and nobody was permitted to buy a ticket for a single event. It was all or nothing. Once the annual subscription drive was complete and the money was in the bank, there was never any doubt as to how much would be available to pay for engaging the artists. The subscription campaign was planned with all the strategy of a presidential race. Nothing was left to chance. It lasted about a week and involved a gala banquet, speeches about the benefits of culture, much doorbell and phone ringing, and tantalizing descriptions of which artists and attractions could be hired to perform in the local auditorium if the budget met the fees required. After the money was raised, and only then, came the actual booking. It goes without saying that the Community salesmen offered artists under the management they represented, while the Civic organizers similarly looked after their own.

During the middle fifties, the government brought an antitrust suit against these two concert managements for maintaining such organizations with the result that, technically at least, all artists from all managements henceforth became available to be booked on these Organized Audience Series. This is, however, more true on paper than in actuality. I don't think it really matters any more, though, because nowadays things have changed considerably as the level of musical sophistication throughout the country has risen (in spite of Ward French's notions of what the public really wanted), and good music in many forms is vastly more accessible everywhere: there are infinitely more college and university musical series now, and chamber music runs rampant; there is an abundance of young orchestras, and even those that existed twenty or thirty years ago have far longer seasons than formerly; records and tapes make almost all music available effortlessly and inexpensively, usually in several versions, and FM radio provides an important contribution. So, while the Organized Audience Plan still exists (although in a somewhat reduced way), I don't think there is much need for it any more. But during the time we OYAPs were getting our start, Community Concerts was, for lack of anything better, a reasonably valid idea for most small towns, and Organized pap was eagerly suckled by the hungry hinterlands.

After the campaigns were run and the concert budgets determined, certain "attractions" (as the soloists and groups were called) would be suggested to the music associations as appropriate for their particular series. The proportion of groups to soloists seemed to grow from year to year. Of the solo artists, singers—especially coloratura sopranos—were fine, violinists were okay, cellists were poison, and, thank God, pianists were the most popular and there rarely was a series without one. The glowing brochures which described our amazing talents to the would-be subscribers also served the purpose, we hoped, of titillating the sales representatives upon whose enthusiasm we imagined a good part of our income depended. In addition to the printed word, there was the annual conference, or convention, for the representatives' education, which took place in New York and at which we were regularly called upon to demonstrate our wares. Each year, one or another of us would be expected to play about twenty minutes' worth of our most razzle-dazzle repertoire for what was, in effect, an audition for the Community sales staff. We'd put on our afternoon formals and our company manners and hope that they meant half of what they never failed to say about our astounding and unique gifts.

Exactly who was appropriate or available to exactly what series in what cities actually depended on the way routing could be most conveniently scheduled. This was more important than what the representatives truly thought about us. With the major solo artists, the Community availability was predicated on filling in any gaps between important engagements, and with the groups it was, of course, economically essential that the tours be routed to proceed in an orderly fashion. There was also a special category of solo artist, whose entire and usually brief career consisted almost exclusively of Organized Audience engagements. He often drove himself from date to date and therefore, as with the groups, his itinerary had almost Rockette-like precision. With the OYAPs though, there was a certain amount of arbitrary decision: we were pretty much peas in a pod, so it didn't really matter who went where, as long as every place was covered. Thus, one year I'd be told, "You're not going to the Coast next season because you were there last year. But you'll be available to West Texas and Northern Ohio instead." (They had the country sliced up into neat little sections.) Actually, this was all perfectly sensible, and the intention was certainly to arrange our Community concerts in such a way that travel time and expenses were minimized. As with most noble efforts, though, it didn't always work. And even in cases where the routing turned out to be ideal, there might be a hole in our concert schedule which would leave us with three days to kill between cities like East Lynn and West Lynn, Alabama.

But they tried hard, these doughty purveyors of culture, and Lord knows we needed every penny we could net. From our fees for ordinary, non-Community concerts (referred to as "straight sales"), we paid, in addition to all our expenses, a management commission of 20 percent. For Community concerts (never referred to as "crooked sales"), the management commission was only 15 percent. The catch lay in something called "the differential." This was a margin between our normal concert fee, which was paid by the local Community association to Community Concerts, and an established lower fee which eventually found its way to us. For example, in my early days, I would be "sold" to a Community series for my normal fee of $400, but I would actually receive only $250, from which would then be deducted the 15 percent commission. The margin contributed to the running expenses of Community and was, in other words, the razor strop on which the organization's blades were ground so smoothly. These margins were (and indeed still are) on a sliding scale. But the scale is inversely comparable to taxation in that the lower the fee, the larger the percentage of differential. It figures that an artist whose manager is having no trouble filling his tours would just as soon not get involved with Community, unless, of course, he raises his Community fee proportionately higher than his normal fee to make up for the differential that subsidizes Community's coffers. I guess the simplest description of this cumbersome procedure is that the fees are akin to wholesale and retail: Community associations pay the top retail price, and the manufacturer, or rather, the artist, gets the wholesale price for his merchandise.

And there's no doubt that merchandise was exactly what we were to the Community sellers and buyers. Some of us were packaged brightly and some were perhaps a bit shopworn, but one thing applied to all of us: we were a commodity to be purchased, consumed and disposed of. No matter how we might triumph on the stages of those high school auditoriums; no matter how wildly cheered we were during our nightly standing ovations; no matter how effusive the compliments delivered over punch and cookies at the receptions afterward or how ecstatic the reports transmitted to the home office next day, the chances of our ever returning to that particular concert series again were virtually nil.

"Graffman?" the president of the local association could be heard to muse a while later. "Oh, yes. He was here a few years ago." (Brightening.) "He was simply sensational!" To the logical next question, however, the answer was inevitable: "Oh, we all simply loved him. But of course we can't use him on our series next year. You see, we've already *had* him."

As Cecil Smith described it, "An artist, like a case of measles, was something to be experienced once in a lifetime."

On the other hand, there were a thousand towns—actually— which subscribed to Community at that time. So, at an average of twenty Community concerts per season (more than I ever played, although I do remember someone who broke ninety-five and then disappeared forever), the supply of new cities in which to be "had" was as endless as the supply of artists.

Playing the Community circuit had very little to do with music. Success depended not so much on how you played but on how you behaved. The key was charm: charm before, during and especially after the concert. The sponsors would never fail to send a report back to New York, and repercussions were felt if the slightest lack of charm was detected. "Smile when you bow!" Ruth O'Neill admonished me. To be fair, my stage presence must have left a good deal to be desired in any city. I remember playing a recital in the then-new Grace Rainey Rogers Auditorium at the Metropolitan Museum in New York around that time. We had been fussing with rugs and drapes onstage all afternoon because, as with all new halls, something seemed not quite right with the acoustics. During the intermission, Mrs. Isaac Stern strode into my dressing room and, in what I can only describe as a Stern voice, spoke. "There's something I must tell you *now*," she said firmly. I thought my playing had thus far been okay, so I assumed it had something to do with the acoustics. "It really can't wait until the end of the concert," Vera continued. "Gary, you simply *must* keep your legs together when you bow!")

Although our Community report cards very often had nothing to do with how we played, they almost always had a great deal to do with *what* we played. It was made clear to us by our managers that for these concerts certain music, certain types of music and above all music of certain lengths, was frowned upon. The magic length was seventeen minutes. Programming any longer composition was severely discouraged—even something as familiar and inoffensive as *Carnaval*, which, I recall, was often a bone of contention. Ward French, ever co-operative, suggested that with cuts it might be acceptable.

In my early days as a Community OYAP I was learning the "Wanderer" Fantasy (twenty-one minutes), and of course I delighted in ignoring all guidelines as to repertoire then considered appropriate for the boondocks. I felt strongly then, as I still do, that it's not the length or type of music but the way it's played that keeps or loses the audience's attention. Besides, these towns were ideal testing grounds for pieces one was breaking in for a New York or Chicago recital. So I insisted on my Schubert over the advice and protests of my mentors, who grimly forwarded my program to the printers' with many a "Don't say I didn't warn you," and eyes rolled heavenward. I must admit that no piece could really be forbidden. As we were fond of pointing out, we artists employed our managers and not the other way around. But the fact remained that the number of Community concerts we were granted was in no small part due to the way we played the game.

Brave Eugene had the audacity to program the *Carnaval* one year, and when the cuts were proposed he reacted as if an Aztec had threatened to remove his vital organs. He held fast to every note and every repeat in spite of the fatherly advice ("Look here, Istomin, you play ball with us and we'll play ball with you") issued by Montezuma French, who subsequently extracted revenge by virtually ignoring Eugene's existence as far as Community was concerned.

I got away with my "Wanderer," but it is quite likely that this had nothing whatever to do with the intensity with which I played it, and everything to do with the charm that I oozed at the parties after the concerts, to atone for the program to which I had subjected the hapless subscribers of Hazard, Kentucky. For, in the case of Community, at least, Ned Rorem's definition of a concert as "that which precedes a party" is particularly apt.

Willy Kapell detested the whole routine so much that I think he would gladly have given up whatever income he derived from those concerts if there were only another way for him to work in new repertoire. And he was beastly at the parties. Never one to pretend about anything, he made his feelings crystal-clear. Legend has it that on one occasion when he was, as usual, skulking in a dark corner, undoubtedly seething about the poor piano at the concert and matching nourishment offered at the party, a dowager sailed up to him and smirked conspiratorially. She lowered her voice.

"I paint!" she whispered.

"So what?" responded Willy.

Willy learned the Copland Sonata and first played it at a Community concert. This piece is not, nor was it ever, a particularly inaccessible composition to listen to, and furthermore it is certain that even in his earliest stages of learning the work, Willy must have played the hell out of it. But just the word

"Copland" (if not attached to *Rodeo*) on a Community program was synonymous with "trouble." An executive from the New York office of Community was present at the post-concert party and collared Willy.

"You are not yet of the stature to inflict such a piece on your audience," he lectured. Willy very quietly took his coat and his wife and left the premises.

Although Willy was a terror at these parties, the most classic remark I've ever heard on one of these occasions came from the lips of a European conductor who at the time was music director of a medium-sized orchestra in the Northwest. This was not a Community party, but in those days post-concert celebrations in small towns were all very similar. We went to the reception together and when we saw that the refreshments consisted of ginger ale, cookies and a receiving line of which we were the recipients, we surreptitiously eyed our watches to see if we could decently leave before the last pizzeria in town shut tight for the night. In about ten minutes the conductor nudged me.

"Let's get out of here," he muttered.

"I'd like nothing better," I replied, "but *you're* supposed to be the music director here. Don't you think we should at least wait until we've finished the handshaking?" (I was getting older and wiser by then, and I liked him.) He grudgingly agreed, but became increasingly annoyed as the line of well-wishers continued without end. I could see that his patience was running very thin. Finally, a lady came up to shake his hand and confided, "I play the cello." This was it. The conductor turned to me and in one of those stage whispers that's louder than a shout said, "The cello, the cello. Of *course* she plays the cello. What else could she get between her legs?" Shortly thereafter we found ourselves at the pizzeria and he found himself without an orchestra.

When I first started to play Community concerts, the standard fare at the post-concert party consisted of cookies and fruit punch. After a few years' experience, though, I began to learn where pockets of good food existed. This contributed a good deal to my enthusiasm whenever I heard Ada Cooper shriek, "and next January you're not going to West Texas but to East Quebec!" It may have seemed to some like being consigned to the Arctic wasteland, but I happily endured the blizzards and sub-zero temperatures because I knew what awaited in those little towns along the St. Lawrence. There, at someone's home after the concert, after layers of storm coats, scarves and galoshes were unbuttoned, unwound and unhooked, would stand the good ladies of La Malbaie, Montmagny or Sept-Îles, attired in brightly colored silken raiments, direct from Paris. The food and drink matched, and it was worth a few frozen toes to join in those festive evenings. But normally, in the United States, and especially on the Great Plains, it seemed, I'd look furtively around, stomach rumbling, to see if perhaps what had just been proffered was merely the hors d'oeuvre to a meal that was about to be served in the next room. Not bloody likely. Rarely, and then only on the most gala occasions, were we treated to molded Jell-O salad and perhaps some chicken à la king. This was not lack of hospitality on the part of our hosts, but merely innocence. They had all had their dinners, and I'm sure it never occurred to them that someone could be ravenous at 11 P.M.

Things have changed a good deal since then—for the better —and I like to think that my early sufferings may have played some small part in improving the quality of post-concert life for my younger colleagues. It came about in this way: we had a good friend, Rachael Taylor, who worked in the press department at Columbia Artists, and who wrote the artists' biographical material sent to all concert sponsors. Little vignettes about private lives and habits, called "human interest" stories, were included in the press kits. Rachael described in mouth-watering detail my prowess in the kitchen (not at all true); my love of good and, at that time, exotic food (quite true); and my desire—nay, *need*—for a soul-sustaining as well as body-nourishing meal after a concert (exceedingly true). I remember that she wrote something like, "When Graffman, or for that matter, any pianist, plays, the calories go as fast as the octaves," thus managing to indicate (a) that all performers are almost always hungry; and (b) that even if I had been seen eating a hamburger at a drugstore counter before the concert I was still going to be famished at the party.

This hint worked wonders. Shortly thereafter, hostesses began to vie with each other to see who could concoct the most elaborate and "continental" recipes. At one point I must have been served quiche Lorraine and moussaka on twenty successive evenings. But this was an indescribable improvement over the Jell-O, and the desire to please was touching and most appreciated. Of course I suppose it would be an exaggeration to credit all of this burgeoning interest in ethnic cookery to my Community press kit. Americans, especially Middle Americans of comfortable means, were just then beginning to make their first postwar forays abroad, and although they may have demanded hot dogs in Rome, they, or at least their womenfolk, began to experiment in the kitchen upon their return. By the next decade the post-concert punch-and-cookie routine had pretty much become history, and I began to put on weight.

CHAPTER NINE

Matters of Life and Death

GEORGE SZELL had a reputation for being fierce. It is said that his bite was even worse than his bark. He was completely intolerant of anything he deemed wrongdoing, and this was particularly true when the transgression concerned music. Once, jokingly, someone who knew him well enough to dare it mentioned to him that he treated the interpretation of one short phrase of music as a matter of life or death. "But don't you see," he replied, impaling the speaker with his laser-beam eyes, frighteningly magnified behind ice-cube-thick spectacles, "it is. It *is*."

From what I knew of him, it was clear that he ordered his own life accordingly. Whenever we played together, even the orchestral rehearsals were as carefully prepared for as if they were performances. We would meet a day (or, when a recording was involved, several weeks) beforehand for a most thorough piano rehearsal. Instead of standing over me and beating time, as is often done at these meetings, he would seat himself at a second piano and play the orchestral part—from memory. This applied even to music that he was not terribly close to. Nothing that he chose to perform was dealt with like a step-child, and he gave as much of himself to Rachmaninoff as he did to Mozart. I believe that the first times I performed the Prokofiev Third with him in 1954 as well as the Prokofiev First in 1966 were the first times he had ever done these works. Yet the same procedure, including his playing at the second piano from memory, applied. He didn't do it as a stunt, though; he did it because he felt that was the correct, proper and *only* way to give the music its due.

It was at these sessions that I came to understand the aptness of the German word for rehearsal: *Probe*. It wasn't just a question of running through the score to check that our tempos agreed. It was almost like psychoanalysis. "Are you *sure* that is the way you want to play it?" he would question my phrasing of a certain passage. When, after we had discussed my reasons and he had satisfied himself that what I was doing was out of conviction rather than capriciousness, he would nod, "Fine. I'll have the clarinet do the same." This is not to say that he accepted all my musical thoughts without argument. Far from it. He never hesitated to pinpoint sloppy thinking, and on countless occasions he opened my ears—or I like to hope he did—to infinite nuances of musical interpretation that I had hitherto overlooked. But basically he adopted the atti-tude that I was the soloist; we had to have some common musi-cal meeting ground or he wouldn't have engaged me in the first place; therefore, he and his orchestra would, on this occasion, defer to my ideas.

This was quite heady stuff for the unseasoned performer I was when I first played with him in Cleveland, but luck must have been with me, for apparently I didn't antagonize him as I had Ormandy a couple of years earlier in Philadelphia. He drove me to the train station after the second concert and, in the couple of hours I had to kill before the sleeper to New York came through, treated me to a sumptuous dinner. When

I asked him, over dessert, whether he had any advice for me, he merely observed, mildly, "You don't play any chamber music, do you?" I readily admitted this gap, and the good doctor prescribed a strong dose.

No physic could have provided a more effective musical cathartic than the stringent regime that awaited me at the Marlboro Music School when I finally got there two years later, in the summer of 1952. By then I really needed it. I'd been carousing abroad most of the two years since playing my Leventritt concerts in 1950; and although technically I had been sent to Italy the first year to study on a Fulbright Grant, the conditions were extremely flexible then and most of my studying involved serious sightseeing and even more serious surveying of hedonism throughout Western Europe.

I arrived in Naples on the *Saturnia* with a wardrobe trunk, which everybody carried in those days, a bag filled with foodstuffs that Wanda Toscanini Horowitz had sent to my cabin for me to deliver to the composer Ildebrando Pizzetti as a gift from her father, and an insatiable appetite for everything (except, perhaps, practicing); and I spent my first few months in the Trastevere section of Rome sampling the local delicacies and visiting friends at the American Academy. The Fulbright people had recommended that I enroll in the Accademia Musicale Chigiana in Siena, and on one of my sightseeing jaunts I went over to inspect that remarkable city.

Undaunted by the sight of an awesome, fourteenth-century palazzo, I knocked on the huge door, and was welcomed, to my great surprise, by a friendly-looking middle-aged lady speaking American English. I might have expected to see her because actually she was quite famous. Her name was Olga Rudge and she was not only Count Chigi's secretary but had also been for many years the constant companion of Ezra Pound. She was a violinist who had gone to Europe with George Antheil in the 1920s to play his concerto and had remained there, I believe, ever since. When she heard that I'd studied with Vengerova she became even more cordial: as it turned out, she had shared an apartment for a while in Paris with Vengerova's assistant, Olga Stroumillo.

Madame Rudge sent me to the Vivantes, a family who owned a villa about four kilometers outside of Siena and wanted to have a student boarder. I am not really sure that they *wanted* to have a boarder—student or otherwise—but this was just after the war and things were difficult. I made arrangements to spend the summer there, and this turned out to be a splendid time, as they were a wonderful family of intellectuals with a beautiful daughter.

Before settling in at the Villa Solaia, as the Vivantes' home was called, I went back to Rome, and thence to Paris, where I stayed for a while at the renowned 53 rue de la Harpe. This narrow little building in one of the city's most romantic quarters dated from at least the early nineteenth century and until very recently had seen service (as seems to be customary in old Paris houses) as a bordello. By the time I got there, however, the top, or third, floor had been taken over by a nest of American friends. They would come and go. First Shirley Gabis and her then-husband, Seymour Barab; then Ned Rorem; then Leon Fleisher made headquarters in the apartment, which had two decent-sized rooms. In the front room was a piano, and there Leon was installed, off and on. In the back room, which I'd been lent, there were only a bed, lots of books piled up on the floor and stacks of paintings by friends of Shirley. Between these two rooms was a small area which contained a stove, sink, toilet, shower and bidet, the latter usually heaped high with dirty dishes. (Thanks to Mrs. Leventritt's daughter and son-in-law, Rosalie and Ted Berner, who were passing through Paris then, I had one real bath—at their suite in the Crillon.) On the ground floor of this building was a famous Senegalese night club, the Rose Rouge, which was a rendezvous where Middle Western American white girls met tall, handsome black Senegalese gentlemen. I remember how the deep drums late at night would hypnotize me to sleep. Every now and then I'd be awakened by peremptory knocking at the door of our apartment. Usually it was a French soldier just back from Indochina looking for his favorite. I guess that was part of the place's charm.

A few days before leaving Rome for Paris, I'd had an accident: someone closed a car door on my finger. Although it caused no lasting damage, my nail came out and there was no way I could play the piano for at least three weeks. I made the best of this enforced holiday, and when Eugene came through Paris on his way to Marseilles, where he was to play with the orchestra and Paul Paray, I accompanied him. After sampling just about everything that swam in the Mediterranean, we went together to Prades, where he was to participate in the first Casals Festival. Prades, although in France, was practically on the Spanish border; Casals, a legendary figure even then, when he was only in his seventies, lived there in self-imposed exile from his Spanish homeland. For many years he had refused to give concerts in any country that recognized the Franco government, so he hadn't played in public for a long time, and this festival, marking his return to the concert stage, triggered much excitement. Just before the opening performance I remember seeing Alexander Schneider looking as if he were about to explode. He couldn't take his eyes off Casals, as if the cellist might dematerialize or transmogrify if anyone's back was turned. Instead, however, Casals obligingly drew his bow across the strings of his instrument and produced the same sounds that we knew so well from his old records.

Music-lovers and society people had come from everywhere. The tiny town was crawling with *paparazzi* and their popping flashbulbs following fashionable women limping bravely over the cobblestones in spike-heeled sandals. (Like the brave soul who ate the first oyster, some chic lady eventually dared exchange her death-defying slippers for those rope-soled Catalonian espadrilles, which shortly thereafter became the accepted footgear, accompanying everything from jeans to evening gowns.) While Eugene worked, I had a marvelous two weeks going to many rehearsals, most concerts and all parties.

The nearest I got to a piano, or to participating in any chamber music, was as page-turner on one unforgettable occasion.

This was a recording session that Columbia was doing; and because of what happened I must have repressed what the music was, for I no longer recall it. But I do recollect that it involved six or eight players, one of whom was Sascha Schneider. During the recording, something always went wrong in one certain section of the piece, each time for a different reason. Either one of the performers played something not quite perfectly or there was an engineering problem. Something always happened. At last, things were going just right—until I turned a page in such a way that the music fell down with a *whoosh*. Understandably, Sascha Schneider chased me all the way down the main street of Prades, holding his fiddle high over his head and screaming the most extraordinary curses at me in at least four different languages. There was no question that he would have tried to bash my skull in had he caught up with me; fortunately for his violin, I escaped.

It was really quite a time for me, with my bandaged finger, everybody feeling sorry for me and no responsibilities whatsoever. But I had an Italian Fulbright and was paid my monthly stipend in lire, so it behooved me to return to Italy at certain intervals to pick up my money, if for no other reason. Although I was registered at the Accademia, I didn't go there to study. It was a very splendid place and a fine school, but I preferred to accomplish what work I did on a rented piano at the Vivantes', occasionally zooming into town on my Vespa motor scooter for another round of graduate-level sightseeing.

The year after the Casals Festival was begun at an old church in Prades, the Marlboro Music School opened its doors on the campus (unused in summer) of an agricultural college in Vermont. Its founders were Adolf Busch and his brother Hermann, his son-in-law Rudolf Serkin and their friends and colleagues the Moyse family (Marcel, granddaddy of the legendary flutists; his son Louis, who also played the flute; and violinist/violist daughter-in-law Blanche). They envisioned a kind of musical retreat for the study (or "exploration," as they called it) and performing of the great chamber music literature. It was set up in a most informal, almost family-like, way but the pleasantly rural atmosphere enveloping the converted barns and farm buildings was misleadingly bucolic. When I first saw it, during its second summer, the place was a beehive.

Berlitz may offer "total immersion" language courses; at Marlboro, there was total submersion in chamber music. My first look at the bulletin board where assignments were posted sent me into a state of shock. Within a few days, I read, I was expected to learn, study, rehearse and play for Serkin the Dvořák Quintet, the Schumann Quintet, a Brahms trio and assorted little pieces like the Beethoven D major Cello Sonata and the Fauré A major Violin Sonata. Although I had, of course, heard these pieces many times, I doubt very much that I'd ever seen the music to some of them, much less attempted to study any of them.

I felt like a GI about to start basic training. Indeed, Marlboro was very basic then. We must have been about forty students, all told. We came from everywhere, and the mix was predominantly string and wind players. Most of us lived in Spartan fashion in dormitories on the campus, but were rarely in our rooms. We'd roll out of bed at daybreak and head directly for the practice shacks. Aside from a short break for an institutional-tasting lunch, occasionally enlivened by spaghetti-throwing battles, we worked until dusk, alone and in our assigned groups. We were juggled in various combinations and permutations to prepare on our own all conceivable kinds of chamber music, from sonatas to Brandenburg concertos, which we would then play for an assigned member of the faculty.

Contrary to the Marlboro of later years—the Marlboro which became "a community of equals" (with some, certainly, more equal than others), and which fostered no clear delineation between faculty and students—the Marlboro of early times was definitely a place where students learned from faculty. (This situation caused a couple of sleepless nights, I later found out, for my great friend Claude Frank. Claude was then teaching at nearby Bennington College; and as a former Schnabel student who was well known to and most highly regarded by Rudolf Serkin, he was invited, beginning in the

summer of 1953, to teach also at Marlboro for a couple of days
each week. This was a marvelous opportunity and quite an
honor as well, since he was by far the youngest member of the
faculty. It was only recently that he confessed to me his terror
at the thought of being assigned to teach a chamber group to
which I, his contemporary, might be assigned as pianist—an
event that never did occur at Marlboro, although in subsequent
years I have often been the beneficiary of his wise musical
counsel.)

A few years later the stern lines of demarcation between faculty and students began to pale. Claude claims that his inter-
OYAP marriage to Lilian Kallir hastened the metamorphosis.
(The fact that Claude was born in Nuremberg and Lilian in
Prague did not in the slightest minimize their OYAPness:
They had come to America as teenagers, settling in New York,
where they proceeded to influence us natives at least as much
as we did them.) They spent their first summer as man and
wife, in 1960, at Marlboro, where Claude was busily teaching,
full time by then. But his bride existed in a kind of musical
limbo. She was not on the faculty and yet she was not one of
the students. She was just there: an uncomfortable position for
someone of her capability and experience, not to mention her
firm musical views and determined character.

Indications of the quietly indomitable will that lay behind
Lilian's sweet face and ladylike demeanor had been evident to
her friends ever since the time when, as a most promising
young artist who was also attending Sarah Lawrence College,
she escaped from the school infirmary, where she had been
confined with an attack of appendicitis—it is said that she lowered herself from a window with a bedsheet, but this may be
hyperbole—to play a scheduled recital at the Brooklyn Academy of Music. Although she admits to having blacked out a
couple of times during the recital, I remember both that it was
excellent and that she skipped the post-concert party.

Obviously, it would have been untenable for Lilian to sit
around Marlboro for two months reading cookbooks. So she
was invited to play with the various ensemble groups, neither

as a teacher nor as a student, but simply as a "participant." Gradually, then (according to Claude), it became a custom for the "official" faculty to join with the "official" students for performances, leading to the commingling (or anarchy?) that obtains today, when, it is said, everyone learns something from everyone else, whatever his age or experience.

But in those earlier years, the traditional student-faculty relationship was observed more formally, and we students would prepare our assigned tasks for our assigned teachers seriously, intensely, passionately and, as lesson time drew near, frantically. It was a matter of honor to outdo ourselves at every opportunity: unthinkable to offer less.

Surprised though I was by the amount of accomplishment expected of me in such a short time, I rallied with tremendous enthusiasm when I began to work with the violinist and cellist to whom I had been assigned. Berl Senofsky and Shirley Trepel (to whom he was then married) were both members of the Cleveland Orchestra. Berl was the assistant concertmaster and Shirley, gracing the cello section, was one of the first females in a major orchestra. I had known them casually; as soon as we started to play together, however, we became inseparable. Although at Marlboro it was customary to change chamber music partners regularly, as in a square dance, we insisted on playing exclusively with each other for the two summers we spent there, and undoubtedly made ourselves thoroughly obnoxious in the process. We spent almost every waking moment together those summers, and almost every moment was waking. I can't imagine how we did it, but it seems to me that while practicing our hearts out from morning till night, we also managed to keep a continual poker game afloat and fix elaborate barbecues at the Senofskys' elegantly rustic cottage in the woods.

One of these events involved twenty-seven lobsters. After giving our all to the Brahms C minor Trio and finally performing it at an afternoon concert, we felt we needed to get away for a couple of days' rest and recreation. The Senofskys had a bronze-colored convertible Chrysler and a big bronze-colored dog to match. Naomi was on vacation from her job that week, so we all piled into the car and set forth to visit friends in Maine. On our return trip we decided that the nicest thing we could do for our landlocked friends in Vermont would be to bring them live lobsters. So we stopped at a market in Damariscotta and bought a huge barrel swarming with several dozen hyperactive crustaceans. We had to stop every now and then to replenish the supply of ice, and thanks to this tender care they were still waving their claws around like Leonard Bernstein discovering Mahler when we arrived in Brattleboro at twilight.

The first lucky recipients of our largesse were the Hermann Busch family. We parked in front of their cottage. Berl and I each took two squirming lobsters and banged on the Busches' front door with a foot. Hermann innocently opened the door, took one look at us and our wriggling companions, screamed and ran back into the house, crying for his wife and daughter. He was already safely several rooms away when the ladies arrived, looked at the lobsters with acute distaste and invited us to return another time without them.

Our next stop was at the Serkins', where our gifts were received with wide, if rather forced, smiles. Finally, we gave a goodly batch to the Marcel Moyse family. They seemed genuinely pleased; and, as French people with the highest interest in life's most important things, they insisted we remain until they could relate to us a complicated and superb recipe for preparing a stew of these animals. We subsequently found out that they had an even bigger feast than planned because the Serkins promptly turned over their ration to the Moyses. At least our lobsters came to a good end.

We had an enormous party at the Senofskys' for the rest of the lobsters, prepared à la Moyse. The recipe involved simmering the crustaceans in several bottles of white wine, a couple of bottles of cognac, countless herbs and enough chopped garlic to threaten the choppers—eight of the bravest guests—with becoming what we began to fear was permanently permeated. For at least a week their presence could be detected by smell alone.

But George Szell didn't send me to Marlboro to cook

lobsters, and although during those summers there was a good deal of frivolity indulged in by all concerned (when Peter Serkin, then a mischievous little tot, put the rotten duck eggs under our beds, he was only doing so on the instructions of his father), we did take our music very seriously. Marlboro was very intimate and casual in those days, and although there were regularly scheduled concerts, the repertoire was decided on only just beforehand. If Serkin, or another member of the faculty, felt that a group's performance was good enough to be heard by the public, we'd be so informed. We would then play as if we were in Carnegie Hall rather than in the makeshift auditorium that also served as our dining room for a predominantly local (and very enthusiastic and knowledgeable) audience.

America's burgeoning interest in chamber music got a big boost from Marlboro, with surprising results in the way the musical taste of the Vermonters developed. A few years later (when concerts were scheduled a little more formally than in my day, if less so than they are now) someone called to ask what was on the program that weekend. Serkin himself answered the phone, it is said, and was exceedingly pleased to give the news: instead of Reger or even Schubert, the featured composer was "box office." "This week," he announced proudly, "we're doing the *Tchaikovsky* Piano Trio." "Oh," said a very disappointed voice. "When's the next Mozart?"

If my first summer at Marlboro in 1952 introduced me to the joys of a new kind of repertoire and musical give-and-take, the following winter in New York unexpectedly strengthened my Russian musical heritage through lessons with Horowitz.

I was giving quite a number of concerts by that time, but still continued to play for Vengerova every now and then. Our telephonic communication, however, was much more regular— an umbilical cord that was never cut as long as she lived. She would phone me, usually between students, and although I know she taught incessantly there must have been some gaps because I can remember marathon conversations. This was during the period when I still haunted recital halls. Vengerova went occasionally, too, and would unfailingly call the next day to rehash the previous evening's performance, almost like a continuation of our lessons, as if to make sure that I was getting what she thought I should get out of a great recital. Similarly, she was always curious to know how I reacted to performances that appalled her. She would complain to me about various students (particularly the talented ones who she thought were not doing their best), and would expect me to keep her informed of the activities of all my colleagues—everything from the repertoire they were studying to their love lives.

Vengerova and Horowitz were good friends, and through her I had met him and even played for him a few times when I was a teenager. Now she called and told me that since he was not giving concerts at that time (this turned out to be his longest sabbatical—the one that ended with his return to Carnegie Hall in 1965, when he worried, "Nobody will remember me!" only to learn that eager fans were bivouacked overnight by the box office), he wanted to do a bit of coaching. He told her that he would be willing to give me some lessons.

Strange to say (or perhaps not strange, since I was so stubborn), I was ambivalent about this at first. I admired Horowitz immensely. But as with all great artists, he had such a strong personality. And I had *my* ideas about certain things. I wasn't sure I wanted to be closely influenced by him, and I made all of this abundantly clear to Vengerova, who told me to shut up and go play for him.

His method of teaching me, after the first or second visit, erased irrevocably all doubt in my mind about whether I wanted to be taught by him. At no time did he ever even hint at imposing his ideas on mine. In fact, it was quite the opposite. After criticizing and making suggestions, he tried to find ways within my conception—or what he thought was my conception—of playing a phrase more intensely, or more lyrically, or both. He almost never would go to the piano and say, "Here's how to do it." He showed me how he practiced certain things, and how I could solve certain technical difficulties by practicing in different ways.

Above all, he wanted me to learn how to treat melodic lines

as if they were sung by the human voice, an interesting contrast with Serkin, who, in Marlboro, frequently described different figurations as representing various orchestral instruments. This is obviously an oversimplification, as of course Horowitz conceived of something like the Mussorgsky *Pictures* orchestrally, and Serkin sometimes even sings a theme that he's playing while he's playing it. But nevertheless, in Marlboro the talk was mainly about a left-hand passage representing, say, a cello rather than a bassoon, while a certain right-hand melody might bring to mind the quality of a viola. And I remember the revelation I felt at Serkin's suggestion that some staccato notes that I made extremely short were actually the equivalent of a pizzicato in a stringed instrument and therefore should last *longer*, as the sound of a plucked string vibrates for a while before it disappears. But Horowitz was more concerned with trying to make the piano sound like a human voice, and continually analyzed how a great singer would phrase a certain passage. To illuminate this philosophy further, he introduced me to the recordings of great *bel canto* singers such as Battistini and to operas that I didn't know, such as *Pique Dame*. My lessons covered a lot of territory.

I think I must have played almost once a week for Horowitz for a couple of years, and then about once a month for several years after that. He was a "night person," and our sessions would usually begin at eight or even nine in the evening. Although he might have been considered something of a recluse at that time because he didn't go out much, he was always (in my presence, at least) extremely cheerful, enthusiastic and full of enormous vitality and bounding vigor and energy that left me breathless when, as sometimes happened, it was suddenly two o'clock in the morning and Mrs. Horowitz would come into the living room and shoo me out.

My lesson didn't go on for all that time, though. After the formal part was over—about two hours or so—he would then (like Vengerova) ask me about all of my colleagues, the music business in general, and then on to politics, museum exhibitions and the many other subjects that interested him. He read

voraciously and his curiosity was wide-ranging, his ideas
thoughtful and his way of expression uniquely pungent. But
fascinating though our discussions were for me, I was always
waiting for the moment—usually around midnight—when he
would ask a question like, "Do you by chance know the Sixth
Sonata of Scriabin?"

"No, not really . . ." I would reply apologetically.

Then the evening would begin.

Horowitz would stride to the piano, saying, "It's a very great
work . . . you should hear it. I would like to play it for you,
but of course you understand that I cannot play the piano any
more." Then he would sit down at the instrument. "If I could
play, I would play it for you." His hands would hover tantaliz-
ingly over the keyboard. "Since I cannot play the piano any
more, this is not possible. However, I'll try to give you just an
idea. But please forgive me, because, of course, you understand
. . ." and he would proceed to tear through the piece, often in
a performance so brilliant and so perfect that it could have
been recorded on the spot.

The first piece would remind him of other works by the same
composer that he "could not play," and these, too, were amply
demonstrated during these unforgettable evenings, when he
must have played for me over the years practically all the
Clementi sonatas, scores of Scarlatti sonatas and many works of
Scriabin and Medtner. I hope I am not betraying a confidence
—I don't believe that it was a secret—by saying that he also
played for me some of his own compositions written many
years earlier. They were extremely beautiful and impressive,
and I have no idea why he has always hidden them. They had
their own individual stamp, but also reminded me, not surprisingly, of Rachmaninoff, who was, of course, a good friend of
Horowitz, and whose photo, among a large collection of pictures of relatives and friends placed on the piano, stared som-
berly down at me during those evenings.

Once it did more than stare. I was playing a Rachmaninoff
prelude. Horowitz had suggested to me a different way of attacking a certain passage that was giving me trouble, and when

I tried to play it with the new fingering, every single note came crashing down wrong. As I lifted my hands from the keyboard, there was yet another crash: the photo of Rachmaninoff, alone among all of those on the piano, had fallen to the floor, its frame and glass smashed. Both of us were quite shaken for the remainder of the evening, and we avoided playing any music by anyone whose photo was anywhere in the room.

It always surprised me that Horowitz' active concert repertoire included so few of Rachmaninoff's works for piano and orchestra. During the many years that I heard him play in public, I believe that—strange as it may seem—the only Rachmaninoff concerto he performed was the Third. (In all fairness, I suppose it is quite enough for a mountain climber to scale the Matterhorn on roller skates without tackling every other Alp as well.) Nevertheless, he was, of course, intimately acquainted with Rachmaninoff's other concertos, and I was told that Rachmaninoff played the *Paganini* Rhapsody for him a number of times when it was still a work-in-progress.

It has never ceased to astonish me, by the way, that this Rhapsody, which now seems as firmly ensconced in the standard concert repertoire as the "Emperor" Concerto, first saw the light of day in Philadelphia as recently as 1934, not long before I made my first trip to Curtis. As is well known, however, the instant and enduring audience appeal of Rachmaninoff's music has not exactly endeared it to many of his colleagues, who regard it as beneath consideration.

"How can you play such junk?" were the only words Walter Piston addressed to me after I'd performed the Second with the Boston Symphony (he had come to hear a work by one of his friends on the same program). I wonder how much the fact that Rachmaninoff's music was appreciated during his lifetime, as well as after, has contributed to making him something of a pariah to a certain portion of the musical intelligentsia. If he'd only been neglected, there would undoubtedly now be a group of activists fighting for Rachmaninoff Power. But as it is, most present-day composers revile not only his music but its performers.

"You are the worst! You are the very worst! I tell my students about you and your terrible programs all the time!" David Diamond shouted at me at a party one evening, causing all conversation to come to a halt, when I approached him to say good night. "Do you play *anything* after Bach-Busoni?" he cried, with pain, as if I'd stuck a knife in him. Pleas of mine that a fair amount of Bartók and Prokofiev was in my active repertoire only provoked him further. Ned Rorem, guest of honor at that gathering, also looked anguished, but in his case it was embarrassment, as if some gruesome deformity of mine, usually kept discreetly veiled, had been exposed to the jeering throng. Ned's unfailing good taste and sensitivity have never allowed him, by even so much as a glance, to betray what he may be thinking about players of Bach-Busoni, not to mention Rachmaninoff.

What can I say in my defense? I read through a great deal of new music industriously, but (whether because of my background, training or, for all I know, genes) whenever it came time to add something to my repertoire—something I'd have to practice intensely and live with for years—it almost always (with very few exceptions, most notably the Fourth Sonata and Second Concerto of Benjamin Lees) turned out to be something like another Schubert sonata or Mozart concerto that I hadn't yet studied.

And, as I found out only recently, I did not even escape Stravinsky's wrath. At my first Carnegie Hall recital I played his Serenade in A. Innocently, I followed it with a Rachmaninoff group. Apparently, there is no way to make a composer happy—even by playing his music. Just last year I was shown a copy of that Carnegie Hall program, linking these two masters, which Stravinsky had seen. His notation in the margin near his name left no question as to his displeasure. "What a neighborhood!" was the comment.

Rachmaninoff was critical of his own music as well. Horowitz told me that when the composer played for him the newly created and soon-to-be-famous Eighteenth Variation of his

Rhapsody, with its gorgeous inversion of the Paganini theme, he apologetically mumbled, "Well, maybe it'll save the piece."

The first pianist after Rachmaninoff himself to perform this extraordinary work was, I believe, Gitta Gradova. With her pungent wit and logical, no-nonsense approach to life (with which I became familiar when we sat on Leventritt juries together and, subsequently, when we became fast friends), she must have proved a match for the music in more ways than the obvious.

Despite her exotic-sounding name, Gitta Gradova was brought up in Chicago, where her hospitable parents entertained and looked after visiting performers with, I imagine, the same kindness she and her husband, Dr. Maurice Cottle, have cared for and fed stray and lonesome touring musicians to the present day. It was in this manner that Gitta, as a young piano student, became acquainted with many of the great musical artists of the time. Prokofiev gave her a lesson on the Grieg Concerto. He also introduced her to Rachmaninoff, and her close and lasting friendship with him as well as with Horowitz blossomed from that time.

When, as a young performer, she came to New York to play the *Paganini* Rhapsody with the Philharmonic and Barbirolli, she stayed with the Horowitzes. Her host escorted her to the first concert, and she described with relish (in retrospect, as it must have been horrible while happening) their voyage down Fifth Avenue to Carnegie Hall.

"I wasn't especially nervous—just normally excited," she recalled, "until we got into the cab. And then he started. He wanted to reassure me, of course, but his method was strange, to say the least.

" 'Gitta,' he said, 'in case you feel that you're going to forget . . . that you're going to have a memory lapse . . . just remember that many of the variations begin on A. So if you think you're going to have a memory lapse, just concentrate on A. Simple! That should help, in case you forget. Don't forget!'

" 'Yes, Volodya,' I said, beginning to feel my hands get clammy.

"'So just remember, if you think you're going to forget, just remember A.'

"'Yes, Volodya,' I said, wishing he'd shut up, already.

"'And one final word of advice: In case you *do* forget, don't stop. No matter what happens, *don't stop playing!* Remember, *no matter what happens,* keep on going! Don't stop! *IT'S PROWINCIAL TO STOP!'*

"By the time we got to the auditorium, we were both sick."

In spite, or perhaps because, of their very different temperaments and outlooks, Horowitz and Serkin have always been friends. But I don't think they saw each other very often in those days; Serkin's headquarters were in Vermont and Philadelphia and he toured most of the time, seldom visiting New York except to perform or record. One of the evenings that the two of them were together I'll always remember vividly because it was then that I managed, in one fell swoop, to bend both of these individualists to *my* will.

This came about when Horowitz had started to go out occasionally. He had taken a box for Rubinstein's Carnegie Hall recital, invited the Serkins and then called to ask us to join them, too. We had just returned from Hong Kong, where I'd had a splendid new tuxedo made, and in the same breath with my eager acceptance I inquired, "Black tie?" Horowitz said he hadn't thought of it, but, no, probably not. He detected my disappointment at his reply, and when I confessed that this would have been my first opportunity to wear the new suit, he obligingly said, "Oh, in that case, all right." The evening arrived and we gathered in the box. Serkin looked very uncomfortable in his dinner jacket and stiffly starched shirt which seemed to be scratching him—and with a stud that refused to stay buttoned. Although white tie and tails is, or was, normal attire for concert performers, dinner jackets were neither fish nor fowl, and I have the feeling that when Serkin wasn't wearing his business uniform he would have much preferred his usual civilian garb. Horowitz, on the other hand, looked elegant, as always, if a bit odd in a beautifully tailored dinner jacket, double-breasted and with extremely wide lapels, that looked like something William Powell might have worn in a *Thin Man* movie. He sat down next to resplendent Hong Kong me, smiled confidentially, opened his jacket and let me look at the label sewn in the lining, which bore the name of a famous tailor and the date of 1936. A good year for tuxedos.

CHAPTER TEN

...and Other Such Crises

ALTHOUGH I NEVER did get to wear my snazzy dinner jacket much—until, in fact, Pierre Boulez became music director of the New York Philharmonic and decreed that black tie for performers would be less intimidating than the customary tails (by which time it was no longer so snazzy)—it seemed, during the fifties and early sixties, that almost every memorable recital or concert we attended was followed by a matching party. Many of these, to our delight, were at Rosalie Leventritt's. They were gay and informal and the food was splendid. Among other things to be looked forward to was the far-famed tomato aspic, bursting with huge, succulent shrimp.

When I first met Mrs. Leventritt, around 1948, she seemed elderly (to a nineteen-year-old, anyone over forty is ancient), although I now realize she couldn't have been much older than I am at present. Lovely to look at—even the last time I saw her, when she was in her mid-eighties—she was small, elegant, slender, sweet-faced, with large blue-violet eyes that were usually smiling and always sympathetic. A slight Southern drawl (she came originally from Birmingham) accented her impish humor and softened sometimes needle-sharp observations.

Almost always surrounded by young people—mostly members of her large, close-knit family—she also gave encouragement, advice, moral support and, when necessary, financial assistance to a dazzling array of gifted performers, by no means limiting her enthusiasm to those who had been winners or even competitors in the contest her family sponsored. Murray Perahia and Richard Goode are two examples of the interests of her later years; but I can remember on countless occasions during the quarter century of our friendship entering her celadon-green sitting room to find a budding pianist or violinist (or violist or cellist, for that matter) perched, glass of sherry in hand, by the little table in front of her armchair, pouring out his heart as she listened intently. Delphic oracle, impresario, Southern belle, New England country doctor and mother, she bent over her ever present needlework, only putting it down to emphasize a point, solve a problem, make a joke or answer what seemed like incessant telephone calls from small grandchildren and gigantic conductors, all of whom she chaffed in the same bantering manner. She never at all fit the picture of a formidable *grande dame* of the arts, even though just about every notable performer of a certain musical persuasion was, if not an intimate confidant, then at least a true and loyal friend.

The musical persuasion that persuaded Rosalie Leventritt was emphatically not razzle-dazzle Russian. Although she was never snobbish about Rachmaninoff or Tchaikovsky or brilliant virtuosity, it was clear that her special fondness was for the intimate works of Brahms, Schubert, Schumann, for chamber music in all forms (she was one of the guiding spirits behind the Marlboro and Casals festivals), and for the performers who played the music she liked to hear the way she liked to hear it. Among her great friends were Adolf Busch—the whole Busch family—the Serkins, Horszowski, Steinberg, Menuhin, Martinu, Szell; for the out-of-towners her spacious, cheerful apartment on Park Avenue was virtually New York headquarters. Many of them practiced there, some of them stayed there and all of them at one time or another graced, or were the reason for, the joyful post-concert evenings she so often invited us to share.

Although occasionally, on her birthday (celebrated jointly with her close chum, the violist Lillian Fuchs), there would be a party with music, generally at the after-concert events music was eschewed in favor of good food and talk. One slight exception that stands out in my mind occurred on my wedding night. Serkin had a tradition of giving his annual Carnegie Hall recital around the first week of December, and Naomi and I, taking our approaching nuptials rather casually, decided that if we got married on the day of a Serkin recital we'd always remember, at least approximately, our anniversary. On the day in question, after visiting both City Hall (where the clerk who joined us in wedlock gave a routine performance) and Carnegie Hall (where it seemed that Serkin was particularly inspired), we basked in his post-recital celebration at Mrs. Leventritt's. Everything was fine until, at a certain moment, a hush fell over the party as, to our great embarrassment, Rudolf Serkin and Nadia Reisenberg seated themselves at the two pianos and plunged into a stirring rendition of Mendelssohn's *Wedding March* as a cake was brought out. If we had hoped our deed would escape notice, the jig was up. Several members of the Marlboro Board of Directors had come down from Vermont for the recital and one of these ladies, encountering Naomi, who was wearing a blush to match her Jezebel-red dress, twittered coyly, "And is this the bride?" My wife, cornered, stammered, "More or less," which in those unenlightened days was rather a brazen *gaffe*.

One razzle-dazzle artist whose irresistible charms won him a secure spot in Rosalie Leventritt's chastely Schubertian heart was a gangling Juilliard student from Texas named Van Cliburn. He was nineteen when he played at the Leventritt Competition. Word had gotten around that he was very gifted, but nobody really knew what to expect. And he looked so different. He was so tall—and, well, so *American*. (This reminds me of an experience that befell me several years later at Carnegie Hall. I had gone to the recital of another pianist from Texas—they had proliferated by then—and at intermission, after greeting Van, John Browning, Philippe Entremont and a few other slightly younger colleagues, I heard the voice of Schuyler Chapin hooting at me, "There he goes—the last of the Jewish pianists!") At the time Van entered the Leventritt, however, pianists were Central or Eastern European, or at least of that extraction. It looked so odd to see a *cowboy* play the *piano*. But when Van took over the keyboard, all visions of bucking broncos vanished instantly. The Leventritt jury—and the audience, of which I was one—were astonished by his relaxed yet seemingly limitless virtuosity, and when he finished an electrifying performance of a Liszt rhapsody, there was a good moment's stunned silence before the judges could gather the temerity to ask him to play a little something else. He was still sitting at the piano, awaiting instructions, and I remember that he turned to them at that moment, before beginning the next piece, and shyly asked, "Would y'all mahnd if Ah went and got a glass of WAWtuh?"

The few moments he was gone from the stage gave us all a much-needed breather and the opportunity to shake our heads in wonderment. The jury scribbled busily on little index cards provided for their comments, doodles and reminder notes about each contestant—not that they were likely to forget this one. At the end of the afternoon, after victorious Van had been borne away in triumph, Naomi and I noticed a forgotten note pad on the floor beneath the chair where Talent Scout Arthur Judson—always on the lookout for another OYAP— had been sitting and scribbling busily. We pounced on it and read his sage assessment of the winner's potential: "Not now; perhaps another year."

Van was a very likable kid, and what he may have lacked at that time in musical sophistication he more than made up for in natural talent and genuine love for what he was playing. I have a feeling that the somewhat smart-alecky ways of us East

Coast OYAPs may have grated on his gentle and gentlemanly character; but in spite of our raucous behavior and frequent teasing, we honestly appreciated and admired his quite extraordinary gifts.

Even before he went to Moscow, some four years later, Van was charismatic. As part of his Leventritt award, he made his New York Philharmonic debut at one of the orchestra's Sunday afternoon concerts. Carnegie Hall looked like the Alamo. Planeloads of Texans had come up for the launching. Van played Tchaikovsky, and the place went wild. After the smoke had cleared, we fought our way backstage, bearing with us Rosalie Leventritt. The staircase leading up to the artists' rooms at Carnegie Hall is always jammed after a successful or well-attended concert, but on that afternoon it was worse than the subway rush hour at Christmastime, possibly because Texans are generally larger than IRT riders. We let ourselves be carried along by the crowd and finally found ourselves craning up at a beaming Van. He grabbed fragile Mrs. Leventritt in an enormous bear hug, and would have swept her off her feet if there had been room. "Honey," he drawled, "see all these people?" She nodded. "Well, they all comin' to yo' party," he announced. Mrs. Leventritt gulped.

That afternoon was the only time in the many years of attending her parties that I can remember a certain tenseness on the face of our hostess. Things got off to a shaky start when some helpful soul put the masses of long-stemmed roses Van had sent, together with an appropriate amount of WAWtuh, into the Ming vase that stood on one of the pianos, resulting in a trickle that eventually turned into a cascade. Meanwhile, what seemed like the entire Carnegie Hall audience trooped into the apartment, happy, hearty, huge and hungry. Rosalie Leventritt wandered through the crowded rooms with a glazed look and (although she would never say it) an expression on her face that beseeched, "Family! Gang! Please go easy—I don't think there's going to be enough food!" I nobly denied myself a second helping of the shrimp aspic that afternoon, more than making up for it, of course, on subsequent occasions.

Rosalie Leventritt was often called upon to provide solace for wounds inflicted on some of her great friends by one of her greatest friends, George Szell. Although she shared his impeccable, uncompromising standards, her bronze core was cloaked in soft celadon-green velvet, while his was armored with steely porcupine quills, which could pierce deeply and painfully. He was aware and, I think, even proud of his ogre-like reputation. The day that *Time* magazine appeared on the newsstands with his picture on the cover and an exhaustive profile inside displaying his foibles—warts and all—his delight was boundless. "It's official! It's official!" he crowed. "It's in print—I'm a bastard!"

Extremely articulate in several languages, George Szell enjoyed—in fact, insisted on—saying, in a precise arrangement of perfectly chosen words, exactly what was on his mind. Sometimes these observations were merely apt and maybe just a wee bit prickly, such as his description of America's most powerful concert manager: "A vest-pocket Machiavelli"; a famous Central European conductor's political history: "No, of course not! He was never a Nazi, just a prostitute"; or my wife's hairdo: "Today you look like a toilet brush." But at a certain point each season—usually around the Ides of March—his associates girded themselves for what was cheerfully referred to (by those not affected) as his Annual Fit.

This was usually brought on by a crime against music committed by someone who, he felt, should have known better. The catalyst could be as simple as a tiny blooper played at the beginning of a rehearsal on a freezing morning by a favorite French horn player ("Now, Mike, let's not start *that* again!") or the sound, during a concert, of his first cellist's bow inadvertently knocking against the rear of the piano ("The first time, Lynn, I can understand. It's an accident. It can happen. But the second time, no. IT'S INEXCUSABLE TO MAKE THE SAME MISTAKE TWICE!"). But sometimes, on a very black day, it could involve what Szell considered to be an unforgivable musical aberration on the part of a hitherto beloved soloist, resulting in anything from a piano lesson administered from the podium to, very sadly, a serious and even permanent breach of friendship.

So one always went to Cleveland with more than the normal apprehensions. Even the name of the orchestra's auditorium—Severance Hall—had an ominous ring, and I always imagined I could hear a guillotine whirring as I entered the backstage portals. But (almost disappointingly, considering the august company I would have shared) those porcupine quills never slashed at me—for musical reasons, anyway. This is not to indicate that I was above or beyond criticism (particularly when I remember one of my first performances of the Rachmaninoff *Rhapsody*, after which Szell escorted me to the dressing room in which Naomi was cowering and, with a big smile, shouted at her, "You were *right* not to go into the audience tonight!"), but can only be considered as pure, dumb luck, equivalent to surviving a game of Russian roulette.

Our Armageddon (for of course we did finally have one) occurred on a much less Olympian battleground. It came after our recording of the Tchaikovsky First Concerto, the day we were performing it at Carnegie Hall. (Leave it to Szell to arrange a recording as a warm-up for a Carnegie Hall performance. *He* knew how to order priorities.) We'd finished our rehearsal and retired to the Green Room backstage, where Columbia Records had scheduled a photographing session for the record album cover.

Szell was a bit testy because time had been wasted at the rehearsal by a piano problem. (The Cleveland Orchestra, unlike most others, still had full, serious rehearsals in New York even though the works involved had been rehearsed and performed —and in this case, even recorded—in Cleveland.) The instrument I was to play on, which had been sent to Cleveland for the recording, had just arrived back in New York after its ten-day odyssey traversing the four hundred and sixty-five miles between the two cities. But instead of being at Carnegie Hall, it was resting at a trucking depot in the East Bronx awaiting the moment when a sufficient load would be assembled to make it worthwhile for a truck driver to transport it to the Steinway repository at West Fifty-eighth Street, where it could then be unloaded from the long-distance movers' truck and loaded onto a Steinway mover's truck for the two-block journey to Carnegie Hall. Meanwhile, I had to play at the rehearsal (once it was definitely ascertained that the piano in question could not arrive in time) on the Carnegie Hall house Steinway, which had, earlier that morning, been carefully tuned and then carefully locked. This meant that we all had to wait until someone came running over from Steinway's with the key. Although once it was unlocked there was nothing wrong with this particular piano, it was not the one that I'd be using for the performance, and so the most delicate matters of balance of sound with the orchestra were still left unresolved. These problems, as can be imagined, were not things Szell took lightly.

Nevertheless, he co-operatively arranged his face in a record-album-cover smile; that is, until he noted that Don Hunstein, the Columbia photographer, was nowhere to be seen. We cooled our heels for a few minutes until that excellent, if somewhat eccentric, artist arrived and proceeded calmly to set up his paraphernalia, which was considerable and involved elaborately conceived arrangements of floodlights, reflecting umbrellas and other gadgets, all of which Szell regarded with increasing irritation. Finally, as Don was moving an umbrella for what seemed like the seventeenth time, Szell spoke. In measured tones, quietly at first, he said, "I had a concert last night. I have a concert tonight. I have another concert tomorrow night. I am not a young man. I have no time to waste. And furthermore," here his voice became stronger, more penetrating, and, as he turned to me, utterly chilling: "And *furthermore*, I don't think I want to be photographed with you, Gary, with your hair like that." (I hadn't had a haircut in months. Part of the reason was laziness or, as I liked to think, lack of time; but a good deal of it was because this was the era of the Rich Hippie Look and curls down my neck seemed fashionable. Naomi hated my long hair and badgered me constantly, but I was running with the tide; anyway, Liszt's hair had been even longer. Somewhere inside of me I knew that Szell, too, had been disapproving of my coiffure every time we'd met in the past few months—which was frequently—even though he'd never given the slightest overt indication. But we had all heard the story of his meeting Peter Serkin at the airport in Amsterdam, a few months earlier, and of driving him directly to a barbershop before allowing him to set foot in the Amstel Hotel.) Szell stared at me unsmilingly and repeated, "No, not with your hair like that. Now I want some lunch. And you can either get a haircut or, if you prefer, we will have two separate photos on the album cover. There will be a photo of me on one side, and a photo of you on the other, and," here his lips curled, his eyes narrowed and he bellowed, "*and you can be naked, for all I care!*"

I bolted for the nearest barbershop and a half hour later emerged feeling, if not looking, like a skinned rabbit. When I shamefacedly opened the door to our apartment Naomi let out a shriek that I'm sure was heard the length and breadth of Fifty-seventh Street. At that moment, the phone rang. It was Szell. "Gary," he shouted. "Don't do it! Helene" (his wife) "says she loves your hair long. Besides, she says, it will surely sell more records if one of us, at least, looks like a Beatle. Nobody, she says, will want to buy a record with a picture of two crabby old businessmen on the cover."

"Too late," I replied grimly.

"Ah, he did it already," said Szell to his wife, who was evidently by his side. Loud female cries of dismay crackled over the wire. Naomi then grabbed the phone to assure Szell that he was on the side of the angels, and gave fervent thanks to him for accomplishing what she had been unable to do. His momentary embarrassment at being the cause of such a drastic change in my appearance was instantly overcome by the placating words from my wife, his eternal ally. Regrouping his forces, he roared—with a sound I'll never forget—into the phone, "Mattresses! *Mattresses!! M-A-T-T-RRRRESSES!!! That's* what they look like! That's all I ever see walking down the street these days! Smelly, greasy *mattresses!*" More screams and cries of dismay from the lady at his side, and encouraging, "attaboy" squeals from the lady at my side, our voices blending in a veritable Verdian quartet.

Another photography session was set up for the next day, when Helene Szell's only comment to me was a sympathetic, "Well, it'll grow back. I'll wait." Our serious expressions in the photo that finally did grace the record cover belies the fact that by the time this picture was taken we had all simmered down and, just the minute before, Szell had actually been clowning for Don Hunstein's camera with a fez I brought over to Carnegie Hall for a prop. That series of photos, however, has mysteriously disappeared.

I like to think that the recording session itself was far less disagreeable than our bleak visages on the cover photo would indicate. Of all the orchestras I recorded with, the Cleveland's way of working seemed closest to simulating an actual performance; at least, there was an attempt. Orchestra recordings are sometimes made on a patchwork basis, without adequate rehearsal, with the cynical or (depending upon one's point of view) pragmatic idea that what doesn't work out will immediately be done over, and over, and over until all mistakes are "covered." Then, at an editing session (at which, sometimes, none of the performers choose to be present) the most desirable takes are spliced together, sometimes, of necessity, in very small sections. This is done under the supervision of the record's producer, the Renaissance man employed by the recording company to see the thing through from start to finish.

These producers (or at least the ones I've had the pleasure of collaborating with) are remarkably gifted, and in their own ways as virtuosic as are the musicians whose performances they capture on tape. They, too, are solidly trained musicians who must know the scores thoroughly. In addition, they have to be diplomats, psychologists and, in order to minimize the dread penalties of overtime, army drillmasters. Most important, they are privy to the art, craft and dirty little secrets of sound engineering as well.

The virtuoso producer has, in fact, begun to vie with the virtuoso performer on records. Before the advent of LPs, when records were made in no-longer-than-five-minute increments, the usual way to correct anything was just to do that record side over. Recording onto tape changed all this, and as the producer's finesse with splicing a better phrase or even a single note over a less satisfactory one increased, so did his power.

One of the earliest indications of things to come occurred when RCA transferred, some years after his death, Artur Schnabel's recordings of the thirty-two Beethoven sonatas to long-playing records. Schnabel had never seemed to care particularly about wrong notes, and his famous series of Beethoven sonata recordings had their fair share. At the time of the transfer to LP, the limitless possibilities permitted by the use of tape were just beginning to be explored, and whoever was in charge of the transfer, carried away by the golden opportunities at his disposal, decided to clean things up a bit while he was at it. Many of the sections of these sonatas repeat; and as Schnabel didn't necessarily play a wrong note in the same place twice, it was a fairly simple matter to replace a smudged phrase with the same phrase played cleanly in the repeat. That it wasn't Schnabel any more—because, of course, there might be a subtle difference in emphasis in his performance of the repeated section—wasn't the point; the important thing was that, at last, more correct notes were there. It is said that when this cosmetic surgery had been completed and the finished tapes were heard by the eager young surgeon's superior, a thunderous order echoed through the corridors of the RCA recording studios to *"put those goddam clinkers back!"*

I have long been in awe of Andrew Kazdin, for years the producer of the Cleveland Orchestra's records (among many others), and have watched him accomplish incredible feats involving sleight of hand and ear, not the least of which was eliminating the clank of a double-bass player's cuff links hitting against his instrument (obviously not in Szell's orchestra!) without erasing the double-bass music as well. We all heard the extraneous sounds when the tape was played at the editing session; eventually Andy was able to deduce the cause and develop a strategy for their removal. At his calm and specific instructions the rolling tape was stopped at the offending places and, as I marveled, small triangular (cuff-link-shaped?) pieces of tape were literally cut away, successfully separating the clackety-clacks from the plink-a-plinks. I have no doubt that if Andy were to be presented with a trunkful of assorted sounds played on assorted instruments, he could, like Dr. Frankenstein—or, perhaps, more accurately, Henry Higgins—assemble them in such a way as to create a viable recording of almost any piece of music, thus doing away entirely, once and for all, with performers.

In the beginning, the producer was anonymous. Gradually a mention of his work crept in somewhere on the record jacket. As time marched on his name loomed larger and larger and someday, I think, this will culminate in the ultimate distribution of credit, reading something like:

ANDREW KAZDIN PRODUCES!

and then, in smaller letters,

Zubin Mehta and the New York Philharmonic,

and finally, in the tiniest possible type,

playing the Beethoven Fifth Symphony

A rival company will issue a record of the same music entitled "JOHN PFEIFFER PRODUCES!" which will involve another orchestra playing the same music. On one cover will appear a photo of the producer, with a diabolical leer, operating innumerable asymmetrically arranged buttons and levers on a machine resembling an unidentified flying object; the other record will sport a likeness of the rival producer asleep in a hammock on some remote island paradise.

Discophiles will compare the Kazdin version against the Pfeiffer version, and audiophiles will write learned treatises on "the imperceptibly smooth transitional splices to and from the orchestral and Moog tapes . . . where in the latter the producer was able to . . . more nearly approach the conductor's interpretation than was the orchestra . . . at least in the slow movement, which . . . invites comparison with the earlier, and now classic, Thomas Frost interpretation . . . a breakthrough in its day . . . combining, as it did, four second violins each from the tapes of three different orchestras . . . in order to produce a more stylistically integrated mix." Considering what producers have to go through to produce a record, I think they deserve every bit of credit they can get.

Even in Cleveland, where the serious preparations may have given the actual sessions a more performance-like atmosphere than obtained with some other orchestras, the recordings were nonetheless edited with the most scrupulous and painstaking care. Certainly, in an age when perfection as slick as modern technology will allow is taken for granted, it would be foolhardy to market a product any less idealized than the fashion decrees. Still, the attitude was of prime importance: one tried not to fuss with the basic take any more than absolutely necessary, as opposed to the frequent practice of not even attempting a cohesive performance for the recording machines.

Anyway, by the time Szell and his orchestra were ready for a recording, it was assumed that everything would go smoothly, and that nothing would be left to chance. Lest anyone feel that leaving nothing to chance makes for a routine performance, let me state that I firmly believe that only when nothing is left to chance—when every idea has been thought out and practiced and ingrained—is it truly possible to take *real* chances at a performance or recording session, and to allow the inspiration of the moment to take over. The flexibility must be within certain boundaries, which have clearly been staked out according to the taste of the performer. Otherwise, chaos.

If there was one thing Szell's detractors harassed him for, it was what they considered his lack of flexibility. He was sometimes likened to a bandmaster beating time steadily, come what may. The truth or falsity of this point of view can be argued *ad infinitum* and comes under the category, in my opinion, of subtlety: as mentioned earlier, what is not enough for one person can be far too much for someone else. Nevertheless, Szell was never considered a conductor who allowed a lot of leeway in rhythmic matters. But life is full of surprises. At the Tchaikovsky recording session of which I am writing, when we made a test of the first movement, I played the first series of octaves several times, but somehow the beginning of each series always sounded muddy. Szell explained to me that this was because the sound of the orchestra had not yet sufficiently died away before I plunged in. "The trouble with you, Gary," he said (all of this was being picked up, of course, by the recording microphones), "is that you're playing *too metronomically*." This observation (completely accurate, by the way) from someone who was often called "the walking metronome" caused unbridled hilarity in the control room and throughout the orchestra, which got the session off to a good-natured start.

The only time, in fact, that we heard even a growl from the lion on the podium was after the flute solo at the beginning of the second movement. A visitor in the control room was puzzled to hear the third note of the solo being played as an F, when his Eulenburg score (and the way he was accustomed to hearing it) involved a B-flat. He mentioned this to Andy Kazdin, whose score called for the F, and when Szell came in to listen to the take, Andy asked him about the discrepancy. A rumble like distant thunder was heard deep down in Szell's throat, and although he seemed to be trying to control his annoyance, he finally burst out, "That's the trouble with those petty minds, those pedants, those levelers who monkey with editions. They always want everything the same. They want everything to conform with their niggling ideas of how things should be. Symmetry! Pah! The whole *point* is that this is the only time the melody goes that way." He glowered at the offending score. "This is not the *old* Eulenburg edition. It's a new one! They're always doing those things these days . . . 'improving!' . . . they do it with Dvořák, too. And Mozart. Everywhere. Puerile idiots!" He took a red pencil and made the correction in the score. Later, the visitor reported, he checked eight other then-current recordings of the concerto and found that only one, by the Chicago Orchestra under Reiner, had concurred with the Cleveland and Szell.

Sunshine again, and soon we were finished. "Andy, are we okay?" Szell called to the producer, possibly the only person in the world at that moment who might be able to tell Szell that he was not satisfied with some of the orchestral playing and survive. "Everything seems fine," Andy sang out. "Gary?" asked Szell. I thought I'd done the best I could, and admitted it. Szell's eye then caught sight of Naomi, huddled in a corner with *her* score and an "is-this-all-there-is-to-life?" expression on her face. He approached her and looked down kindly. She raised her face to his, hopefully. Maybe you could just do the whole thing over once more, her eyes seemed to say. He paused until there was complete silence in the room. He made sure he had everyone's attention. He then fixed her with that implacable steel-blue stare, enlarged through glinting glasses to the icy brilliance of twin searchlights at Alcatraz, and boomed, "For the kibitzer, no stakes are too high."

Class dismissed.

CHAPTER ELEVEN

Pianist in the Basement

IN THE EARLY fifties it was still possible to do things on a grand scale. The Steinway piano company celebrated its hundredth anniversary in October 1953 with a gala concert at Carnegie Hall at which ten Steinway concert grands, lined up on stage like the great bulls of Pamplona, were consecutively attacked by several teams of ten pianists each who tore through specially concocted twenty-hand arrangements of rousing music (my role being one tenth of "The Star-Spangled Banner," which opened the proceedings), somewhat on the order of a relay race.

The New York Philharmonic-Symphony was also pressed into service. Toward the end of the concert nine of the pianos were removed and Dimitri Mitropoulos, then the orchestra's music director and also a pianist of note, seated himself at the remaining Steinway and played the Prokofiev Third Concerto, conducting from the instrument. The logistics of maintaining eyeball contact with his orchestra while accomplishing this feat were neatly solved by replacing the ebony piano lid, which would normally have blocked his view, with a see-through Plexiglas one, constructed just for the occasion. As can easily be construed, no expense was spared to make the event unforgettable.

But the climax of the celebration, at least in my opinion, took place after the concert with a sumptuous dinner party at the Waldorf-Astoria for what seemed like a cast of thousands. The beloved Theodore Steinway, grandson of the founder, president of the company, intimate and respected friend of the instrument's immortals, presided. As a businessman, he knew full well that this golden era was drawing to a close, and he startled the assembled multitude, about to begin the banquet, with a solemn announcement.

"Things are not what they used to be," he declared, as waiters scurried back and forth pouring vintage champagne, "and we must really begin to economize. So, my friends, I beg of you: please, just one spoonful of caviar apiece." He then held aloft an enormous, oversized soup spoon, and signaled us to begin ladling. I did not hesitate to follow this invitation and plunged right in, savoring my good fortune at being a Steinway Artist almost as much as I did the juicy black fish eggs.

To be completely accurate, I did not always play the Steinway. From the time I started to study, at around the age of three, until I was accepted at the Curtis Institute of Music, some four years later, I practiced on the family Baldwin, which my father used to accompany his violin pupils. As soon as I went to Vengerova all this changed: she quickly arranged for the Curtis Institute (or rather, the benevolent Mrs. Bok) to have an excellent Steinway sent from the school in Philadelphia to our living room in New York.

Although one of the two pianos in Vengerova's studio was a Mason & Hamlin (at that time a superior instrument, highly regarded by musicians), the other was a Steinway, and this was always the piano on which I played during my lessons. It was typical that Vengerova considered it important for a seven-year-old to practice on a Steinway, too, even though there was a perfectly adequate grand piano in his home. She regarded what she considered the best instrument a necessary tool for building a proper musical education, reinforcing her constant preoccupation with sound for the sake of sound, and the singing, non-percussive tone that she felt so necessary for pianists to acquire.

So this Steinway Model L (the largest of the three baby grand types, appropriately identified as "S," "M" and "L") arrived at our house for what turned out to be a very extended loan. For the next ten years, in my unceasing search for the singing, non-percussive tone, I whanged the daylights out of it. Then, when I was seventeen and about to graduate from Curtis, my father received a letter from the school administrators saying that although they could not continue to lend me the piano once I had finished my studies there, the Institute would sell it to my father if he wanted it. Would $500 be a fair price? Even for those days, and even for my budget-minded father, it was a good buy. Moreover, once it became family property, my father had it sent to the Steinway factory, where, for another $800, the injuries inflicted upon its insides were effaced and it was once again as good as new. That was in 1946. Since then, this instrument has, with one more overhaul at home in 1975, endured another thirty-odd years of my pummeling. It is exactly the same age as I am, and I only wish that I were holding up as well.

I must have been around nine when I was introduced to the makers of my piano. Although the Steinway factory is somewhere out near La Guardia Airport, the New York showrooms and offices for many of the executives as well as the pianos concerned with concert activities were in Manhattan's music neighborhood on West Fifty-seventh Street in the edifice then known as the Steinway Building. I was about to make one of my then-infrequent public appearances, and according to the customary courtesy extended toward the performers who play and endorse the Steinway, I was invited to select an instrument for my recital from the bank of concert grands stored in the basement of that building.

Vengerova took me there. But first she escorted me upstairs to the office of Theodore Steinway. As soon as we entered, he jumped up from behind his desk and clasped my hand warmly, greeting me as if I were someone who played every year with every orchestra in the world and was unquestionably going to continue to do so for all eternity, completely ignoring the fact that I was in short pants. I then met his brother, known as Uncle Bill, who was similarly respectful; and finally Alexander Greiner, called Sascha, the manager of the Concert Artist Department, and the person directly in charge of dealing with the performers who played the Steinway. He, too, paid homage to me, ignoring my bare knees and soprano voice, and together we descended, in a little private elevator lined with charmingly inlaid woodwork, to The Basement.

How can I describe this place that came to mean so much to me, and, I imagine, to most of us OYAPs, for so many of our formative years?

Physically, The Basement—or, to be accurate, the room in the basement known as The Basement (except to Stokowski, who stubbornly called it The Cellar)—is a cavernous chamber, furnished with the accoutrements of a factory workshop, windowless, of course, and drably painted. Exposed pipes involved in the plumbing and heating for the entire sixteen-story building snake across the walls and ceiling, often calling attention to their presence by ominous series of hisses, thuds and clankings. One customarily enters this room by pushing aside with great effort a groaning, heavily weighted steel sliding door. (There's a perfectly normal door, too, but nobody ever seems to use it.) Inside repose several dozen black monsters—nine-foot concert grand pianos—that are not for sale. They are consecrated, instead, to the Steinway Concert Department, which means that, like the houris of a seraglio, they serenely await the pleasure of the Steinway Artist. During the daytime, white-coated technicians minister to their every need: repairing, adjusting, refining, ascertaining that every one of these instruments' twelve thousand parts functions at top efficiency.

It is here that the Steinway Artist may come to select an instrument to use for performance in and around New York City; and to use also—if he can afford it and is willing to invest the extortionate sums now demanded by the Teamsters to ship it out of town—in other cities throughout the country (although heaven only knows, these days, when, if and in what condition it will arrive). Ladies of the evening, these concert pianos are, to put it crassly, available for one-night stands. Although many are revisited by the same artists time and again, woe unto him who becomes too attached to any one of these slippery black beasts! For the relationship can rarely be monogamous, is almost never permanent, and Fifty-seventh Street often resounds with wailing and gnashing of teeth when the piano's makers decree, for one reason or another, that some particularly favored instrument's Basement days are over.

They may look alike, these enormous pianos lined up in the big room, but they do not sound alike. Nobody really knows why. Various theories are advanced: perhaps the relationship of certain parts of the instrument to its sounding board; perhaps even the specific wood used for the sounding board itself— every piece of wood is different, after all; mysterious acoustical reasons; alchemy. But the fact remains that while each Steinway piano has its characteristic "Steinway sound," each instrument, for a number of indefinable acoustical reasons, also has its own unique voice. And the greater the instrument, the more individual and unique its voice. It only remains for the artist to find the particular instrument that speaks best for him—the instrument that he feels will allow him the greatest freedom of expression.

It is in search of this ideal instrument that pianists flock to The Basement, a seemingly endless stream of them: from the Juilliard debutant to the season's Soviet lion; from the white-haired patriarch to the bare-kneed prodigy. Most frequently one sees them scuttling (after nightfall, when the technicians have left and the offices are closed) like nocturnal scavengers, down a flight of service stairs at the rear of the building, near the overflowing trash cans.

That is the normal way we go to The Basement. On my first

visit, though, at the venerable age of nine, I was carried gen-
teelly downward by the private elevator, encircled by my retinue of human Steinways. When we entered the big room, even
I, who took almost everything in stride, was awed by the sight
of a veritable dragon pit squirming with huge black pianos.
Theodore Steinway introduced me to The Basement Nibelungen who guarded the golden sounds produced by these
craggy and capricious monsters. The head Nibelungen at that
time were appropriately named Hupfer, Schnaper and Messer-
schmitt, and they, in turn, proceeded to make further introductions.

"Mr. Graffman," said William Hupfer, the head technician,
"I would like to introduce to you CD 18, Rachmaninoff's
piano. Here, sit down and see what you think of it." Said
Greiner, "You were at the Hofmann Jubilee concert, I know.
Here is the instrument he used for that. Why don't you give it
a try? . . . Aha! what about this one? Schnabel will play it at
Carnegie Hall next month. Now, let's see, when is your recital?" (Turning to another piano:) "Oh, too bad, this will be
out on tour with Rubinstein at that time, but why don't you
play something on it anyway, and tell me what you think of
it? . . . This one is with Serkin; that one is already reserved by
Casadesus. So, of the pianos that are here now, you may choose
from these ten. We'll write down the numbers for you." And
he proceeded to show me how to identify the different instruments. "And if you wish to come back again next week,"
Theodore Steinway added, "there'll be a few more pianos available that are out at the moment. So come back and see what
suits you best. This is not a decision to be arrived at lightly,
you know!"

Although I continued to encounter Theodore Steinway casually over the years, one of my great regrets is that I never had
the opportunity of becoming as well acquainted with him as I
did with the various other members of his family it has been
my privilege to know. They are a wonderful bunch, and share a
common heritage of passionate individualism as well as the

ability (among the males, at least) to build a piano from scratch.

Several members of this clan spent the summers in a compound of cottages overlooking what in Massachusetts is known as a "great pond"—anywhere else, it would be a lake—and in the summer of 1959 we took over the Chapins' cottage while Schuyler and Betty (Theodore Steinway's daughter) and the four boys got away from it all to an even more isolated spot: the island of Eigg, in the Hebrides. At the end of August they came home with tales of chopping coal each morning to light the stove for tea (and of Goddard Lieberson's overseas phone call to Schuyler at Eigg 002 wooing him away from Columbia Artists to Columbia Masterworks). We, for our part, countered with detailed descriptions of the rainiest summer on record. I was doing some heavy practicing and had had sent up from New York an item that the Chapins overlooked in furnishing their cottage: namely, a Steinway. After about a month of almost incessant rain, everything turned green with mold, including the piano. Maybe that is an exaggeration, but it certainly is no overstatement to say that every key was sluggish and many were stuck, in spite of electric light bulbs and other dehumidifying devices inserted inside the long-suffering instrument. One Saturday morning, however, we were overwhelmed to see a blue sky and bright sunlight. We quickly brought all our damp clothes and slimy shoes outside, where we saw two Steinway brothers, John and Fritz, advancing on us with a purposeful air. (It was particularly lucky that this sunny day occurred on a weekend, when they were both on the premises.) They marched into the music room, took apart the piano, removed its innards, and carried them outside into the divinely dry heat. There, placed gently on the cocktail table facing the pond, the piano's interior mechanism sat like a sunbathing skeleton while the mushy felts and swelling wood dried out for a few hours before the next month's onslaught of rain closed in on us.

It was during that summer—about five years after Theodore Steinway's death—that we first became friendly with his

widow, Ruth. She had by then left New York and installed herself more or less permanently in this piny New England retreat,
where she was one of the pillars of the community, as befitted
the *Mayflower* descendant that she was. She also gardened,
swam (every day, it seemed, except when the pond was frozen
solid), read everything in sight, watched birds, kept turtles, involved herself in amateur theatricals, careened down back roads
in her bright red convertible Volkswagen, cooked fish chowder
for multitudes ("only haddock will do, of course") and in the
summer at tea or cocktail time on her breeze-swept brick terrace overlooking the calm waters, regaled us with vivid stories
of life between the world wars with Sergei, Josef, Myra, Arthur,
Olga and practically every other legendary pianist whom she
had known so well.

She also genuinely loved to listen to other people's stories.
She made every guest feel (and I think she really meant it) as
if *his* was the visit she had been waiting for. That year, and on
subsequent summers, when we made our annual return—as
visitors—to the Chapins' cottage, we eagerly looked forward to
her invitations. (The houses were separated by no more than a
few hundred yards of woods, but one never "dropped in.")
After successfully slithering along the worn-slippery pine-
needled path to her terrace, we would carefully lower ourselves
into the hard wooden dark green Adirondack chairs to the welcoming exclamations of our hostess: "Gary! Nayomi! Isn't this
nice! Now. Tell me *everything!*" She reveled in travel tales and
was an inveterate traveler herself, each year inspecting another
far-flung part of the world with keen-eyed enthusiasm. Her son
John usually accompanied her on these jaunts, although the
time she went to Timbuktu she took a Chapin grandson,
Miles, instead. John, she explained, liked his comfort, and she
felt this trip might be a little rough. One didn't know what the
accommodations would be like and, as she put it, "John likes to
know where he'll lay his head at night. As for me, I don't especially care."

She saved her caring for more important matters. One of
these was the sterling reputation of Steinway & Sons, and I sus-

pect that she was never reconciled to the company's purchase by CBS. This acquisition, which took place in 1972, was hotly disputed by some family members, giving rise to a moving plea by two more Chapin grandchildren, Samuel and Theodore, to veto the merger. In an impassioned yet well-considered letter to the stockholders, they cited the well-known case of the Fender guitar, the quality of which apparently deteriorated shockingly after its acquisition by CBS, and warned that although "the Steinway name will live on . . . no one can be sure it will be affixed to a product equaling the quality of the piano on which the Steinway tradition has been built." This, nevertheless, was a minority view; and while one cannot truthfully claim that Sam and Ted's worst fears have yet been realized, I do fervently wish that the Steinway family still owned—and ran as it was run when I first became a Steinway Artist—the company that bears its noble name.

Not that I didn't complain about pianos while Steinways were still in charge. As a teenager, I learned that to play concerts outside of New York City was to gripe. One of the first facts rudely brought to my attention then was that, once away from the bosom of The Basement, the condition of the instruments at a touring pianist's disposal would be, at best, unpredictable. A good tuning was the most one could hope for.

Nobody thinks it at all odd for a violinist to take his Strad to a violin-maker for frequent adjustment and repair. Yet it was (and still quite generally is) a common misconception among even the most sophisticated concertgoers that tuning is all a piano needs to keep it in condition. Would that this were so! Tuning a piano is like having the tires of one's car properly inflated: without doubt, most important. But to make sure that the car runs properly, one does have to peek at the engine every now and then as well. And changing the pressure in a tire any number of times is not going to help a faulty transmission one iota.

My initial reaction of shock and dismay when confronted by pianos in less than perfect health evoked sympathy but not much more. The white-coated Nibelungen who clucked and

fussed over Basement gold had nothing to do with the Steinways that languished and turned to dross in other cities, and I
soon discovered that first-class piano technicians, even in the
days when good craftsmanship was more prevalent than it is
now, were an endangered species.

"The sad truth is, Gary, that good technicians are few and
far between," Sascha Greiner explained, "and sadder yet is the
fact that even where there may be someone who really knows
how to take care of a piano, there is no guarantee that he'll be
the one who's engaged to look after the instrument you'll be
playing on. Good tuners you'll find—there are enough of those;
but a technician and a tuner, as you must know by now, are
two different animals." (Although a technician can also be a
tuner, it is rare indeed to find a tuner who is also a first-class
technician.) "In most cases you'll find that it's the tuner who'll
be in complete charge and, with all the good will in the world,
he can make a botch of things when he tries to do more than
tune. This is a great pity, because a concert piano requires constant vigilance and attention. Changes of temperature and humidity, careless movers, accidents such as a glass of something
being overturned, not to mention the parade of pianists assault-
ing it (you'll forgive me, Gary, if I use that term) . . . it's too
bad, but we have no control over who is hired to attend to our
pianos in the field. So hold your breath, and hope for the best!"
Thus, OYAP Lesson Number One, learned at Sascha Greiner's
knee: It is not enough to know how to play well on a piano in
good condition.

Lesson Number Two was also provided by Uncle Sascha, or
more specifically, at his suggestion by Uncle Bill Hupfer, then
and for many years the chief Basement technician, who gave
Leon, Eugene and me a quickie course in the rudiments of
pianology. He showed us everything, starting with how to take
the damned things apart. He introduced us to the mysterious
rites of "regulation" and "voicing"—the painstaking processes
by which a piano's mechanism and sound are brought to their
highest peak. Watching and listening to Bill Hupfer at work
we observed that skill, experience, patience and dedication

were not enough; a top-flight technician also had to have an ear at least as sensitive as a musician's in order to voice the instrument properly. We learned that it was, in fact, up to the technician to determine the characteristic sound of the instrument in question and to realize its full potential. To accomplish this, he must first ascertain that the hammers are striking the strings at precisely the most advantageous place on which the strings should be struck, and he must then be able to mold, literally as well as figuratively, each of the eighty-eight felt-covered hammers with files, pins, irons and sometimes even a shellac-like liquid to produce the desired results. And after this job is completed, he must go through the entire procedure once again with the shift (or left) pedal depressed, as this causes a different part of the hammer to strike the string. Following this "voicing with the soft pedal down," as it is called, he must check to make sure that he has not inadvertently undone his original work.

All of this intricate voicing, we discovered, was undertaken only after another series of elaborate and difficult operations had been completed—that of regulating the piano's action properly, by judicious manipulation of many parts, thus ensuring that the pianist will be able to depress each key throughout the entire keyboard by exerting the same amount of weight; that as each key is being depressed, the same complicated activities will occur within the piano at the same extent of depression for each key; and that each key will continue to function normally even when repeatedly depressed at great speed. Elementary as this may seem, it was rare even then to find a piano on tour that was regulated evenly (not to mention well voiced), and we soon became painfully aware of how crucial it was to make adjustments in our playing to compensate for lack of same in our instruments.

Sometimes I feel that my real schooling in piano playing began only when I was turned loose among those ill-tempered beasts west of the Hudson. I had to learn, above all, how to Scheme. After analyzing the problems presented by the particular instrument snarling up at me at any given moment, it was necessary to plot a safe course through its minefields in order to avoid untoward explosions during the performance. These explosions might come about for any number of reasons, some as obvious as a loose pedal's almost falling off (I remember supporting one such pedal with my left foot throughout an entire Rachmaninoff concerto in Minneapolis)—but most of them stemmed from more complicated maladjustments. The insights Bill Hupfer gave us into the inner workings of these instruments enabled us at least to understand what caused the problems that beset us, and to deal more realistically with the local tuners/technicians (how they must have hated us!) regarding what improvements, if any, might safely be attempted. I gradually came to realize that if my piano of the evening had been ineptly regulated, it was far safer to say absolutely nothing to the person in charge than to give him another crack at making the instrument even worse.

Although a pianist's tinkering with the mechanism of the piano on which he's supposed to give a concert is, if not strictly forbidden, intensely frowned upon, this drastic step is sometimes necessary simply to make the performance possible. I don't pretend to be able to undertake serious or extensive adjustments myself, but occasionally I can do a little something to a piano in desperate straits. With the aid of Bill Hupfer's graduation gift of a small set of technicians' tools, I learned to correct certain problems on my own pianos, as well as to become quite adept at replacing strings. On my first trip to Southeast Asia, John Steinway presented me with a set of treble strings (these are the ones that break most frequently) to take along, just in case; replacements for such things were not easy to come by in far-flung ports of call. However, I have always found more problems closer to home.

One April Fools' Day not too long ago I came to a rehearsal in a medium-sized city on the North American continent to find that the first F above middle C on the piano I had to use that night would simply not go down unless I whomped it with such force that it sounded like a pistol shot. This was not very appropriate for the first, and frequently recurring, note of the main theme of the slow movement of the Mozart D minor Concerto, which was what I was attempting to play. The local tuner made no pretense of having any idea of what to do. In this case, actually, a temporary solution was quite simple. I merely removed the action of the highest note of the keyboard (which is very seldom used, and certainly not in Mozart), and traded it for the offending action of the essential F. As each note's action is interchangeable, this posed no problem. During my labors, the orchestra and conductor began to rehearse the rest of the program, although I noticed that they were covertly watching while, armed with only a screwdriver, I soon had the insides of the instrument strewn all over center stage. My sleight of hand with the mechanism of the piano impressed them far more than anything I could ever do by merely playing the infernal machine; so much so, in fact, that when I returned to the city and piano in question a couple of years later, I discovered that nothing had been changed.

When I say "nothing had been changed," I mean, of course, that the borrowed action of the piano's topmost note remained where it had been temporarily installed. On the other hand, the piano itself had, not surprisingly, deteriorated even further in other ways. But by that stage of my life I had come to terms, more or less, with what to expect. Lesson Number Three came long after Sascha Greiner and Theodore Steinway had departed for a better world, and it was: Very rarely does anything get any better.

After Theodore Steinway retired, the company began experimenting, like all other manufacturers, with replacements for natural materials that were becoming more expensive or increasingly difficult to obtain. Nowadays it seems as if everything, everywhere, is synthetic. With the Steinway pianos, it was the ivory keyboard that was the first to go. At present, just about all pianos have plastic keyboards, and they are, I admit, of considerably higher quality than the earliest replacements for this scarce (and eventually forbidden) material. I've adjusted to them, as one, sadly, adjusts to encounters with Formica tabletops and Princess telephones. But there are some pianists, especially those whose hands perspire heavily, who have considered the added pitfall of slipping off those slick, non-absorbent plastic keys to be the proverbial last straw, and have seriously thought of changing professions. I imagine that there would have been a way, if anyone responsible had cared enough, to salvage enough ivories from old Steinways (because up until the mid-fifties all Steinways, including uprights, had ivory keyboards), or to use all the ivory that was still available to the company only on the relatively few concert-sized pianos being produced (around three hundred a year), since it is only at a performance that something like this is critical.

I am sure that many changes made in pianos in the name of progress were never noticed by any pianist, and as long as they work, there is no reason to grouse. The trouble is, though, that they often don't. If the composition of the glue which holds parts of the piano together is altered, the only way a pianist becomes aware of it is if that which has been glued becomes unglued. I have, unfortunately, observed this phenomenon several times in the past five years—although never during the previous thirty—when, as I am going about my business in the usual way, a black key has come flying off the instrument. (There must be *something* good about this new glue, however, because thus far the key has come apart only at rehearsals.)

Another synthetic replacement inside the instrument that all too often makes its presence known these days is something called a bushing, formerly made of felt, and now made of that horrid material known as Teflon. The reason for replacing the felt, apparently, was that the natural material expanded and contracted with changes in humidity and temperature, while Teflon remains constant. But the Teflon bushing surrounds a wire placed into wood which, God bless it, continues to expand and contract as it always has. The Teflon remains stubbornly unco-operative, and while the wood behaves normally, the Teflon just sits there, with the result that nasty little clicking sounds can often be heard. This has caused untold anguish not only to pianists but to piano technicians all over the country, and often gives the latter a good excuse to quash any complaint a pianist may have with, "Well, what do you expect, with those goddam Teflon bushings?"

It is a sad fact that no matter how knowledgeable someone may be in the art and craft of piano making, if he is not a pianist himself he can honestly not realize what a difference—and what hazards—these so-called innovations can cause. During the period when experimentation with new materials and methods of production was just beginning at Steinway's, some pianos began to appear in The Basement with black keys that were narrower than normal. It was not long before the word went out among pianists: "Watch out for CD _____; it's got a great sound, but narrow blacks." Eventually, this infiltration became frightening. "Life is tough enough," we OYAPs grumbled. "First they make the white keys slippery and now they're also increasing the odds for missing the black notes we're trying to hit. What *is* this, anyway?" At first our queries were turned aside as being the usual pianists' delusions. Finally, however, a battalion of us marched upstairs to the executives' offices and dragged our tormentors back to The Basement with us. Producing an accurate measuring instrument, we proved beyond the shadow of a doubt that there were at least three different widths of black keys on the various instruments. It turned out that three different companies manufactured black keys for Steinway pianos. Although they were all supposed to be identical, the product of each manufacturer varied by just a tiny bit —not enough to be noticed by a non-pianist, but just enough to drive a pianist as crazy as he is generally accused of being.

We've come a long way since the days when Steinway factory technicians proudly signed their finished work. This is not to say that the Steinways being manufactured now are, even with the synthetic materials, necessarily inferior to the older ones. For me, they're still the best pianos. Hordes of piano buyers seem to agree, and herein lies the cause of an insidious problem: In order to meet consumer demand for its product, the Steinway factory often allows its pianos to leave the factory before they are quite finished. By this I mean that the final regulation and voicing (perhaps two days' work in all) is fre-

quently just not done before the instrument is sold and on its
way to Iowa or California. Without these finishing—and ultimately crucial—touches, the piano doesn't sound as good as it
could or as good as it should. Some of the newer instruments,
therefore, have a bad reputation. However, in my opinion, they
are not defective; they're just premature. Everything for a first-
class instrument is in there somewhere, but, ripped untimely
from the factory, the piano, like a seven-month baby, is just not
fully developed.

Those pianos that are lucky enough to be chosen for The
Basement get incubator treatment and a good start in life, at
least. But the others have to exist generally without any assistance, and thus they rarely attain optimum condition. It is a
real shame. A ray of hope in all this gloom is the fact that a
good technician can not only repair almost any deterioration or
destruction of a basically fine instrument, but he can also finish
that which has been left undone by the manufacturer. It is
therefore completely possible to return or bring "unplayable"
or "unfinished" Steinways to their peak quality. I have seen
this happen. Before my very eyes and ears a new piano which
had been considered hopeless by its owners and those pianists
unlucky enough to have grappled with it (actually playing on it
without the aid of a sledgehammer was out of the question)
was turned into a first-class instrument. It took exactly two
days of painstaking work by a superb technician and the result
left nothing to be desired. (To be completely accurate, I
should say that the job took exactly two nights, as this particular technician, Roger Clemens, who looks a little like Abe Lincoln, lives in a ghost town on an Arizona mountaintop and in
general marches to the sound of his own drummer, prefers to
work his magic between dusk and dawn.) It was he who said to
me, with real sorrow, after the operation, "It's such a pity. I
shouldn't have had to do this. I should be spending my time restoring and maintaining old instruments, not finishing new
ones. I didn't do anything that couldn't or shouldn't have been
done before this instrument left the factory. What a sin that
these people have to pay for a job that shouldn't have been

necessary!" Be that as it may, they did, in the end, have an excellent instrument, and I was in luck for that concert.

Nevertheless, one learns to roll with the punches. Around 1967 I began to keep a card file of the pianos I played in every city on my tours, and have faithfully charted their ups and downs ever since. I really don't know what masochistic tendency keeps me doing it, since I rarely have any control over the situation even if I know what to expect. At best the notation warns me of a lemon that can rarely be circumnavigated and at worst I cheerfully arrive in a city expecting to find what I'd noted to be a fine piano, only to discover that neglect or mistreatment has mangled it beyond recognition. However, this card file does serve as a record of sorts. My friends nicknamed it the Truth Box, and although some of them suspect that the notations are actually coded telephone numbers and attributes of various acquaintances-on-tour, they do occasionally request piano information therefrom or mordantly offer snippets of their own, ranging from the specific ("In Denver, request CD 166 from warehouse—although note that keys have no lips— better than CD 258 in auditorium") to the general ("Miami stinks").

Oddly enough, the situation at present is looking up (in a few major cities, at least). This is largely thanks to enlightened concert managers and piano dealers who are becoming increasingly aware that Steinways, like Strads, require continual care of the highest quality. They have also become reconciled to the concomitant fact that maintaining this high standard is not cheap. Happy examples are provided by two former disaster areas, where I squandered a small fortune over the years, shipping pianos from New York: in Chicago, where the orchestra recently bought a fine instrument and has it kept in top condition; and in Washington, where both the local Steinway representative and the concert managers understand what needs to be done and have at their disposal a top-flight technician to do it.

More variety for the touring pianist's itchy fingers is provided nowadays by a gradual infiltration into North America of the more or less forbidden Hamburg Steinway. Within the past few years several major orchestras and concert presenters have imported these instruments, and now an enterprising dealer has set up shop in a few cities with rental pianos from Steinway's German factory. These pianos have arrived by devious means, as Hamburg Steinways are not normally available in North America—somewhat odd, considering that the Hamburg establishment is a branch of the New York Steinway company. But in theory and in most cases in practice as well, the New York factory supplies North America with Steinways and Hamburg takes care of the rest of the world.

According to the manufacturer's New York headquarters, the theory behind keeping each factory's product within its own sphere of influence has to do with climate. We are told that the German Steinway, although a magnificent and superbly crafted instrument, cannot survive the rigors of North America. One might well ask, then, why the Hamburg-made instruments are enthusiastically sold—with guarantees—to buyers in every conceivable climate on earth. These pianos flourish in hot, damp parts of the world, like the Brazilian jungle; cold, damp parts of the world, like northern Europe; hot, dry parts of the world, like Saudi Arabia; and cold, dry parts of the world, like Siberia. But New York, Chicago, Atlanta, Los Angeles? Out of the question. American central heating—American air conditioning—some mysterious, indigenous American climatic force would wreak vengeance in a trice, and it is darkly intimated that the unfortunate American owner of a German Steinway will awake one morning to find, instead of a piano, a pile of wood shavings and tangled, rusted metal scraps decomposing on his music room floor. (I must be lucky. My Hamburg Steinway, which has nestled compatibly with its New York counterpart in my overheated, overair-conditioned living room for over a decade, shows no particular symptoms of decay.)

Although American and German Steinways are basically very similar, there are some significant differences. Most noticeable to a pianist is the action, and it is usually obvious to a player by the response or "feel" of the instrument whether it has been supplied with a German or an American action. (This is not accidental. The actions are manufactured to slightly different specifications. And to confuse the issue further, I have recently seen in the New York Basement some American Steinways with German actions.)

The casual observer can easily spot a Hamburg Steinway—or almost any German-made piano, for that matter—by its super-shiny, almost mirrorlike black finish. For while the Hamburg Steinway factory has managed to avoid for a longer period many of the synthetic interior trappings adopted by New York (especially the accursed Teflon), it does, in deference to the prevailing Middle European taste in furniture finish, cloak its instrument in glossy coats of polyester.

To the serious listener, the most apparent characteristic which sets the Hamburg Steinway apart from its New York brother is the type of sound produced. This difference, as with the action, is intentional. The quality of sound sought by the Hamburg technicians—if one dare generalize about something so personal—seems to be somewhat mellower and perhaps less brash, particularly in the bass, than the quality of tone that is the hallmark of the New York instrument. Nowadays it is becoming fashionable to praise this "Hamburg sound" at the New York pianos' expense. I disagree. Although I have played on some memorable Hamburg Steinways, I prefer the New York sound, which I feel offers a far wider range of possibilities —if the instrument is in optimum condition; as I have made abundantly clear, this is usually not the case with the New York pianos. On the other hand, it seems that the Hamburg factory has, so far, been able to hew to a generally higher standard of quality control.

Of course, it is always possible to find on tour a splendid New York Steinway in fine condition. It is also possible to encounter a dog of a Hamburg Steinway in dreadful shape. This fate befell me when I played for the first time in Japan—at the

Osaka Festival, with Szell and the Cleveland Orchestra. I found myself at rehearsal faced with an instrument that was both dull *and* ugly—a rare combination. After the first movement of the concerto thudded to a close I peered into the darkened auditorium for Louis Lane, Szell's associate conductor, who could always be relied on for as piercingly honest an opinion as that of his older colleague. I spied him prowling around and called his name. He frowned up at me with an expression of intense distaste.

"Does this piano sound as awful as I think it does?" I asked him.

"Actually, Gary," he replied in measured tones, "I can hardly hear you at all. But I must say that when I *do*, I wish I hadn't."

When the rehearsal was over we approached the Japanese gentleman in charge of the concert. "Isn't there another Steinway we could try?" we asked him.

"Yes," he replied, looking forlorn and embarrassed.

"Could you take us to it?" I prodded, for time was short, and it seemed that he wasn't going to move. He looked utterly miserable, and remained motionless and silent. I tried again:

"Is there no other Steinway in Osaka?"

"Yes," he repeated, becoming increasingly agitated. Then he led us to a little room backstage in which stood a Yamaha and a Bechstein. Shortly thereafter the problem was explained to us. It is not good form in Japanese to say, "No." So this gentleman was merely replying to my question most accurately: "Yes . . . yes . . . yes, there is no other Steinway in Osaka."

I played that concert on a Yamaha.

In general, however, the Hamburg Steinways I have played on in the United States and Canada do seem to be in better condition than most of the New York Steinways placed throughout North America. Part of this must be due to their healthy start in life. Perhaps also it is because their owners are among those who realize that pianos, like automobiles and people, need regular checkups.

Paradoxically, then, while the standards of quality control at the Steinway factory may not be as impeccable as they once were, pianists today actually may stand a better chance, in some places, of finding an instrument in satisfactory condition than they did in the Good Old Days—or Dark Ages—when, it seems to me, OYAPs trod an uphill treadmill all the way.

After our experiences on the road, it was always with a great sense of relief that we OYAPs returned to The Basement and, so to speak, pulled the covers up over our heads. Although nowadays a nocturnal visit requires almost as much preparation and identification as might a call on Fort Knox or the Kremlin, when we were OYAPs there was no particular security surrounding either The Basement or its precious occupants. No pianos were locked. Even those instruments that had been prepared for a concert and were to be delivered to the auditorium the next day simply displayed a scribbled note saying something like "Fixed up for Serkin. Please don't touch." And it was unthinkable to put a finger on that keyboard.

In order to spend an evening there, playing through concertos or browsing among the concert pianos, one simply made an appointment with the Concert Department for practice time—usually available to Steinway Artists from the end of the technicians' working day at four-thirty until eleven at night—and one had the run of the place during the allotted period. Of course, during the high concert season practice time at The Basement was at a premium, and during the 1950s we OYAPs often pooled our allotments so that, with judicious appointment-making, it was quite possible for Eugene, Leon, Jacob, Claude, Lilian and me to tie up the place every evening from about seven o'clock until closing for several weeks running.

It was not always a simple matter, however, to depose the Steinway Artist who had settled in directly beforehand. The accepted procedure, when one heard sounds emanating from behind the heavy sliding door as one approached, was to wait until that particular passage had been traversed and then sloooowly push the groaning door open and peek inside. This

LEFT, "I? Kick Godowsky in the stomach?" With my parents, 1936. (Graffman Collection)
RIGHT, *Life* magazine used the following caption on this photo in 1938: "The Most Familiar Scene in Music: Boy at Piano, Teacher Watching. Here at Curtis, Isabelle Vengerova Watches 10-Year-Old Gary Graffman." What I was thinking is unrecorded. (Credit: Fritz Henle)

My debut with the Philadelphia Orchestra, 1947. This photo proves that I was not entirely oblivious of the conductor. (Credit: Adrian Siegel)

RIGHT, Ormandy and soloist search for
the missing cadenza, 1947.
(Credit: Adrian Siegel)

BELOW, the Stephens College plane takes
me from St. Louis to my recital on the
campus and I discover that playing the
piano has great side benefits, 1950.
(Credit: Hope Associates Corp.)

LEFT, OYAPs Three (Eugene Istomin, me, Leon Fleisher) pose for publicity photo, 1954.
(Credit: Louis Mélançon),

BELOW, office party, 1953: My bride and Schuyler Chapin enjoy a relaxed moment amid Naomi's messy files.
(Graffman Collection)

"Is *this* the right note?" The Brahms D minor with Munch, the Boston Symphony and Old 199. (Credit: John G. Ross, courtesy *Life* magazine)

Before the haircut. Rafael Druian, then concertmaster of the Cleveland Orchestra, tells the boss what's on his mind; Andy Kazdin (upper left) beams while I brood. (Credit: CBS Records)

"You're drowning out my orchestra!" Recording the Tchaikovsky Second Concerto with Ormandy and the Philadelphia Orchestra on CD 283, the piano that sounded like a squadron of dive bombers. (Credit: CBS Records)

Listening to playbacks of the Rachmaninoff *Paganini* Rhapsody with Leonard Bernstein. Something tells me that we did that spot over again. (Credit: CBS Records)

I can't have the real thing, so the Steinways present me with a replica of CD 199. (Naomi, Theodore Steinway, John Steinway, Ruth Steinway, Henry Steinway, me, Polly Steinway, Fritz Steinway, Cassie Steinway.) (Credit: courtesy Steinway & Sons)

Author (r.) and scribe. (Credit: Boris Goldenberg)

Choosing pianos in The Basement. Somehow, I always gravitated toward Old 199. (Credit: Roy Stevens)

Some of the pots I brought back from the dig in the Philippines. (Credit: Don Hunstein, CBS Records)

Julius describes his latest triumph (1951). (Graffman Collection)

After a New York recital in 1967. I was so overwhelmed to see Rubinstein (and Mrs. Rubinstein, center) that I never gave him a chance to say anything. I just kept talking the whole time. (Credit: Alfred Statler, courtesy *Time* magazine)

was usually enough of a hint—the person hunched behind the Steinway (if not one of our buddies) arose somewhat apologetically, nodded, exchanged a bit of small talk and fled. Sometimes, however, when the ensconced pianist was stubborn, it took a few glowers and harrumphs to unseat him—or her. On one such evening all my glowering and harrumphing failed to intimidate a small, rather unprepossessing, dowdily dressed lady who, oblivious to my impatience, continued playing rather provincial-sounding finger exercises with the aid of a metronome. I placed myself squarely in her line of vision, and slowly undid my scarf, which I ostentatiously arranged on top of a nearby piano. She continued to play her scales and arpeggios. I then removed my coat, folded it and put it on top of my scarf. No reaction from the pianist or her metronome. Then my jacket. Still no response. Finally, I started to walk loudly around, checking the identification numbers of various pianos to find the ones I was scheduled to try—really a most impolite thing to do while someone is working. But after all, she was working on *my* time. Finally, she stopped playing, looked up and decided to be sociable. "So, young man, you are giving a concert soon?" "Umph," I replied. "And where will you be playing?" "Nggggg," I told her. "And what is your program?" "Lady—" I was about to snarl something like, "Ionlyhavetwohourstopractice*threeprogramsandfiveconcertosso PLEASE!*" when she interrupted sweetly, "And do you play abroad? If you ever come to South America, you must look me up in São Paulo." At that point, I shuddered with the awful realization that the next words I would, and in fact did, hear were, "My name is Guiomar Novaës." Incredibly, the same thing happened to me several years later when—once again—I failed to recognize the reigning Queen of the Keyboard.

When we OYAPs gathered in The Basement, as we did so often during our early years, we used it as our workshop but also, in a way, as our clubhouse. Friends joined us there as audience for our run-throughs. Colleagues slid open the groaning door and criticized us fearlessly. Gossip of all kinds was disseminated from this headquarters. Once I even found, on one of the pianos I was to try, a letter with a foreign postmark addressed to

Mr. Piano Player Gary Graffman
Steinway Basement
57th Street
New York City, USA

Best of all, there awaited us a tempting array of instruments, some old, some new, but all in the splendid condition that displayed their individual charms most effectively. Picking out a favorite among these beauties was one of the great pleasures of that era.

CHAPTER TWELVE

A Boy and His Dog

CHOOSING A PIANO is similar to tasting wines. If a wine is crude or has gone bad or is simply undistinguished, one can tell immediately. If, however, one is dealing with wines of the highest level, comparing, let us say, several of the first- and second-growth Bordeaux of the same particularly good year, then the only way to appreciate them fully and to detect their individual characteristics and complexities is to try them side by side.

On a few memorably festive occasions it has been my good fortune to undertake this type of experimentation with great Bordeaux from the legendary cellar of the Alfred Knopfs. Opportunities to perform similar research with pianos in The Basement of the Steinways occur a bit more frequently, although with perhaps a trifle less festivity, when a batch of concert instruments both old and new are lined up for comparison tests. As with selecting first-class wines, it is, in the case of choosing among these pianos, more a question of individual preference for certain characteristics above others. While it is true that I could easily prefer one instrument over another according to the repertoire I plan to play on it (for big, Romantic concertos it is certainly desirable to have a more brilliant-sounding instrument than may be necessary for a recital of Schubert sonatas), the over-all idiosyncrasies of the kind of piano I prefer include an extremely deep, resonant and almost angry-sounding bass; a rich middle register with a viola-like quality; and a treble that combines this richness with a shimmering sound that is almost like a very vibrant "ping." This is a tall order, and it is rare to find an instrument with all these attributes in perfect condition. However, miracles have happened.

One evening, I think it was in the fall of 1953, I was prowling restlessly around The Basement, trying out various passages of music on the pianos that had been assembled for my inspection. When I am choosing pianos, I like to play the same phrases on all of them to compare the qualities of the different instruments. After years of experimentation, I have found one particular test piece that shows the most about them in the shortest amount of time. This is the section in the slow movement of the Brahms B-flat Concerto from the place where the piano makes its first entrance until the orchestra returns. In these few bars one is able to hear everything from extreme softness to powerful loudness in all sections of the piano, including exposed single notes in the upper middle register, which often proves the most dangerous area, as it has a tendency to sound somewhat percussive in all but the most beautiful of pianos.

At the time of which I am writing, however, I had not yet discovered this Brahms ploy, and my rather haphazard struggles to decide which piano I preferred at any given moment would, more often than not, leave me limp and confused. My cruising among these pianos that evening was directed by the list of available instruments which, as was customary, had been left for me by one of The Basement Nibelungen—in this case, the master tuner, Morris Schnaper. (Concert Steinways—the largest-sized, or Model D instruments destined for concert use —are generally identified by the letters CD followed by a one-, two- or three-digit number. This identifying mark is observable as a golden decal on the lid of the piano, and for good measure it is also painted on the plate where it can easily be seen. Completely arbitrary, these numbers are sometimes changed around, and when a piano leaves the Concert Department, the CD number is removed, eventually to be bestowed on another instrument designated for concert use. These CD numbers have no relationship to the six-digit serial number of the piano, which is permanently engraved or stamped in several places inside the instrument, and indicates its exact age. The serial numbers went to six digits in 1901, when the 100,000th Steinway was made. And in 1953, after one hundred years of manufacturing, the number 340,000 was reached. In recent years, the manufacturer of these instruments has been playing cat-and-mouse with the serial numbers of the CD pianos—they become increasingly harder to find—for the reason that it is believed a pianist will automatically reject a newer instrument for an older one. Although by no means always the case, there is more than a grain of truth to this, perhaps because the older instruments were in fact more carefully made than the newer ones. But in those days, The Basement's treasures, old or new, provided us with an embarrassment of riches.)

Morris knew my habits. I was likely to vacillate among the proffered delights, running back and forth from one to the other until I became utterly confused. So, along with the list, he'd scrawled on a separate sheet of paper the stern injunction: "Gary: Picking a piano and STICKING TO IT!" which he plopped down on the lid of one of the instruments. Never let it be said that I didn't follow his advice. The piano on which the note, probably inadvertently, had been placed became the instrument I used whenever possible for the next twenty years.

Whether CD 199 (or 338944, made in the vintage year of 1952) had all the qualities I ascribed to it, or whether, because I *believed* it had those qualities I was inspired to play my best on it, is as insoluble a question as that of the chicken and the egg. The enormous bass, the luscious middle register and the gleaming treble were all there, but it always seemed to me that there was yet something more, something different from even the best of the other pianos. This was mainly apparent in the length of time its sonority continued to hover in the air after a note was struck. A piano's curse is, after all, that it is a percussion instrument; its player's curse is the unending battle to minimize this basic characteristic. On 199 I felt almost as if I were playing a stringed instrument—as if it were possible, even, to make a crescendo on a single note. This was, of course, completely illusory. But illusion and fantasy are the ingredients that make a performance soar, and something within that piano (or within my imagination) allowed me to lose myself completely in the music whenever I was seated at 199.

Every pianist carries in his head the sound of an ideal instrument, and although many of my colleagues enjoyed playing on 199, I don't believe that any of them were quite as mesmerized by its seductive charm as I. To them it was merely an excellent, even splendid, piano. But even if 199 lacked to their ears the magical properties that I attributed to it, this particular instrument did become the OYAPs' favorite for at least a decade. Our common dependency upon it reached such proportions, in fact, that for a couple of seasons in the mid-fifties, four of us—Leon, Eugene, Jacob and myself—joined forces and figured out a way to have 199 shipped around the country to meet us for our most important concerts, sharing in the transportation costs as well as in the security of having it around when we needed all the help we could get.

To accomplish this complex task, we analyzed our touring schedules and agreed, with remarkably little fuss, about which of the concerts any of us might be playing on a given date was most worthy of the services of 199. Thus, if I were giving a recital in, say, Toledo while Eugene was with the orchestra in Chicago, it would unquestionably go to him. But if one of us was in Boston while the other was in Philadelphia, compromises had to be made. Factors to be considered were what other pianos would be available in those cities; the type of repertoire being played; the amount of nervousness engendered by that particular engagement; and not the least of it, the fact that it takes longer to move a piano than a pianist, occasionally necessitating compromises for purely logistical reasons.

Naomi contributed a little engagement book from Columbia Management, the kind in which each artist's dates are inscribed, and we labeled it "Leogene Grafteiner" and marked within it the tour of CD 199. It was quite a hectic itinerary, and now that I think back on it, I'm amazed that so few disasters occurred. The worst of these incidents, indelibly etched into my memory, was precipitated by, of all things, Eugene's gallantry.

The distinguished Romanian-Swiss pianist Clara Haskil was making her first United States appearances that particular season and Eugene, who knew her through their mutual friendship with Casals and was very fond of her, had arranged her visit and acted as her unofficial host in our country. He fretted over her comfort and the organization of her tour so intently that we began to refer to him as "Clara Haskil's mother," notwithstanding the fact that she was at least forty years his senior.

One day he informed me that it was our duty to pitch in to make Mme. Haskil's visit as easy and pleasant as possible. I agreed. "Then you will surely not object if 199 goes to Boston for her debut; it's the least we can do for her." When he told me the date, I pointed out that I was making *my* Chicago recital debut the following week. As that city was notorious for the poor condition of its pianos, I felt that this in itself warranted special consideration. Eugene understood completely, and after doing some research advised me that the piano-moving department at Steinway's had assured him that there was nothing to worry about—199 could go to Boston for Mme. Haskil and still arrive in Chicago in plenty of time for me. The whole thing would be so simple. Impossible for anything to go wrong. Eugene made it absolutely clear that any hesitation on my part would be churlish beyond belief, setting the reputation of American manhood back by at least a century. What could I do? Hiding my misgivings, I reluctantly spread my cloak across the muddy gutter for Mme. Haskil. I soon learned that chivalry does not pay. The freight train carrying 199 from Boston to Chicago was derailed, and while I galumphed through the recital on whatever miserable instrument was available in Chicago, my better half was lying on a siding in Erie, Pennsylvania. The good news that 199 had escaped with only minor scratches sustained me through the performance although, in retrospect, I think I should have canceled.

In general, however, Leogene Grafteiner's tours worked out to the satisfaction of everyone but the Steinway bookkeeping department. The transportation billing got so complicated that eventually they just shoved everything into an envelope and sent it to us to unsnarl as best we could. So each month there was a day of reckoning when all the bills were assembled and we attempted to prorate the moving costs, a mind-boggling mathematical feat that I can't believe we did without the aid of a calculator. Still, the system worked surprisingly smoothly, and it was only in the early sixties, when shipping costs began to escalate outrageously, that the joint venture was gradually abandoned, and the touring of CD 199 became limited to our most pressing individual needs.

Even though this meant that the piano seldom ventured farther west than Chicago after that time, it continued to travel regularly along the Boston–Washington corridor and was, of course, booked solidly for engagements in and around New York City. This constant use, common to most Concert Basement pianos, meant that every now and then an overhaul was required, and 199 would be *hors de combat* for a while. As the time drew near for any kind of serious repair work on this instrument, I would become increasingly fretful. One never knew for sure how it would react. Even the most routine operation has been known to wreak a personality change within a piano. So I always felt a pang of dread whenever my friend Fritz Steinway (Theodore's youngest son), who was head of the Steinway Concert Department from the time of Sascha Greiner's death in 1958 until he joined the old-new Arthur Jud-

son management in 1963, broke the news of an impending
overhaul to me in his most sympathetic manner: "Sorry, old
boy, she has to go to the hospital for a face-lift; nothing serious
—just a little chin-tuck—but she'll be out of commission for a
couple of months." (Fritz had a tendency to anthropomor-
phize pianos even more than the OYAPs, and although there
was never any question in my mind that CD 199 was female,
somehow I always referred to her as "it.")

Routine overhauls were usually scheduled for the summertime, or whenever the piano's services were least required. And
each time 199 was returned to The Basement after its visit to
the factory in Queens (or, for that matter, after a smaller job
done in The Basement workshop), I approached it tentatively
and tried it with great trepidation, which gradually turned to
even greater relief as I heard those familiarly mellifluous sounds
once again. Fritz, who was as always standing by in time of crisis, would chomp on his pipe, grin broadly and say teasingly,
"When are you gonna trade her in for a new model? One of
these days she'll collapse like the One-Hoss Shay. Man, that
damned thing is held together with spit and Scotch tape!"

I tried desperately to postpone any overhauling of CD 199.
It got so that I began to believe that anything done to any part
of it might alter the magic sound, and that if I so much as let
it out of my sight it would be whisked away to the factory and,
for all I knew, lobotomized. My paranoia dated from an experience that befell me in 1955 and that, although I didn't fully
grasp it at the time, must have signified the beginning of the
end of the Good Old Days.

One Sunday evening, just before my first recording session
ever, I went to The Basement to play over the piece I was
about to preserve for posterity—the "Wanderer" Fantasy—on
CD 199, which, first thing next morning, was to be transported
to Webster Hall, an old barn of a place conveniently adjacent
to Lüchow's restaurant, where many RCA recordings were
made. Jacob, my audience and critic for the evening's run-
through, was waiting for me with what, I realized in retrospect,
was a sick expression. I approached 199, sat down, lifted the lid

of the piano and was horrified to see, leering up at me like a set of cheap false teeth, an artificially shiny, unfamiliar keyboard. Gone were the friendly, mellow, warmly yellowed ivories I so loved to tickle, and in their place was this monstrously grinning expanse of synthetic glossiness. "*Plastic!*" I shrieked. Jacob, who had already seen the keyboard, nodded calmly. He could afford to be calm. He wasn't making the record. (He had already done the last Beethoven sonata—Opus 111 being one of his warhorses since his teens—for Columbia, so he was a veteran of the mysterious, adult world of the recording studio.) I, on the other hand, having never encountered a microphone head on, panicked like a horse confronted with a rattlesnake, and bolted for the nearest telephone. It was around dinnertime, and I am amazed that Henry Steinway, then president of the company, was summoned to answer my frantic call, because I must have sounded like a raving lunatic.

"Plastic! Plastic on 199! You put . . . you . . . plastic . . . on my piano . . . how? My piano, plastic! You? Why me? My 199 has *plastic!* Take it away!" I bawled into the receiver.

"Calm down, Gary," said Henry, when he could get a word in edgewise. "Take it easy. We'll put the ivory keyboard back on 199. Everything will be all right. I promise. Don't worry. We'll put it back tomorrow. But tell me, Gary, how did you know it was plastic? Who told you?"

"Plastic, plastic! Who *told* me?" I spluttered. "*Forgodsakes,* it's *plastic!* On my piano. On 199! Feels like shit! Take it off! Off! Offa my piano! Aaaaagh!"

"Now, Gary," Henry spoke with the firm, sweet reasonableness of a policeman who is trying to coax a would-be suicide off a railing of the Brooklyn Bridge, "don't you worry. We . . . will . . . put . . . the . . . old . . . ivories . . . back . . . immediately. But now, you must do *me* a favor. Please come into my office tomorrow. I want to talk to you about this, and I'll explain everything then. But really, it was supposed to be a secret. Who told you?"

It was incomprehensible to me—and still is—that anyone could have imagined for one minute that a pianist could not

see (or for that matter sense from a mile away) the difference
between ivory and plastic keys. Nevertheless, the next morning
I obediently presented myself at Henry Steinway's office. He
called in Bill Hupfer and Sascha Greiner; and, as he grilled me
on how I was able to detect the replacement of my keyboard, a
secretary took down every word I uttered. Some of the more acceptable ones were, "glaring, shiny, synthetic-looking, artificial
—in short, *plastic!*—cold and slippery, slimy like the skin of a
greased eel, and *not what I am used to.*"

For his part, Henry explained to me that the company was
experimenting with substitutes for ivory; that they had tried
several other kinds of plastic for keyboards and thought this
was the best; that they felt that if a pianist were told in advance what was being done he would automatically reject the
new material. They realized that it could be disastrous to
tamper with a piano that was about to be used at a concert performance, but they knew that a solo recording session could be
postponed without too much hassle, if necessary, so that
seemed like the safest way to carry out this necessary test. And,
as I happened to have a recording session when they were ready
with the new keyboard, I became the guinea pig. As it turned
out, however, nothing constructive came of that particular trial,
because I was so upset that, as promised, the old ivory keyboard
was immediately returned to CD 199, where it remains to this
day.

But the plastic replacement for ivories had to come sooner or
later, and my fit only postponed the inevitable—for other pianos, if not for 199. I was determined to keep *my* piano un-
sullied, however, and continued to protest vigorously any proposed alterations. This applied even to its exterior. A concert
pianist doesn't notice how the case of a piano looks. I think we
are completely oblivious to this aspect of our instrument. Even
the fussiest of us, who will not suffer an ashtray unemptied or a
sofa pillow unplumped, looks through, and does not see, the innumerable nicks and gouges on his concert piano. The beat-up
condition of some of these pianos' cases is not at all surprising,
considering the amount of moving they endure. Practically

daily, Basement pianos are put on their sides, their legs and pedals are removed, they are thrust into trucks, they are bumped around the streets of New York, they are dragged out of trucks, they are hauled onto stages, their legs and pedals are shoved back in and they are set upright once again, only to undergo the same procedure in reverse a day or two later. And in spite of (or perhaps because of) the efforts of no less than six (as required by the union) husky movers who surround the instrument like the Sleeping Beauty's fairy godmothers, it is subject to astonishingly brutal treatment. Almost all of these pianos, I have been told on good authority, have at one time or another been dropped. Small wonder, then, that CD 199 seemed to have more than its share of nicks and scratches and gouges. But I was so sensitive about it that I terrorized anyone who suggested even the most minor beautification, and after a while no attempts were made to remove even the most horrendous scars. Eventually, this extended even to dusting; for who knew? Perhaps just that one milligram of gray fuzz was responsible for retaining the sound an instant longer. Thus it was always easy to spot 199 anywhere in The Basement because of its distinctively unappealing exterior. It looked, among those sleek, well-groomed state-of-the-art concert beauties, like a mangy hippopotamus just returned from an afternoon's wallow in the mud pond.

I remember once arriving at the auditorium of the Library of Congress in Washington, where I was playing a sonata recital with CD 199 (and, incidentally, also with Henryk Szeryng), and being happily reunited with both of them at our rehearsal session. Szeryng, by the way, was among the many non-pianists captivated by the extraordinary sound quality of CD 199—so much so, in fact, that he agreed to accept the Big Stick Theory, at least for our performances together. (Traditionally, a piano lid is not opened all the way—it's kept on the "half stick" or "small stick"—when a pianist is performing with other instrumentalists, even if it is for a sonata recital, where the partners are theoretically equal—notwithstanding the fact that Beethoven entitled some of his violin sonatas **"GRAND SONATAS**

FOR PIANO FORTE with Violin Accompaniment"—because it is assumed that the sound emanating from the piano will be less. This is not at all the case, as Rudolf Serkin was the first to point out to me. If the piano lid is not all the way open, the pianist will often hear a muffled or pinched sound—more so, perhaps, than the audience—and this will cause him to force and not play naturally. With the lid all the way up in normal concert position, he will immediately hear the full volume and extent of the instrument's sound-lasting properties and will (if he is listening) instinctively adjust to a lower dynamic level and employ a more subtle palette of sounds. It is virtually impossible to convince a string player of the truth of this theory, but there is no question in my mind, both as a player and as a listener, that it is indisputably correct. Szeryng was typically dubious at first, but he became so enamored of the sound of 199 that he not only insisted that the instrument be opened all the way, but after the first movement of the Brahms D minor Sonata during that concert turned to me and whispered—so piercingly that I was sure the broadcasting microphones must have picked it up—"What a gorgeous sound that piano has! Don't hold back! Don't hold back!"

Anyway, after our rehearsal for this performance, a lady from the Library's concert department called me aside and asked, "Mr. Graffman, are you satisfied with the piano?" "I should hope so," I replied, thinking of the rather large transportation bill that would be awaiting when I returned to New York. "After all, I chose to have it sent here." "Yes, yes, I know," she said, "but we were worried that perhaps they shipped the wrong one. You see, when it came out of its packing box it looked so awful that we couldn't *believe* anyone would want to play on it!"

Slovenly harridan though it may have looked, CD 199 (or Old 199, as it eventually began to be called) was "my" piano for better or worse, in sickness or health, even though it belonged, of course, to Steinway & Sons. Leon, Eugene, Jacob, Claude and sometimes Lilian (although she claimed it was not a "woman's piano" and said that she never really felt comfortable with it) continued to use it off and on during the ensuing years. One reason for Old 199's popularity was its extraordinary versatility. In its heyday it could roar with me through a Tchaikovsky concerto in the vast reaches of Central Park's Sheep Meadow with the same ease as, under Eugene's ministrations, it meshed with the elegant sonorities of Isaac Stern and Leonard Rose in trio concerts at Carnegie Hall; or, with Claude at its (ivory) keyboard, it movingly illuminated the complete cycle of Beethoven sonatas at Hunter College. My piano did get around. Sharing its favors with close friends, though, was not in any way distasteful to me. But sometimes other artists—strangers!—played on it too (although only if none of us had reserved it), and I tried to contain my jealousy, not to mention worry, when I knew that CD 199 had been sent off to some mysterious assignation. For my part, I remained faithful whenever possible, except for one notable fling.

I first met CD 283 in The Basement in the summer of 1963. Unlike my muddy hippopotamus (which was then having one of its periodic "chin-tucks" in the factory), it looked as sleek as it sounded, and on our first encounter it bit me. That happened as I reached underneath its keyboard to undo the padlock (which, somewhat like a chastity belt, prevented any unauthorized persons from tampering with it, and was by then standard equipment on Basement pianos) and ripped a finger open on some sharp protrusion. It bled so much that I had to run home—fortunately, just down the block—to bandage my wound before I could dredge out the magic gold secreted by this crotchety Rhinemaiden. Bumptious and brash, CD 283 (soon nicknamed Christine, after a prominent playgirl with similar characteristics, then much in the news) made up for in power what it may have lacked in refinement. But it had a gorgeous, rich, glossy tone, too. In short, it erupted sounds that were a cross between the Mormon Tabernacle Choir and a squadron of dive bombers. Playing 283 made me feel, simply, like God. I became thoroughly infatuated with this instrument, and for a couple of years played all my big, juicy Russian concertos on it. Christine's enormous volume of sound could be

overpowering. When that piano accompanied me to Philadelphia to record the Tchaikovsky Second Concerto, I remember Ormandy's saying rather pathetically (and only half in
jest), "Please, please take it easy! You're drowning out my orchestra!"

Eventually, however, the unflagging exuberance and basic
callowness of Christine began to exhaust and even bore me,
and I longed once again for the warmth and sympathy of Old
199. Before a complete reconciliation could take place, though,
ample revenge was exacted. As mentioned earlier, *La Campanella* had been, since boyhood, my surefire success piece.
Ever since I'd trotted it out in the Salle de Champagne at the
flutter of a blond waitress' eyelash, I could count on its coming
through for me in any number of awkward situations. A clinker
in *La Campanella?* Impossible! CD 199 and I had romped
through it so many times together that I could practically put
the piano on automatic pilot and sit back to enjoy the effect.
Thus, although I am always somewhat uncomfortable at tele-
vised performances, I had no apprehension at scheduling this
piece—and my return to CD 199—for "The Tonight Show."
But Old 199 had other plans for me. I don't know what happened, but what came out of that piano that night was a mess.
And I'm sure I was playing the same notes that I always did. I
could never get over the scary feeling that Old 199 was paying
me back for my peccadillo with Christine. And if it was illusion, caused by my guilty conscience, then the illusion, as always, commanded my fingers.

And so we went through the years together, Old 199 and I,
each of us, on occasion, needing a bit of repair. Gradually,
though, 199 began to suffer from a number of ailments which
caused it to behave erratically. It has been explained to me that
when a piano is new, its sounding board is convex. When the
piano ages the sounding board begins to sink, minimizing the
volume of sound the instrument can produce and reducing the
sound quality as well. This can be rectified, but it is a major
job. Another problem that routinely affects much-used pianos
has to do with something called a pin block. This is a block of

wood into which the tuning pins are set. The strings are wrapped around these pins, which must be turned by the tuning hammer each time the piano is tuned (which, for a concert piano, takes place before each performance and usually before each rehearsal as well). Sooner or later the holes into which the pins are set become enlarged, causing the pins to slip and the piano to become untuned. To keep this problem at bay for as long as possible, tuning pins are made in several sizes, and as the smaller size becomes loose in the pin block, it can be replaced by the next larger size, and so on. But, because of all this wear and tear, it finally becomes necessary to replace the pin block itself—another mighty job. These problems were among the complaints that plagued Old 199, and by the early 1970s, it became evident that Fritz's "spit and Scotch tape" could no longer keep the One-Hoss Shay together.

Although a certain amount of rebuilding is done to the most popular of the hard-living Basement pianos, after a while these continual major operations become financially impractical. The time and effort spent on restoring one of these instruments can, obviously, be spent more sensibly and profitably on making several new ones. This is only good business practice, logical and realistic, and one cannot fault Steinway & Sons for disposing of those of its concert instruments that have reached a condition of extreme delicacy, to put it politely. I understand; I understand as well as the next crazy pianist. Nevertheless, it came as a horrible wrench for me to be asked, when I arrived at The Basement one afternoon in January 1974, "Do you want to go over and say goodbye to your friend? It's just been sold." There, in a corner, stood my dusty hippopotamus. As I approached, I saw that it had already suffered the final indignity: Stripped of its proud Concert Basement identity, CD 199, it had now become plain old 338944, revealing to the world its age but giving no hint of its illustrious past. "Go on, go on—play a little on it," I was urged. "It'll be for the last time. Lucky you dropped by today—the piano's going out first thing tomorrow." I found I couldn't bring myself to touch it.

Naomi, informed of what had happened, did not behave at

all as one would expect of a wife when told that a longtime
mistress had been abandoned. She burst into tears and remained inconsolable until I agreed to try to rescue the condemned one. In our distraught state, grief soon turned to rage.
(Even now, when I think of it, my blood boils.) How could
they sell *my* piano without even offering it first, at least, to me?
Preposterous! But, to be practical, if we had been offered the
chance to buy it, where would we keep it? Concert grands take
up a considerable amount of space, and we already *had* two big
pianos in our living room. And to replace one of my workhorse
pianos with (now ex-) CD 199 would be foolhardy, and surely
not provide the honored retirement it deserved. But something
had to be done quickly, it was clear; and the first step, as always, was to voice my displeasure to the owners of my piano. A
hasty telephone conversation, while not exactly cheerful, resulted at least in their agreeing to hold up the sale for a couple
of days while I tried to find a suitable home for my faithful
companion. Naomi and I measured every empty space in our
apartment and cursed ourselves for having accumulated the
clutter of furniture which prohibited even the thought of introducing another substantial-sized object. Where could it go?
Wild schemes of buying the monster and donating it to some
nearby auditorium, where it could slumber peacefully in the
wings and, perhaps, be used on special ceremonial occasions,
ran through our heads. But nothing that we could think of
seemed really feasible. Suddenly, as happens in the movies, the
phone rang.

"Graffi?"

Thundering hoofbeats of the great horse Silver carrying the
Lone Ranger to our rescue could not have brought more relief
than the ebullient voice of Ruth Henderson, who, hearing no
reply, asked again:

". . . Graffi?"

How could we have overlooked the Hendersons? Our great
friends, Ruth and Skitch (also very close to the Steinway family), had recently moved their headquarters from East Sixty-
first Street to a rambling farm in rural Connecticut, and they

had been searching for over a year for a good piano that Skitch could use in the studio Ruth had fixed up for him in their barn. (Calling the Hendersons' barn a "barn," by the way, is a little like describing the palace at Versailles as a garage.) We had looked at a number of pianos together; just the previous month, in fact, we had accompanied Ruth from the farm to the showroom of a dealer in Danbury in response to his excited call that he had at last found "the perfect piano." This had turned out to be an instrument of some unknown make which had absolutely nothing to recommend it except a very shiny case. We were annoyed at having made a long drive on a snowy night, and did not hide our irritation. The piano dealer shrugged and explained to Ruth that they'd never find a satisfactory piano as long as I was around. "Your friend," he said unpleasantly, jerking his thumb in my direction, "the trouble with him is, he's a Steinway snob."

Almost incoherent with haste and excitement, I babbled our story to Ruth: CD 199 was, for the moment, waiting in limbo for salvation. Before I had finished, she cut through my tale of woe with a crisp announcement. "I want it," she said. "Next week is Skitch's birthday. It's just perfect. He loves that piano. Nothing could be better. He'll be thrilled." The happy ending was complete when, at our joint insistence, the Concert D number was officially restored, repainted and re-decaled, and 338944 became once again, and for all time henceforth, the one and only CD 199.

My old friend sits in splendor among the rolling hills and fields of Connecticut. It is dusted—even polished—regularly, and looks quite respectable, especially when a vase of fresh flowers and rows of family photos hide some of its more hideous scars. It's played on tenderly, and I have visiting privileges. Even Horowitz, for a while a neighbor of the Hendersons in Connecticut, has paid it court; and Franz Mohr, Steinway's current Chief Nibelungen, comes to give it a checkup every now and then. CD 199 has even begun, in a minor way, a second concert life, as Skitch has taken to letting it out of the barn occasionally for some local concerts in nearby New

Milford. There's no use pretending, though. I miss it, and I'm still playing the field. I've never found a replacement that has, for me, quite the same magic, and I guess I'll always regret not having grabbed the chance to keep it for myself, somehow—restored, of course, to its past splendor. The topic occasionally comes up in conversation by the fireside with the Hendersons and Old 199 in Connecticut; but, strange to say, if I ever voice my sorrow at what I didn't do that desperate afternoon, they seem not to hear, and, staring dreamily off into the flickering flames, unfailingly change the subject.

CHAPTER THIRTEEN

God Is a Brazilian

MY FIRST FOREIGN concert tour began in a most auspicious manner.

I had been invited to South America by an impresario in Buenos Aires via an impresario in New York. (Not Columbia Artists, for this was 1955: the dollar ruled supreme, and the big New York concert agencies didn't waste time negotiating with managements in countries where the currencies could be shaky and the financing shady. Anything south of Texas was regarded with deep suspicion, and tales of unfulfilled contracts and stranded orchestras were rampant. One thing was certain: Nobody would ever leave for that part of the world without having a round-trip ticket in hand.)

My South American impresario's counterpart in New York was a Russian who looked like the bear in *Petrouchka*. He spoke Imperial Russian, very peculiar English and, I believe, scarcely a word of Spanish. But he did have a working relationship with the existing South American managers. By this I mean that he would write, cable and phone and occasionally his persistence would be rewarded by a reply. All the details concerning tours of this type remained amorphous until the absolute last minute. So, typically, the day before I was to leave, authorization for the airplane tickets still had not arrived. My impresario finally lumbered over to the offices of Aerolineas Argentinas in person. I don't know what he screamed at them, nor in what language, but he did get the prepaid tickets. Triumphantly he departed, neglecting to open the door, and thus leaving an impresario-sized hole in the glass. I am told he didn't even notice anything was amiss, so indignant was he. The tickets were then delivered with a note of instruction from my impresario to Naomi, who, apparently, was to coach me in appropriate behavior on foreign soil. It read, in part:

> I wish that you tell Gary as follows:
> 1) He could be a well dressed there
> 2) Second he should not be confused and losing—he should be firm, gay and etc.

The DC-6 took off on schedule. Its first stop was pre-Castro Havana, and everything seemed normal. But by the time we reached the second stop, Caracas, there was some sort of commotion among the crew. Still, nobody made any unusual announcement until we arrived at our next stop, Rio. There we were told the flight would terminate. The reason: "Problems in Argentina." We were all to be put up in a hotel at the airline's expense. The "problems" in Argentina turned out to be the revolution that overthrew Perón. The airline personnel didn't know from day to day when the Buenos Aires airport would reopen, and so my first foreign tour began with an unscheduled week's vacation, free, in Rio de Janeiro. At that point I decided I had chosen the right profession.

When I finally arrived in Buenos Aires, I was taken through sandbagged streets to the Hotel Claridge, where I found an American ballet company, a German opera company, several chamber music groups and the pianist Wilhelm Backhaus, all of whom had been trapped in the hotel. During the week I had been gorging on Brazilian delicacies, they had been huddled in the Claridge basement, receiving rations of the only food the hotel still had available: white bread and Swiss cheese. Had I been scheduled to leave New York twenty-four hours later, my visit, of course, would have been canceled; worse yet, had I left twenty-four hours earlier, I would have spent the week huddled with these unfortunates and their cheese sandwiches.

Since I was in Buenos Aires anyway, the local impresario asked me to play just one of the scheduled concerts, which took place at 5 P.M., before the night curfew. I did so, and then agreed to come back the following year to complete the tour.

When I returned the next August, this time with Naomi, who had never forgiven me my bachelor week on the beach at Ipanema, the first concert was scheduled for Montevideo, capital of Uruguay. The last stop before our destination was Buenos Aires. We got out to stretch our legs and had a short conversation that sums up what a South American tour is all about.

A redheaded gentleman approached us breathlessly and said in English, with a slight German accent, "You are the Graffmans? I am Uhlfelder from Conciertos Gerard. I am not your manager. I am here to meet Senofsky. Where is Senofsky?" We assured him that Senofsky was not on the plane with us. Uhlfelder was philosophical.

"Ah, well, then he will surely be on the *next* plane," he said. "Meanwhile, I have a message from your manager, Don Bernardo Iriberri. He asked me to give you his greetings and tell you that your concert in Montevideo is a day later than you thought; that you are playing not the Prokofiev Third but the Beethoven Third; that the conductor is not González but Tevah; and that the hotel is not the Palacio but the Victoria Plaza." With that he gave a cheery wave and trotted off.

Since that trip we have made many tours of South America. I learned early that the repertoire list submitted should be the smallest possible and consist only of works ready to play at a moment's notice: Almost never does the final program bear any relationship to the original. Some of the changes can only be reacted to by a shrug. Such was the case when I arrived once in Caracas expecting to play the Rachmaninoff *Paganini* Rhapsody, which I had practiced diligently the week before in Rio, thus cutting in half my time at the beach. I should have known better. I was greeted with the news that instead of Rachmaninoff, it would be Mendelssohn. Okay, okay, but why the hell didn't anybody tell me?

"Well," said the local manager, pulling a long face, "when the guest conductor arrived, he looked at the program and said it was impossible. He said he just couldn't do the Rachmaninoff because the last time he conducted it his best friend died."

Uruguay in the late 1950s was known as the Switzerland of South America. The exchange rate was four pesos to the dollar, and Montevideo was a pretty little city, clean and reasonably tidy, with waving palm trees, lots of parks, two charming concert halls and a generally pleasant ambience. I don't recall that either my concerto, the conductor, the date of the concert or the hotel was changed any further on that visit. However, during the recital that I gave after the orchestral concert, a man dressed like a stagehand or janitor ambled across the stage. I was playing Chopin. I saw out of the corner of my eye that he stopped and studied me for a moment. I nodded to him. He nodded back. Then he continued past me and past the piano, off the stage on the other side. I never saw him again and nobody seemed to know who he was.

(Montevideo has changed—as what hasn't?—in the past twenty years. The last time we were there it looked like a stage set for a melodrama about a seedy banana republic. There were sentry boxes everywhere, 25-watt bulbs in the best hotel and little saucers strategically placed to collect rainwater from the leaky roof of the lovely old opera house.)

Buenos Aires reminded us a bit of Paris, with its wide boulevards and cosmopolitan atmosphere. I was scheduled to give a number of concerts there on my second trip, and so we were put up in a suite at the elegant Alvear Palace Hotel. A baby grand piano—white, no less—was installed in the little sitting room under an elaborate crystal chandelier which tinkled in time to the music I was practicing. Surprisingly, nobody complained about the noise the chandelier and I were making. Our close friends, Leon and Dorothy Fleisher, and Berl Senofsky (who proved Uhlfelder correct by indeed appearing on the next plane), were also staying at the same hotel, as was the Soviet pianist Eugene Malinin, with whom we soon became friendly. One or the other of us four performers had a concert almost every night. Afterward, we assembled in my suite with assorted guests, and ordered what seemed like the entire room service menu. Then, and only then, did the serious work of the evening begin. The cards were shuffled, and until such time as one of the wives present said, "Enough, already!" we played poker. Malinin, who spoke only Russian, claimed at first that he didn't know anything about poker, and I explained everything in detail, even making a little chart of the sequence of hands. He studied this carefully and said he thought he would remember. An hour or so later, he asked me, "Can I check and raise?" He learned fast.

Malinin supplemented our feasts from room service with an unlimited amount of first-quality caviar and Soviet vodka, which was supplied by the Soviet Embassy. In exchange for my poker instruction, he taught me how to open a bottle by slamming it on the floor in such a way that the air pressure forces the cork to pop out. I recommend other methods, but that's how he opened our vodka every night. Would that Leon and Berl, each of whom had recently won first prize in the Brussels Competition, had been similarly blessed with equivalent gifts from our embassy!

My subsequent tours of Latin America have been under the management of Conciertos Gerard (Gerard being Gerald Uhlfelder of the red hair, and his partner Werner Wagner, who was one of our original poker circle). From their offices in Buenos Aires they control a network of command posts stretching, it seems, from Mexico to Patagonia. Almost all of their little army bear similarly native names, such as Frischler, Wohlmuth, Guttfreund, Tesch, Loewy, Arensburg. These good people, with their Central European backgrounds, do their utmost to impose at least a semblance of businesslike demeanor upon the frenetic and unpredictable behavior of their hot-blooded Latin colleagues. They strive for order in chaos. It's a losing battle, but they fall bravely.

Heinz Frischler, the Brazilian, seems, however, to delight in the bureaucratic horrors that confront him with the dawn of each new day. This may be "gallows humor," but whenever a horrible mix-up is about to occur and it becomes evident that there is no way to avert catastrophe, his eyes begin to twinkle even more than usual and I get the distinct impression that he can hardly wait for the house of cards to come tumbling down. Exit visas at short notice are his specialty, but he's game to be amused by anything unexpected. (Frischler recognized in Naomi a kindred spirit as soon as he discovered her penchant for completing immigration cards by assuming a variety of adopted maiden names. These ran the gamut from Abramovitz through O'Reilly to Zensetsu, and she claimed never to have used the same one twice.)

Once I was scheduled to play a pair of concerts in São Paulo with orchestra, in two different auditoriums. The second concert was to be in the afternoon, and telecast. The piano was to be transported from one auditorium to the other. On the afternoon of the second concert, I arrived at the auditorium a half hour early to warm up and found that the piano was not yet there. Nobody seemed particularly concerned, and neither was I. I had found, for an exorbitant sum, a dog-eared Sunday New York Times only a week old, and was quite content to work my way through it until such time as I had to go onstage. At the end of the overture, however, the piano still had not arrived. The concerto had been scheduled next, but, simply, the program was reversed and the symphony that had been planned for after the intermission was played instead. By the end of that piece, however, there was still no piano. Now things were getting a bit hairy and the guest conductor, an Argentinian who was originally Polish and therefore had a sense of dignity and order, was not very happy. He kept repeating, "Brazilians! Brazilians! *Brazilians!* Aaagh! Brazilians!" Frischler pretended to be distressed, but I could see him smacking his lips in anticipation of a particularly juicy disaster. Intermission came and went. Still no piano. What next? All the lights went out. A power failure had struck that part of São Paulo. Such localized power failures were commonplace then, and they were usually brief. The audience was requested to remain seated, which they did. Naomi and I calmly read the *Times* in the sunlight from our dressing room window. The Argentinian-Polish conductor tore his hair. Frischler chuckled. In fifteen minutes or so the lights went on again and the piano truck was seen tearing around the corner. The piano was thrust onstage, untuned of course, but still, the piano. I played the concerto as if nothing had happened. After it was over, the conductor, clutching his stomach, screamed, "Never again will I come to this crazy place!" Frischler merely smiled wisely.

"This just proves it," he said. "God is a Brazilian."

From that moment on, I became considerably more suspicious about pianos that had been promised but were not actually on the premises. Once, in Buenos Aires on a Fourth of July, circumstances warranted the explosion of a few firecrackers.

That city boasts one of the greatest musical auditoriums in the world, the Teatro Colón. When I am on the stage there I have the feeling that I am playing in a large living room, although the hall seats about 3,500 people. There are even hanging lamps onstage with rose-colored shades and fringes. (In truth, many cities in Latin America have beautiful halls, both for looking and for listening. Come to think of it, are there any nineteenth-century musical auditoriums that don't have good acoustics? There must be, but I've never encountered them. And for that matter, is there a Greek theater in which one cannot hear clearly everything said on the stage from the farthest reaches of the stone amphitheater? It seems that acoustical problems only appeared with the advent of acoustical experts.) Anyway, I love the Teatro Colón. I had given several recitals

there during my first few visits to Buenos Aires, but the first
time I was to play there with orchestra I spent the evening
sulking in the bathtub of my hotel room instead.

We had already been traveling for a number of weeks, and
while obviously one must embark on a tour of South America
ready to be amused rather than annoyed, there comes a point
past the limit of tolerance, and I must have reached it by then.
I was to play the Brahms D minor Concerto at the Colón,
which, fittingly, possessed one of the few decent pianos on the
entire continent. Just before the rehearsal I went onstage and
warmed up a bit on this beautiful instrument.

As soon as I started to play, somebody from the orchestra
management came up to me and said, "Yes, you may use this
piano for the rehearsal, but of course you understand that you
will not be playing it at the concert tonight."

"?????" said I.

"We'll have a beautiful Baldwin for the concert, but unfortunately it has not yet arrived, so you may rehearse on this
Steinway even though, of course, you may not play on it at the
concert."

"?????????????" I repeated, more emphatically.

"Well, you are playing with the Orquesta Nacional."

"?"

"That orchestra is supported by the federal government,
whereas the Teatro Colón is under the jurisdiction of the City
of Buenos Aires. Therefore, you can surely comprehend that it
is totally impossible for the Teatro Colón management to permit the use of its piano."

As is often the case with people who live in close proximity
to each other and who find life boring, the Colón management
was making it as difficult as possible for the Orquesta Nacional
to function in its hallowed precincts. But this was the Fourth
of July, and so I asserted my independence.

"No," I said.

"??" replied the manager.

"No, I will not play on a piano that I've not rehearsed on;
and no, I cannot play on a Baldwin, anyway. *I* am a *Steinway*

Artist," I said, waving my piano-affiliation flag proudly and concluding, "But I will be happy to rehearse on this lovely instrument while you figure things out."

After the rehearsal, the music director of the orchestra, who had been hastily summoned (I was playing with a guest conductor), patiently explained the whole situation to me again.

"Of course you understand, and of course you will play on the beautiful Baldwin we will have for you this evening," he said soothingly.

"No," I replied.

At this point, Werner Wagner, who shares Heinz Frischler's dry humor and was doing his utmost to keep a serious expression on his face; the orchestra's music director, who was doing *his* utmost not to cry; and I marched into the office of the director of the Teatro Colón and tried to persuade him to make an exception.

"No," he said.

"Then I won't play."

"Of course you will," he aswered patronizingly.

I left.

After great and sincere apologies to the guest conductor, with whom we then shared a huge lunch at a nearby Chinese restaurant, I returned to my hotel. I really wanted to play that concert, and I certainly wanted to play on that lovely piano, but there was no possibility that I could consider playing on an unknown instrument which hadn't even arrived at the theater and, for all I knew, might not arrive until after the concert. Besides, one has one's principles, particularly on the Fourth of July.

As soon as I was in my room, the phone rang. It was the music director of the orchestra.

"My dear, that was very charming, what you did before. But of course you were not serious." His call began in a most pleasant, almost playful, vein as he tried to cajole me into playing. Then came a gradual crescendo of pleadings, threats and insults, ending with "I never want to talk to you again!" and a slam of the receiver. Five minutes later, the phone rang and the entire process began anew.

"My dear, have you reconsidered?" he cooed silkily. Then, mounting rage. Finally, a shout which sounded like "And goodbye forever, you bastard!" Bang went the receiver. The entire afternoon passed in this manner. Eventually, as concert time approached, a symphony was substituted for my concerto, I retired to my bathtub with a good book and life went on.

As things turned out, life went on a bit differently because of my stubbornness on that glorious Fourth. The following morning I learned from headlines and editorials in all the Buenos Aires publications that I had unwittingly exploded a festering pimple. I became, for a week or two at least, something of a folk hero to pianists of that city. They were thoroughly disgusted with being victimized by the federal-civic feud but, having to live with it, hadn't dared make a scandal. Apparently, though, from that time on, any pianist playing at the Teatro Colón had the privilege of playing on its piano as well.

Another seemingly cosmopolitan center where mysterious and primitive rites take place in concert halls is Mexico City. One evening, just before my performance in the Bellas Artes theater, a lovely Art Nouveau auditorium, I was sitting in my dressing room when I gradually became conscious of strangely inappropriate sounds nearby. The Bellas Artes theater is in the middle of the city, but I could swear that what I heard was the bleating of sheep. I was right. I opened my dressing room door just in time to see a huge flock of them being shepherded into the elevator. Some sort of pageant had just concluded which required their services. The sheep departed, but the start of the orchestra concert was delayed for almost an hour by mopping-up operations.

The first one of this series of concerts, incidentally, had taken place in Toluca, about an hour's drive from Mexico City, the night before. The conductor invited us to drive with him to Toluca. He was young and a bit wild and liked fast cars, and so he had trained his driver to make this winding and mountainous journey in about half the time it should normally take.

After the Toluca concert, we planned to drive back to Mexico City together. The conductor suggested, however, that we first stop "for just a few minutes" at a supper party given by one of the orchestra's sponsors at a hacienda "not far from Toluca." Not far from Toluca, but in exactly the opposite direction from Mexico City. When we arrived, we found ten people seated at a long dinner table, halfway through an elaborate meal. Places were hastily arranged for us, and we were fed. None of the other guests had been at the concert, and it almost seemed as if we had wandered into the wrong party. Nobody spoke to us. In fact, nobody spoke. They just ate silently. It looked like a scene in a surrealist film. But after supper, our host became exceedingly gregarious, and after he showed us through the enormous hacienda, he and our conductor friend settled down for a game of chess. One game led to another, and when it was discovered that I knew how to play, nothing would do but that I had to play the winner. By then it was 3 A.M. Our conductor friend couldn't tear himself away from the chessboard.

"I'm going to stay here overnight," he announced. "You are welcome to have my chauffeur drive you back to Mexico City."

The chauffeur was not only a reckless driver, but he looked like a thug and spoke no English. We nevertheless got obediently into the car. He was instructed to drop us at our hotel, and we zoomed into the night. The darkness didn't faze him in the least. Up mountains and down gorges, he never took his foot off the gas. Finally, when we were in total wilderness about halfway between Toluca and Mexico City, and everything was black (I think we were in a forest), he slowed the car, flipped on the overhead light and reached into the glove compartment. There was a click.

This is it, we thought. We are about to be held up at gunpoint. Or shot. Or both. He turned off the light and we clutched each other wildly. There was another sinister click and a moment of silence. Then, "BaROOM, baDAMMMM, BOMBA-BOM-BOM"—we were surrounded by Bruckner, *fortississimo*. Our driver had inserted a stereo cartridge, undoubtedly as he did for his boss on these long midnight drives.

The symphony continued, *fortississimo* (as we didn't dare ask him to turn the music lower) until we reached our destination. I can imagine what the night owls leaving the hotel must have thought as this gigantic Bruckner Machine—a strange new weapon from a James Bond movie—entered the driveway. I often wonder if the driver turned it off when we left.

There is always pandemonium at any airport in Latin America. No matter how few or how many planes may be flying in or out, how beautiful or how awful the weather, how many flights may have been diverted, canceled or just plain forgotten, the disorganization is on a truly monumental scale. The first time we arrived in Bogotá, we forced our way through an almost impenetrable wall of humanity and finally arrived at the baggage area. There we were confronted by a large and rather distraught-looking lady, to whom was appended a much smaller gentleman.

"You!" she exclaimed, pushing her finger into my chest. "You Graffman?" I admitted I was. Long silence. Then:

"Spika Yiddish?"

"No," I said, "I'm sorry, I don't."

She now regarded me with suspicion.

"You Graffman?"

I reaffirmed that fact.

"But you Joosh," she observed.

"Yes," I agreed.

"You no spik Yiddish."

"No," I repeated. She now tried another approach.

"Fleisher spik Yiddish! Zeitlin spik Yiddish!" She pounced accusingly. "You Graffman, you Joosh, and you no spika Yiddish?" I again gave her my regrets. She then addressed me in German, or at least I think that's what it was, even though it still sounded like Yiddish. Then her husband, the small man, came to the rescue by addressing me in Czech. I parried the thrust in Russian. His eyes lit up. We were saved. For our entire stay in Colombia, whenever there was a problem (and there were many), I would tell Izzy the problem in Russian;

Izzy would tell Trudi in Yiddish; and Trudi would grapple with the authorities in what she assumed was Spanish.

Bogotá, unlike Montevideo, is more pleasant now than in the 1950s. I remember at that time being taken to someone's home on a hilltop. Dusk was falling. Our hostess drew back the draperies of her picture window with a flourish, and we saw millions of twinkling lights from the hovels below.

"Look!" she said proudly. "All of Bogotá is before us!" Naomi muttered that she wished it was behind us, all the more so because our room in the best hotel was shared with an enormous and friendly family of cockroaches.

In Bogotá that time we met a little man who looked so much like photos one sees of Colombian Indians that it was strange to see him in the business suit, starched white shirt and correct tie he always wore. He was the press person for CBS Records. He was eager and enthusiastic and seemed to be everywhere at once. He saw us off on the plane to Medellín, another Colombian city where I played, and I am positive that he also greeted us there when we arrived. (He was most anxious for us to like Medellín because it was his home town, and he took us on an extremely thorough sightseeing trip. The only problem was the weather. It was pouring rain—an absolute deluge. But that did not deter our companion. At every point of interest, the car would stop, we would obediently debark, look at the sight, and, drenched, squish back to the car.)

On this first visit to Colombia, I was not told I'd need an exit visa until it was almost time for my exit. This became a nearly insurmountable obstacle. Trudi grappled nobly with the authorities, but the fact remained that it was Thursday; we were about to leave for Medellín where it was not possible to complete the formalities; and when we returned to Bogotá to take a morning flight to Rio, it would be the weekend, when, of course, nothing at all is possible. We were not particularly upset, though, knowing that at the chaotic airport it would be assumed that we were tourists, who needed no exit visas. We planned to melt into that enormous and anonymous crowd.

All of this was changed, however, by our lively CBS friend,

who was determined to use his influence to make things easy for us.

"I will, of course, escort you to the airport and see you through all the formalities," said our friend. "I will explain to them that you are a very important recording star and I will tell them all about your huge successes giving concerts in our country." Our hearts sank.

When we returned to our hotel room in Bogotá, we frantically phoned the U. S. Embassy and were put in touch with an official to whom we explained our predicament.

"We must leave tomorrow morning, and there's no way we can get permission before Monday," Naomi wailed. "The concert manager says that they'll put her in jail." (She never told us what "they" planned to do to us.) The man from the Embassy seemed to take all this in stride.

"You *tried* to get your exit visa, didn't you?" he asked.

"Yes," said my wife. "Exactly—but they told us to come back Monday."

"In that case," advised the diplomat, "I think you've played the game long enough. I would suggest you just leave."

Like Alice in Wonderland crying out, "You're just a pack of cards!" all we had to do was ignore the rules and, since no exit visa was required of tourists, not present one. The only problem was that we couldn't do this with CBS banging the drum. So, at dawn we awoke, and a couple of hours earlier than necessary we sneaked off to the airport, leaving a sad farewell note at the hotel for our forsaken publicity man.

It is not always so easy to leave one of these countries without an exit visa. In Brazil things are infinitely more complicated, and tales are often told of touring artists missing concerts for lack of the proper documents. But what *are* the proper documents? It is hard to tell. Apparently, if one is in Brazil for less than fourteen days, one does not need an exit visa. But some authorities insist that the fourteen days include Sundays, and others are just as positive that Sundays are extra, and that it's fourteen working days. But then again, what are fourteen *working* days if there happens to be a holiday during one's

stay? These refinements are discussed with the utmost seriousness by all concerned.

In order to go to Brazil to give concerts, you must first obtain a special kind of visa. This is not the visa for businessmen;
it is the visa for sportsmen and artists. (I can see a kind of
crazy logic to this juxtaposition.) Before you can obtain even
the application for the visa, you have to present the contract
for your concerts, a letter from your doctor saying that you are
in fine physical and mental health, and a police certificate stating that you have not been convicted of any crime, which ne-
cessitates a trip to Police Headquarters to be fingerprinted. The
only silver lining to this irritatingly black cloud is that in New
York City the Police Headquarters is near Chinatown and—assuming one has the time—it can be arranged to visit the police
and a *dim-sum* luncheon teahouse on the same trip.

Many of these details I must attend to myself, for although
my travel agent is immensely resourceful and imaginative, he
has not yet found a way to get fingerprinted for me. (On the
other hand, Sergiu Comissiona reports that when it became
necessary for him to be fingerprinted in Rio—I'm not sure
whether this was in order for the Brazilians to check that his
fingerprints matched the ones he had given his local police in
Baltimore, or whether it was a new form of autograph collecting—he arrived at headquarters in full dress, explaining that he
was on his way to the concert hall to conduct a concert. He
confided to the police chief that it was all most inconvenient,
as the sticky ink takes quite a while to remove. "Oh, no problem," said the police chief, who obligingly dipped his own
fingers in the ink and stamped them on Maestro Comissiona's document.)

It goes without saying that very rarely does anyone actually
look at the stuff you have so painstakingly collected. Except
when there are exceptions.

One fine day in Rio we set forth to the Varig Airlines office,
documents in hand, to reconfirm our ongoing journeys. (Reconfirmation of flights in Brazil, as in most South American
countries, cannot simply be accomplished by a phone call.

Even if one could get through on the phone, which is highly unlikely, in order to be assured that you will be allowed on the plane for which you have a ticket and a reservation, you must present, at least three days beforehand, all sorts of documents including passports, entrance visas, exit visas, police certificates, health certificates. None of this, of course, in any way guarantees that you will convince the Varig agent—shrewd and cunning creature that he is—that you are entitled to board his aircraft. But without it, don't even try.)

The sight awaiting us at the airline office was most strange. Each of the ten or so agents was sitting at a desk, immobile, telephone at ear, with glazed eye and slightly open mouth. We thought we had wandered into a wax museum. We vainly tried to attract attention, but the catatonic agents appeared paralyzed. Finally, one of them put down his phone, shook his head like a dog emerging from the water and focused on us.

"What happened?" we asked.

"We've just, finally, had our computer system installed," was the reply. "Today is the first day, and now they've all gone dead. There's no way we can do anything," he added apologetically, "until the system is repaired. So leave your tickets with us and come back tomorrow." We did, and upon our return the next day, after waiting in line for the requisite hour or two, were given back our tickets. It was not until we had left Rio that we discovered that, through a computerized error, all of our continuing flights—and there were many—had been canceled.

Amazingly, we managed, somehow, to rebook most of the flights, although some had to be changed to less convenient ones. Nevertheless, our ultimate goal was reached, and as soon as we arrived I began to wonder why. Guayaquil, which even the consistently optimistic Fodor's Guide (referring to centuries of ravages by "fires, earthquakes, swarms of termites and brutal pirate attacks") describes as "not attractive," was spread before us, sleaziest of the sleazy. Hot and humid, the whole city smelled of rotting bananas and worse. Our hotel suite—for I recall that there were at least three ghastly rooms—reeked of a moldy tomb, and the bathroom fixtures were falling out of the walls. It was in this environment that, feeling like Dracula, I dressed in my white tie and tails for the concert. We were to be picked up in front of the hotel and driven to the auditorium. I usually disguise my strange outfit even in hot climates by a raincoat, but here, where I was drenched with sweat before even tying my tie, it was simply not possible. I bravely went downstairs. Naomi was with me, but as often happens on such occasions, she didn't know me. She stood far enough away to make it clear to the onlookers—and there were many—that she had nothing to do with this lunatic. As luck would have it, our driver was late, and there was nothing for me to do but stand in front of the hotel feeling like someone who has lost his pants at Buckingham Palace. By the time the jeep arrived to take us to the hall, I was surrounded by curious and hilarious urchins. They didn't want money; they just wanted to touch me to see if I was real.

The only thing I remember about Paraguay was that my recital program in Asunción included the Benjamin Lees Fourth Sonata and the Schumann *Carnaval*. The Lees was just before intermission; the *Carnaval*, after. During the intermission, a lady who introduced herself as the music critic came to tell me that she had never heard such beautiful Schumann. Of course that can happen anywhere, and is not as indigenous to Latin America as is the problem of dealing with airlines.

The last time we left Brazil, though, we felt strangely secure. First of all, the new Rio airport is so elegantly and professionally designed that it seems impossible for the customary turmoil to take place within its sleek confines. Secondly, we had all documents, and for once, no matter how anybody figured it, there was no way I needed an exit visa. Until midnight that night, I would have been in Brazil only thirteen days, and our plane was scheduled to leave at 11 P.M.

We arrived early at the airport and went immediately to check in at Varig. The agent looked at her computer and said, "I am sorry, but we have no record of your reconfirmation. The plane is, of course, full. All our planes are, of course, always full. You will have to go to Window Fifteen and wait until everyone has checked in. Then, if there is room, we may let you on." After my protestations that we had reconfirmed our flight three times in three different cities and that furthermore I had to be in Boston the next day were to no avail, I played my trump card.

"My visa expires at midnight. If I'm not on that plane, you'll be responsible for harboring an illegal visitor. You know that if I don't leave before midnight I'll have to get an exit visa, but I won't be able to get an exit visa because it has to be applied for before it is time to exit." A supervisor was called, as my voice was rising a bit. The supervisor shrugged and said, "So you'll spend a day on the beach and we'll take care of your visa."

"I don't want to go to the beach, I want to go to *Boston!*" I shouted.

"Go to Window Fifteen," she replied.

Suddenly, the enormous Rio airport, which had been virtually deserted when we arrived, began to swarm with activity. Apparently, all international flights from Rio leave at almost the same time. Therefore, if the place is not totally empty, it is jammed. The night's performance had begun. Shrieking children played Dodge-Em with the baggage carts; shouting adults argued with all agents of all airlines as, one after the other, they were all told that all their reservations were null and void. (It seems that this is standard procedure, and every planeload starts with a clean slate. Everyone goes to Window Fifteen and waits.) Naomi went to Pan Am, which also had a plane to New York at the same time as the Varig flight, and saw a well-dressed Italian, his iridescent silk suit shimmering, squeezing the throat of the Pan Am agent and screaming, "EEEEMMM-BAYYY-CHEE-LAYYY!" He was sent to Window Fifteen.

Of course we were eventually allowed on our plane and of course there were a goodly number of empty seats. I was exhausted, but Naomi, who must have some Brazilian blood in her, seemed to find the evening's sport curiously refreshing.

CHAPTER FOURTEEN

Twin Beds and Spaghetti Sandwiches

"Double or twin?"

This was—I swear—the first question put to me by the Australian Broadcasting Commission representative once the contract was signed for my tour, which was to take place under its sponsorship some three years later. And that was only the beginning. Nothing, but nothing, could be left to chance, and my nostalgic memories of charmingly improvisatory South American itineraries quickly faded in the sternly correct glare of mimeographed questionnaires, forms, lists, rules and schedules which began to clog my mailbox fully two years before the projected visit.

The frankness expected of me in advising the Australians of my preferences in everything from practice schedules to bed sizes was, to be fair, reciprocated. They told me everything. And after coping with amorphous Brazilians, there was no denying the comfortable security of knowing that twenty-four months hence, on June 13, 1958, at 11 A.M. (local time), I would be picked up at the Sydney Town House Hotel, taken to rehearse the Brahms D minor Concerto (during the second half of the rehearsal); thence to a luncheon interview in the Main Dining Hall of the Hotel Australia (near the auditorium); immediately after which three hours of practice time (as requested) had been assigned to me in Studio B of the Broadcast House (at King's Cross). I was also notified what the orchestral portion of the concert that evening would be.

Although the government-sponsored concert agencies retain their incomparable efficiency to this day, Australia and New Zealand have changed considerably since our first visit so many years ago. Now that the world has been homogenized by jets, television and supermarkets, Sydney could just as well be a handsomely situated California coastal city and Melbourne a smallish, somewhat younger Philadelphia. I don't mean to say that there is no longer any individuality to these places—certainly each has (and will, I hope, always retain) its own special quality. But that feeling of isolation, of being almost in another time period, that permeated our first visit is gone forever. A mixed blessing. When I look back on it now, the customs of those two countries as we found them in 1958 seem quaintly eccentric rather than appallingly boorish, and their very remoteness more conducive to a holiday spirit than to the desolate sense of exile we felt at the time.

Our first inkling of what lay in store came in Darwin, Australia's northernmost city, where our chug-a-lug Super-G Constellation stopped to refuel on its twenty-four-hour flight from Manila to Sydney, our destination. We got out to stretch our legs and found that a local ABC representative had been sent to greet us. He was a tall, lanky redhead, who looked and was dressed more like a cowpuncher than a broadcasting company executive.

"Welcome tew Dahwin," he smiled warmly, "the city wiv the 'ighest sewercide ryte in the world."

When we reboarded the aircraft, it was with a sinking feeling. Our tour of Australia and New Zealand was to take three months, and something (the impatience of youth?) told us that it was going to seem a hell of a lot longer.

As the plane droned on to Sydney, we contemplated the vast empty spaces below and our awful fate. Yet let no one say we hadn't been warned. Eugene, one of the groundbreakers in our crowd, had just completed a similar tour and had cut short a vacation in Hawaii at the end of his trip to see us before we set forth in order to offer practical advice. It covered just about every conceivable subject, but began with dry cleaning. He arrived in our apartment while we were packing. Threading his way around mounds of clothing, he picked up my tail suit (newly made to order by Hawes and Curtis of London "from the same bolt of cloth that we used for Milstein and the Duke of Edinburgh, sir"), and asked, "And what is this I see?"

"My new tails, you idiot."

"Aha. And where are your old ones?"

I indicated the closet. Without a word, he removed the new suit from the suitcase and replaced it with the second-best.

"You will thank me for this one day, young man," he said. (I did. For although it has turned out that the bolt of cloth that encased Milstein, the Duke of Edinburgh and me is impervious to everything from sweat to overfriendly cats, it did have a happier start on its long life by remaining in the closet while its already threadbare companion endured the rigors of the forthcoming journey.) Eugene, by the way, was not alone in sounding the alarm about mangled wardrobes. Josef Krips also offered the benefit of his experience in Australia. He told a tale of woe about a suit that eventually required cleaning so desperately that there was no alternative. He bid it a fond farewell and sent it to the cleaner's. A few days later it was back, amazingly, still recognizable. But something was wrong, a little strange. Eventually he realized what it was. Every button had come off, and although each had been carefully replaced, they were different buttons, and no two buttons matched. "And watch out for the laundry at the hotel in Sydney, too!" cautioned Maestro Krips. "I told them I didn't want any starch in my evening shirts—it is impossible to conduct when they are so

stiff—but I tell you honestly, Gary, when they came back I
thought it was a package of matzohs."

Laundry and cleaning do not a civilization make, and that
we realized even as far back as 1958. But food and drink do
have a great deal—if not everything—to do with the quality of
life on tour and we'd heard about the *plat de résistance* of Sydney: something damp and reddish combining watery tomato
sauce, overcooked pasta and soggy white bread, known as a spa-
ghetti sandwich. ("Eat only oysters!" exhorted Eugene.) We
also knew that although Australian wines were justly famous,
the licensing laws were so strange that the only hours one could
legally imbibe alcoholic beverages were precisely those that by
normal standards would be considered inappropriate. No wine
could be served in restaurants after 6 P.M., while in some states
the pubs were wide open at ten in the morning. We were also
aware of something even more ominously indicative of the temper of Australian society, and that was the scandal, currently
raging, in which a well-known conductor had been arrested and
jailed upon his arrival in Sydney for "smuggling" into the country (interleaved in the score of a Brahms symphony) the sort of
photos that appear today in *Penthouse* magazine, by which I
mean the sort of photos that Brahms probably would have
been amused to find in his symphony score. We began to feel a
little nervous about the volumes of Proust and Durrell in our
luggage.

Depressed and weary after an interminable flight, we finally
staggered from the plane in Sydney. No sooner had we reached
the ground than we found ourselves encircled by what seemed
like several dozen eager-looking people clutching pads and pencils. They were reporters. Could it really be us that they were
seeking? It could be and it was. Why on earth were journalists
interested in a less than legendary concert pianist? My sort of
animal is generally not news, as long as he sticks to his trade,
that is. But in those days, as we were soon to find out, the rest
of the world barely existed as far as the Australians and New
Zealanders were concerned. Local news filled the papers, and
that was mostly gossip. The reporters interviewed and reinter-

viewed any and all visitors, hoping to unearth something private and preferably titillating or unpleasant to write about. They also continually solicited information—in this case preferably pleasant—about the standing of their institutions and services in relation to those elsewhere on this planet. The newspapers doted on articles and letters describing substandard meals in Paris, bungled theatrical productions in London, earthquakes in Tokyo, violent muggings in New York; in short, anything to assuage what must have been a whopping sense of insecurity with proof positive that life on the Outside was worse. Thus, instantly upon our arrival, the information these reporters sought from us centered mainly on (1) 'ow we liked Austrylia and (2) 'ow their orchestras compared with those of Boston, Philadelphia and New York. Fortunately, I was able to reply truthfully that I couldn't answer either question yet, so the interrogation turned to other momentous subjects, such as the weather.

Next stop, Immigration. More questionnaires to be completed. One of the documents requested information as to my race. Under the blank to be filled in a few examples, like "European, Bantu, Chinese, Japanese," were given. I took the hint and gravely inscribed, "Caucasian." The immigration clerk looked at the form, looked at me and said, "That should be European." I told him in that case to write "American."

"American is not a race," said he.

"Neither is European," said I.

The clerk seemed perplexed rather than angry. I stood my ground. Eventually, he waved me through, but I suspect that he later crossed out what I'd written and substituted what he thought was correct.

We were then driven to the offices of the Broadcasting Commission, where we met the director, Charles (later Sir Charles) Moses. Tall, silver-haired and ruggedly elegant, he reminded me a bit of a younger Judson. I was also reminded of his historic Stanley-Livingstone encounter with the pianist Solomon, who had toured Australia some years earlier. At their first meeting, the English pianist extended his hand and said, Britishly,

"Solomon." The ABC director introduced himself in kind: "Moses." Said the pianist, who had no idea that he wasn't being teased, "I don't think that's funny at all!"

The real reason for our hasty visit to the ABC headquarters soon became apparent. A large safe was opened, and it was suggested that we put our passports inside, since we wouldn't be needing them for two months. "Artists are *so* absent-minded," we were gaily reminded. "And this is much simpler than trying to replace them when they're mislaid!" We obliged, of course, and only several weeks later, after a particularly dismal stay in Adelaide, did we realize that this stratagem had been devised to foil any thought of escape before the tour was completed, as, apparently, had happened several times in the past.

It would have been difficult to flee even if we'd had our passports, because from that moment on we were seldom without a companion from the ABC charged with seeing to it that we adhered to the schedule so painstakingly arranged several years earlier. Although our keepers were themselves most pleasant and extremely helpful, we could not help feeling that they accompanied us mainly to make sure we stayed put. Artists were definitely odd; harmless, perhaps, but nevertheless to be supervised closely at all times, for their own good, like toddlers.

My first concerts were in Melbourne, and it was there I learned that, unaccustomed as I was to public speaking, this would be precisely what was expected of me when I was not playing. Speeches, usually following luncheons, were as crucial a part of concert life in Australia as parties were to Community concerts in mid-America. With horror I learned that I was not only supposed to listen to them but to deliver some, as well. It was only a simple little thing that was wanted: just a few gracious words to thank whoever had made the preceding speech for whatever he'd said, and to tell everyone how happy I was to be in whatever city I happened to be. But I just couldn't do it. I have never been at a loss for words in normal conversation, but put me in a position where I have to rise and utter platitudes to an audience and I wither away. I'd rather play three concertos.

In Melbourne I was scheduled to play with a Belgian conductor whom I'd never met. He was about our age. His name was Edouard van Remoortel, and it turned out that he liked good food and wine and poker and other worthwhile things, so we immediately struck up a friendship that lasted for the rest of his all-too-brief life. Edouard also liked practical jokes, as quickly became evident at the symphony-sponsored luncheon before our first concert. We were the co-guests of honor, and someone—I think it must have been the lord mayor—made a long and flowery dissertation introducing Edouard, who was about to guest-conduct the orchestra for several weeks. When he finally finished, the conductor, whose English, though lightly accented, was flawless and fluent, arose to reply. He stood for a while, silent, seeming to collect his thoughts. He bit his lip. He fussed with his tie. Finally, he spoke:

"Ladies an' zhentlemens . . . ahhh . . . regret *infiniment* zat ma Angleeesh . . . I cannot . . . *alors*, ma good fraaand, Monsieur Grrrafffmannn . . . weeeel speek wiz you eenstad."

And then he sat down, the bastard.

Melbourne, idyllically located beside a lovely river, has become a bustling, cosmopolitan and, to us, thoroughly charming city. But to our jaded young eyes in 1958 it was a dreary little town consisting of a main street that looked a bit like the set for a Wild West movie: mostly two-story wooden facades, many with arcades to protect the pedestrians from what seemed then like interminable rain. I don't think the climate has changed particularly, but I suppose that as a city becomes more interesting, the weather is noticed less. But at that time there really didn't seem to be much else in Melbourne to occupy our attention, although I gave about a dozen performances, alone and with the orchestra, as was generally the custom on those ABC tours. We were there for about three weeks, and it seemed like an eternity. Our hotel, the Menzies, considered the best in town, was a rather cheerless spot, to put it mildly. It was demolished shortly after our stay.

One lesson we learned on that trip was that if you answer "Double" rather than "Twin," you have as cozy a time during the day as you do at night. The sad fact is that hotel rooms with one bed generally have less space than rooms with two. In our chamber, a smallish bed and a largish wardrobe occupied almost all the floor space, and Naomi and I had to work out strict traffic patterns to avoid constant collisions with each other and/or the furniture. There was also a rickety table littered with postcards (some of which bore a photo of a koala bear with an uncanny resemblance to Leopold Godowsky) on which Naomi dashed off nasty notes to everyone she could think of, thus venting some of her spleen; but which had to be cleared off each evening to receive our meal from room service. We had to resort to room service on concert nights. Even if we had preferred to dine out, the hours of restaurant service did not coincide with our schedule. Before the concert was too early for whatever eating establishments existed in the city then, and after the concert they were already closed. So we were visited almost nightly by a mournful-looking waiter who set before us two bowls of gruel that looked and tasted identical, no matter what we had ordered, and fled before he could hear our groans of despair.

I vented *my* spleen during the day by engaging in marathon practice sessions. By the time I finished, it was already dusk. Mid-June is the heart of the Australian winter, and the days were short and bleak. We had brought a suitcase full of books that we'd always wanted to read, but were frustrated by what seemed like constant darkness or, at best, twilight. It was impossible to arrange the lighting in our room so that we could both read comfortably at the same time. The main source of electricity came from a small, naked bulb that hung down from the ceiling at the exact center of the room, which happened to be at the foot of the bed. As there was no place to move the bed, the situation became awkward. There was no television then (or not in our hotel, anyway), and the four movie theaters in town never changed shows during our entire stay. So after we saw the four movies, we paced up and down the deserted streets on my free evenings, like caged animals, and occasionally snarled at journalists.

For the press was still with us. In fact, the press became our main contact with the world. The press called to ask the most inane questions. Nothing was too piddling for its typewriters. One morning, on a concert day, we were awakened rather too early by a lady reporter on the phone.

"What are you going to wear to the concert tonight, dearie?" she asked Naomi. It was cold and damp in Melbourne, and no place was well heated, so Naomi had taken to huddling in the same thick woolen garment night after night. It was a black-and-white knitted number that we both grew to hate.

"My dress," she mumbled thickly.

"What colour is it?" persisted the reporter.

"Black-and-white stripes."

"Aow, like a zebra, sort of?" I heard the reporter's shrill voice. Then I heard my charming wife reply, "No, actually more like a prison uniform," before she hurled down the phone and burrowed back under the pillow.

Things cheered up somewhat when the New York City Ballet came to town. At least we had friends again. We exchanged horror stories. They had come to Australia with a minimal orchestra, as per the local musicians' union regulations, which obliged them to engage local players to supplement their own people. These, of course, were not the members of the Melbourne Symphony, and apparently their work left a bit to be desired. As it turned out, a good deal of the ballet's repertoire had to be changed at the last minute because the pickup orchestra just couldn't handle the music. Stravinsky was completely beyond their abilities. It seemed that the most they could cope with was *Swan Lake*.

For their part, the Melbournians wasted no time in criticizing almost everything the ballet did. After one of my concerts there was a reception at which high government officials were present. The wife of one of the highest sidled up to me and purred, "I enjoyed your concert very much, Mr. Gaffner. I hear your ballet is not too successful, though." I asked her which productions she had seen. "Oh, I haven't gone yet," she replied. "But my hairdresser told me that they were *most* disappointing."

Ravenous after only the tea and cookies provided at this post-concert shindig, I lashed out at my assailant with the observation that almost all the programs had to be altered because *her* orchestra couldn't play the scheduled repertoire.

"Are you aware, Lady B_____, that the auditorium is so cold that the dancers can't feel contact with the stage?" I continued. "Can you imagine what it must feel like to be freezing while you are dancing? Do you realize that they've all got the flu, and that most of them have twisted ankles because of that impossibly cold stage floor?" I guess my voice must have been rising because I soon became aware of a general silence around me and Naomi tugging at my sleeve. But I was inspired. If speeches were what they wanted, speeches they would get. *"And furthermore, Lady B_____"* (I began to see red) *"the girls tell me the place is not only freezing but filthy. HOW WOULD YOU FEEL LIKE DANCING IF YOU HAD TO SHAKE COCKROACHES OUT OF YOUR SLIPPERS?"* Lady B_____ gasped as two bravely smiling equerries led her away. I wolfed down the rest of the cookies and stalked out into the night.

Amiable Melbournians existed, too. We were eventually befriended by a number of cheery and warmhearted souls. One of them was Willy Serkin, who had received a visa for Australia at the same time that his brother Rudi acquired one for the United States. Willy was a chemist who, on weekends, painted misty watercolors of the pallid landscape surrounding the city. The same wave of westward migration that brought the violinist Tossy Spivakovsky to the New World also carried his brother, pianist Jascha, Down Under; he performed and taught and had evenings of chamber music in the family's big old mansion on the outskirts of town. Most of all, though, Ewart and Marie Chapple—he was then head of the Melbourne ABC —took pity on our Menzies-bound existence and gave us the run of their home. Mrs. Chapple even invited Naomi (who loved to cook and was missing her kitchen, especially her sharp knives) to prepare a dinner of her choice, with the hostess assisting as scullery maid. The marketing took hours, for much improvisation was necessary (there being very few of the ingredients we considered staples, such as sour cream and dill, available), but Naomi made do with a variety of judicious substitutions.

It was at the Chapples' the day after the Battle of the Ballet that we met the distinguished dancer-choreographer-director Robert Helpmann, then in Melbourne leading a touring company of Noel Coward's play *Nude with Violin.* Although he had lived in London for many years, Helpmann was Australian by birth and upbringing and was still familiar with local characters and intrigues. When we related the incident of the previous evening, he calmed Naomi's embarrassment by assuring her that Lady B_____ was well-known for her *faux pas* and that, in effect, she had been insulted by far more important personages than I. I, in turn, was consoled by the fine dinner, and we returned to our dreary hotel room feeling considerably less distressed.

Preoccupation with food seems to affect most musicians on tour. Those of us who eat to live are most often upset physically, and those of us who live to eat are almost always upset emotionally. In the city of Adelaide, which we visited after Melbourne, we had an unforgettable first meeting with the Amadeus Quartet, who were traveling a similar circuit. We heard their concert, and afterward were taken backstage to be introduced to these four Londoners. Sigi Nissel, the second violinist, on hearing that we lived in midtown Manhattan, sighed wistfully, "Oh, what I would give to be eating a pastrami sandwich in the Sixth Avenue Delicatessen!"

"Actually," I answered, "I would have no objection to joining you, but I really prefer the pastrami at the Carnegie Delicatessen."

"Absolutely not!" replied Mr. Nissel vigorously. "Perhaps the corned beef, that, yes—but certainly not the pastrami. The Sixth Avenue's is far superior."

"You're dead wrong. The Carnegie, any day!"

"Sixth Avenue!"

"Carnegie!"

We nearly came to blows.

A truce was declared in Perth, where the Amadeus boys awaited us with smugly triumphant expressions. They had found what we all agreed was a good restaurant. It was owned by an Italian named Rudi, who grew oregano—the only oregano in Australia—in a window box. Rudi was a forerunner of the Central and Southern European, as well as Oriental and Middle Eastern, émigrés who came to settle in large groups during the next decade and became known locally as "New Austrylians." It is largely thanks to them, I am sure, that the profile of that part of the world has changed so dramatically. When we were last in Australia, Melbourne had a respectable number of good Greek restaurants and an excellent Chinatown, while Sydney's King's Cross neighborhood was like a smaller London Soho.

But in 1958, life in the bigger cities, where the inhabitants opted to do things as they'd been done "back home" (meaning mostly provincial England in the nineteenth century, when their ancestors left it), was dull indeed. As for smaller towns, on that tour we saw only one: Geraldton, a dot on the West Coast, where I gave a recital.

We made a quick visit from Perth, some three hundred miles away. An entourage consisting of our tour manager, an engineer (for the broadcast, as the main purpose of the Australian Broadcasting Commission's concerts was, of course, the broadcast), an accountant, a piano tuner and a press representative to keep the newshounds at bay accompanied us. We piled into a tiny plane and eventually descended onto something that the pilot identified as the landing field. We were met by a suitable delegation, and the welcoming speeches commenced.

It was raining heavily, and apparently had been doing so for a good while. As we stood listening to our hosts, we felt ourselves—and, indeed, saw the entire party—sinking slowly but

inexorably into the mud. The lord mayor made what must
have been the shortest speech of his entire career, and for once
my barbaric habit of responding with no more than a muttered
"Thank you!" seemed to be greatly appreciated. We extricated
ourselves from the mud and made our bedraggled way into
town. There a surprise awaited us, and I began to understand
why we had been accompanied by such a large retinue.

Geraldton appeared to be the brightest spot in Australia. It
was so far away from anything that a frontier spirit prevailed.
This meant a considerable relaxation of the usual rules. The
bars remained open after sundown! We made the rounds with
our keeper, eventually picking up a Latvian barmaid who,
when her establishment closed, led us down a muddy path to a
large, dark barn. Flinging open the door, she proudly took us
into a jammed and smoke-filled room where considerable food,
drink, dancing and good cheer were being dispensed. And it
was almost midnight. We played canasta and felt sinful.

I regret that the next day I repaid this unexpected hospitality
by making an awful fuss about the piano. It was of some unknown brand (which doesn't necessarily mean bad, although in
this case, "bad" was too kind a word), but it was the only
piano in Geraldton. I couldn't refuse to play the recital—that
seemed terribly unfair, considering the lengths these people
had gone to for their evening's entertainment. But I was
damned if I'd let the recital on this tinny harmonium be broadcast the length and breadth of the country. So the engineer
had the night off, and although I don't think the ABC was
very happy, it seemed the only solution. I remember afterward
an excellent supper of huge local crawfish, more canasta with
our Latvian friend and a desperately urgent, handmade DO
NOT DISTURB sign that we taped on our bedroom door to
avoid being "knocked up" for early morning tea—another of
those ancient British customs so passionately adhered to in the
most far-flung corners of the Empire.

Back to Sydney, where everything—even movies—turned off
on the Sabbath. On our last Sunday before leaving for New
Zealand, some kind people took pity on us and invited us to

their seaside home for the day. I brought a coconut, limes and
a bottle of rum, planning to make exotic drinks. I neglected,
however, to bring appropriate coconut-opening equipment, and
had to use an ice pick provided by our hosts. After a major
struggle I succeeded in dissecting the coconut and incidentally
in piercing the fifth finger of my left hand. First things first: I
continued to make the drinks, and I still remember how good
they were. Only after we had drained the pitcher did I become
conscious of my swollen and throbbing finger. Off to a doctor
we went, and my last act in Australia was to get appropriate
shots and a serious-looking bandage.

I arrived in New Zealand the next day with a bandaged and
painful finger. The pain disappeared rather soon in the finger,
only to reappear immediately in my left buttock. (I and, I assume, many of my colleagues find it prudent to have needles,
when necessary, jabbed into the gluteus maximus rather than
the more usual spot on the arm.) Apparently the doctor in Sydney who gave me the tetanus shot managed to hit something
he shouldn't have. My first visit in New Zealand, therefore, was
to a doctor who told me to get a hot water bottle and sit on it.

New Zealand was even more off the beaten track than Australia at that time. Auckland and Wellington, the biggest
cities, were more like small towns, and the hotels were like
boardinghouses. Here there were far fewer pretensions:
Freshness and innocence had not yet been sealed over by a
veneer of gentility. This place was so isolated that there seemed
to be no use in anyone's trying to catch up with the rest of the
world, and our tour became fun—until the novelty wore off.

The scenery was staggeringly beautiful. I had a few free days
here and there when we rented a car and drove the empty
roads of the two major islands which comprise this country.
The terrain was remarkably different from its giant neighbor to
the west. Volcanoes belching smoke, enormous chains of Alp-
like mountains, Scandinavian fjords, sinister caverns, vast fields
of sunny mimosa, bubbling hot-mud springs, the largest lake
trout I've ever seen—name it, and New Zealand has it. We
flew in a tiny plane to Milford Sound, a spectacular gorge

which could not then be reached by road. The pilot snaked his way not above but between the mountains, making abrupt hairpin turns at what seemed like the last possible second. On the return journey he developed a strange tic (we were sitting right behind him and could see everything he was doing), as he kept brushing his hands in front of his face. We had been joined in Milford Sound by a swarm of mosquitoes which, after the plane took off, visited the cockpit.

Volcanoes, fjords, caverns, mimosa, mud springs—and newspaper reporters. New Zealanders were even more starved for gossip than Australians. At our first press conference a lady reporter kept buzzing around Naomi, who was wearing black tights. As the reporter's Melbourne counterpart had put it, Naomi was "dressed for comfort rather than fashion." Tights were new in those days and nobody in New Zealand had ever seen or heard of them. The reporter insisted on learning how extensive they were, and Naomi showed her. The next day, under a banner headline announcing that YOU DON'T HAVE TO WEAR PANTIES WITH THEM, there appeared a photo of my smirking spouse. Shortly thereafter she had to retire the tights; her black legs marked us, unmistakably, as "that American piannerplayer and his wife."

Naomi and the newspapers also got us into trouble with the United States Ambassador. He, by the way, had a dog who could do a wonderful trick. If asked, "What would you rather be than a Republican?" the dog rolled over on his back with his feet in the air and played dead. The ambassador was annoyed because, after several weeks of boardinghouse food that made the Hotel Menzies' room service gruel seem like ambrosia, my tactful wife had enlightened the press about the many ways of preparing chicken. She had concluded with the observation that if chicken *had* to be roasted (the only way it was served, it seemed), perhaps the roasters could find a way to do it without causing the roastee's skin to acquire the consistency and taste of wet cardboard. More headlines. The ambassador scolded her: "As a representative of your country, you may think these things, but you must never say them." She rolled over and played dead.

The traveling companion assigned to us for most of this trip, an experienced tour manager named Phil Maddock, had accompanied all sorts of performers from sopranos to snake charmers. Although (or perhaps because) he was patient and long-suffering, we didn't make life easy for him, particularly when he had to pick up the pieces after some of Naomi's more colorful interviews. He took revenge of a sort in Dunedin, where the local delicacy was a kind of smoked fish. He bought a huge one to take home, and thenceforth refused to be parted from it. It was naked and unashamed and several feet long, and it followed us everywhere. We made an interesting foursome, emerging from our plane in the capital city of Wellington, our next stop—Naomi, me, Phil and the Fish. Phil was undoubtedly trying to tell us something, I now realize, but was too polite to put it into words.

Another of Rudolf Serkin's brothers, Paul, had settled with his family on a large farm outside Wellington. A skilled cabinetmaker, he had become something of a local celebrity for having introduced the wooden salad bowl to New Zealand. "Can you imagine? It was by accident I found out. Nobody had ever heard of a salad bowl. They think I invented it!" he confessed to us sheepishly, flashing the familiar crescent-moon Serkin grin. "So I've been doing a tremendous business—*everybody* needs one now." He gave us a beauty, which we carted around with Phil Maddock's dead fish.

We drove and ferried and flew to all sorts of places in New Zealand and slept in lodgings both ramshackle and reasonably elegant. In some of the hotels we were ushered into suites, quite modest by world standards, but very charming, and not at all typical of what we had come to expect. We had Queen Elizabeth to thank for that. She had toured the same route shortly before our visit, and all sorts of renovations, including fancy bathrooms, had been installed for her and her party. On some of our drives in the less-populated areas we frequently spied by the side of the road little huts, something like telephone booths, sporting the royal coat of arms on their sides. These huts formed a network of chemical toilets installed in strategic spots for the royal visit and not yet removed.

Arriving in the city of Auckland, I went for my practice session in the auditorium. When I opened the piano lid I found a note, addressed to me in Russian. It was from our friend Malinin, the Soviet pianist who had become such a poker virtuoso under my expert tutelage in Buenos Aires two years earlier. He was now touring New Zealand, too, and I was delighted to learn that our Auckland visits overlapped. We immediately made arrangements to dine together that night, which, since we were staying at different hotels, was not as simple as it sounds.

The boardinghouse hotel system that prevailed required not only that all meals be consumed at specified hours (dinner was served from six to seven and if you arrived at six-fifteen you had missed the soup—not necessarily a bad thing), but that you consumed them in your own hotel dining room. No running about from plyce to plyce, 'ear? It was quite a job to convince the manageress of Malinin's hotel dining room that he would not be coming to dinner there that evening; once that was accomplished, we had to plead with the manageress of our own hotel dining room for permission to entertain guests. We eventually sat down to an effusive reunion. Malinin was with an interpreter and, as my colleague still spoke virtually no English, the conversation was in Russian, with occasional asides to Naomi. As we got merrier and merrier and louder and louder, the waitresses became curiouser and curiouser. Eventually one of them came up, tapped me on the shoulder and inquired shyly, "If you would excuse me, sir, we've all been wondering— hearing your talk, and all—would you mind telling me what country it is you're coming from, sir?" "Why, America, of course!" I smilingly answered, and continued jabbering in Russian to Malinin, as the poor girl backed away looking extremely confused.

Malinin, who had been in Auckland for several days, told us that he had met a young lady who played the piano, and that he had promised to listen to her and advise her that evening. He asked us to join him. So after dinner we found ourselves at the girl's parents' home, where the young lady and a group of friends and relatives nervously awaited us. We were seated around the room on various sofas and settees, and she started to play the well-known E-flat major Impromptu of Schubert. Almost as soon as she began, she played a wrong note. It came in the first quarter of the third bar, when she hit a G-flat instead of a G-natural with her left hand. Malinin and I, sitting across the room from each other, exchanged sympathetic glances, assuming that the poor girl's nervousness had caused her to lose control. But no. The next time the figuration appeared, she made the same error. It sounded weird. She repeated this misreading each time the phrase recurred. It sounded *very* weird. The piece assumed a slightly ludicrous aspect. None of the girl's friends seemed to notice what was happening, although the piece she was playing was one of Schubert's most popular. It began to seem like a dream. Malinin, his interpreter, Naomi and I, scattered on our settees at the four corners of the room, began to cringe each time the fatal phrase approached. Then we got the giggles. We tried desperately not to look at each other. We swallowed. We gasped. We took out handkerchiefs and blew our noses. The poor girl plowed along, and we bit our lips and tried to think of other things. At last, she finished. I slunk off to an adjoining room. After all, it was Malinin who had been summoned for advice, not I. I should have known that he wouldn't let me off that easily. Someone called me back to the torture chamber. "Mr. Malinin wants you to translate for him because you know musical terminology better than his interpreter," was the excuse. The following conversation ensued:

Girl's mother (to Malinin, via me): "What do you think my daughter should do now?"

Malinin (in Russian, for me to translate appropriately): "Well, she certainly wouldn't stand a chance in a two-kopeck whorehouse."

Me (in English, to girl's mother): "She must continue to practice."

Girl's mother: "Should she change her teacher?"

Malinin: "She could change her ass for all I care, but she'd still be full of shit."

Me: "No, she's doing just fine right now."

The mother asked several similar questions. Malinin continued to answer in the same spirit, as did I, in my translations. Meanwhile, the real interpreter and Naomi, who understood enough Russian to follow the gist of the conversation, were suddenly overcome by some mysterious respiratory disease which caused not only violent coughing but running eyes.

This was only the beginning of what turned out to be Salute to Russia Week in Auckland.

There was in that city a local impresario, a rather pompous person, known as the Abominable Showman. It was he who had brought Malinin. A few weeks later David Oistrakh was to play under his sponsorship. He was determined to greet Mr. and Mrs. Oistrakh in a manner befitting their exalted status—and preferably in their native tongue—and so he importuned Malinin to teach him a few appropriately gracious words of greeting. Malinin was only too happy to oblige. He carefully and thoroughly drilled the manager in memorizing some phrases, most of which are so vulgar as to have no English equivalent—not in common usage, anyway. The Abominable Showman was joined by many Auckland music-lovers in practicing these phrases with what can only be described as boundless enthusiasm. Everything had to be perfect for the Oistrakh welcome. They experimented on each other endlessly, and of course on Malinin, his interpreter and me. Thus, strolling in downtown Auckland, I would often, during that week, hear a friendly shout from across the street advising me in Russian to "go fuck your grandmother." I would ceremoniously bow and thank my well-wisher.

Eventually I left Auckland, and so did Malinin. But his memory lingered on. When the Oistrakhs arrived and the obligatory flowers were thrust into their hands accompanied by the Russian phrases so diligently memorized by these good people, there was a moment of stunned silence (as I heard in Moscow some years later). The Oistrakhs' only comment to each other was a tersely muttered, "Oh, yes, of course. Malinin was just here." I understand that Oistrakh later complained to Malinin, "You didn't do a very good job—their pronunciation was so God-awful that it was almost impossible to make out exactly what it was they were trying to say!"

Although there were times when we thought the day would never come, my last concert was finally finished. We found ourselves, hardly daring to believe our good fortune, on the plane to Honolulu. Another endless trip, but one that we were only too eager to endure. The plane stopped to refuel at Canton Atoll. We had never been on an atoll, so of course we left the plane to walk a bit on this ringlike coral island, to see what we could see in the mysterious predawn darkness. As the frighteningly red sun began to rise, we became increasingly conscious that the ground on which we stood—as well as the ground all around us—seemed to be crawling. When it finally became light enough for us to make out what was going on, we saw billions of tiny crabs marching purposefully back and forth from lagoon to ocean, from ocean to lagoon. The sight was overwhelming, and gave me the shuddery feeling that our H. G. Wells Time Machine had taken us even further in the wrong direction, all the way back (or was it just a few years forward?) to primordial earth. Naomi, meanwhile, stood transfixed, watching the progress not of a crab but of a U. S. Army truck lurching slowly toward us. It was clearly on the right-hand side of the road. To her, this signified a safe return to the real world, at last.

CHAPTER FIFTEEN

About Chinese Paintings and Julius

JULIUS KATCHEN WAS amazing. Being an OYAP wasn't nearly enough for him. He was a scholar of distinction and his interests were endless. As soon as he graduated from college, in 1946, he shook the red dust of New Jersey from his feet and sailed for Paris, which became his home until his cruelly early death twenty-three years later. Although he barely made it to middle age, he didn't waste a minute.

Julius' secret was to focus white-hot concentration on whatever he was doing. He radiated enthusiasm. The intensity of his piano practicing was such that if one was within earshot, one was forced to concentrate with him—impossible even to scan a newspaper. Every pianist has a different system for practicing music that he has already learned—music in his current concert repertoire. Some of us work more, some less; but we all have to keep this stuff in shape somehow. Our habits are conditioned by our early training to a great extent. My upbringing makes it necessary—or makes me think it is necessary—to go over everything slowly, carefully, hands separately, voices separately. Naomi calls it my "N.P."—neurotic practicing. I suppose I could play without this daily workout if I had to, but the fact that I think I need it makes me need it. Julius often fussed over my practicing habits like a cranky parent.

"If you *concentrated*, Gary—if you really used your *brain*—you wouldn't have to spend so much time waggling your fingers around," he was fond of lecturing me in his most schoolmasterish voice. I, on the other hand, was aghast at the thought that on the very day Julius was to play both Brahms concertos at Lewisohn Stadium he had spent hours in earnest research with a Japanese *netsuke* dealer and had barely touched the piano.

We knew a great deal about each other's habits. Although no more than acquaintances during our school years, we became close friends when I was living for a while in Paris during 1950 and 1951. Incredibly warm-hearted as well as managerial, Julius not only introduced me to his friends but virtually took over the launching of my European career several years later by persuading his London manager, Wilfrid Van Wyck, to present me in orchestral and recital debuts in that city pretty much on his say-so. Julius was already well-known in England and on the Continent, and thanks to his help I began to make frequent European tours, journeying to that part of the world several times each season.

After Julius married, he and his marvelously attractive, deliciously acid-tongued French wife, Arlette, and Naomi and I became an inseparable foursome whenever we were in the same

city. The Katchens bought a splendid apartment near the Eiffel
Tower. It extended through two floors of a five-story Belle
Époque town house. On the top floor was an immense studio
with a ceiling that must have been at least twenty feet high.
There was a little balcony at one end of the room from which
one could peer down through the spidery arms of a huge chandelier at the two grand pianos dwarfed below, imagining the
glittering events that must have taken place there in bygone
days. It was said that Kaiser Wilhelm had bought the house
just before the First World War with plans to install his
mistresses in these opulent quarters after his triumphal entry
into the City of Light. Although this never came to pass, we
were happy to accept the Katchens' hospitality and lodge there
whenever in Paris.

I'm sure that the Katchens were better and more thoughtful
hosts than Kaiser Wilhelm could ever have been. Julius rear-
ranged his work schedule at the piano so that my need for what
he considered excessive practicing was indulged. Arlette, born
in Hanoi and at home in any number of languages, coddled
Naomi, who was terrified (with good reason) of trying to communicate in French with Parisians. Together they explored the
city with us as fervently as if they were seeing it anew. We
walked endlessly, we visited museums, went to concerts. But
the high point came once a year for about a week, at
Christmastime, when the four of us systematically ate our way
through the best restaurants of Paris as if we were Michelin in-
vestigators.

God bless those days of the almighty dollar, when even our
minuscule bank accounts could finance visits to the most legendary restaurants. *Quenelles* at Lasserre? Splendid, we agreed.
Pressed duck at La Tour d'Argent? Overrated, we decided. Best
of all? *Toast de crevettes* and wild boar at Le Grand Véfour,
where the Léoville Barton '47 was poured by a fatherly *somme-
lier* who steadfastly refused to serve any Americans who wanted
Scotch before their meal.

We were still young enough then to digest those indescribably rich meals, with appropriate wines, for a week run-

ning without serious ill effects, although I do remember Arlette's dispensing various French potions and powders at bedtime to prepare our livers for the following day's onslaught.

However, New Year's Eve dinner—the *réveillon*—was always at home, and for this Arlette prepared a sumptuous feast, which involved countless trips to many little shops to find just the right morsels. For the first course alone, she haunted the neighborhood seafood stalls, choosing the very finest that each had to offer: "Ah, yes, the *Belons* are fine and fat here, but the *praires*—" (sniffing)"—better at the place around the corner . . . *oursins?* No, not here, let's try the shop across the street." Nothing but the best would do.

Julius presided over all of this like a true emperor, albeit an extremely benevolent one. He looked a little like an intellectual prizefighter, square and muscular, with shrewd eyes twinkling behind thick, rimless glasses. He bustled and supervised and organized and belted out snatches of operatic arias; gossiped, criticized, advised and seemed utterly delighted with his lot in life. Although he spoke the language of his adopted country effortlessly, he never made the slightest attempt to *sound* French. Ironically, he sounded more American when he spoke French than when he spoke English. Like so many Americans who live abroad, Julius spoke in a "continental" way: He used a broad "a," yet he never would have been mistaken for an Englishman. On the other hand, nobody would ever guess his New Jersey origins from hearing him talk. I think Americans sometimes thought he sounded affected because of this accent, but I believe it was completely natural.

Julius was completely natural in his attitude to just about everything, and that included his analysis of his own playing. He never wasted time on false modesty. "Last night I gave the most *magnificent* performance!" he would crow at the breakfast table, and thus began a note-by-note description of the concert, frequently interrupted by Arlette's no-nonsense observations. Occasionally, when a piano had an especially good sound and when Julius was particularly inspired, he allowed himself the liberty of lingering perhaps a fraction of a second longer than absolutely necessary over a lovely phrase. Arlette referred dryly to these slight excesses as "magic moments." But none of her little asides would in any way inhibit Julius' delight in recounting his triumphs. On the contrary, I think they rather encouraged him. Nevertheless, he was an extremely sensitive critic of his own as well as others' playing. When one of his performances did not meet his exacting standards, he would groan in mock despair, "An unmitigated disahster!" and proceed to detail everything that went wrong with as much gusto as he described his "magic moments."

Being with Julius was like standing in a swiftly flowing river. The enthusiasm—the sheer energy—he lavished on whatever caught his fancy inevitably swept his companions along. The force of his excitement affected us all. This was how, in Paris, we first became conscious of his growing obsession.

I don't remember exactly how it began—perhaps during a trip to the Orient that he made around that time—but I'll never forget how it developed. He bought a few Chinese antiquities (and some fakes, as we all do)—ceramics and scroll paintings. Then he discovered *netsukes*, and things were never the same again.

Netsukes are little carved toggles, mostly made of ivory or wood, which were part of the paraphernalia attached to the garment of well-dressed Japanese gentlemen of yore. They were attached by a cord to an *inro* (a small, decorated medicine case of several compartments) usually made of lacquered wood. The cord went under the *obi* or waist sash of the *kimono*; the *netsuke* above, the *inro* below. The carvings on these toggles can depict virtually anything, but most are of animals or people. Some are handsome, some charming, some comic, a few erotic; and although they are still made today, the prizes are those of several celebrated carvers of the seventeenth, eighteenth and nineteenth centuries.

Julius, who never did anything halfway, became a fanatic collector. Elegant Japanese-style curio cabinets were installed all over the apartment, and soon they became filled with these little toggles. Julius knew everything about every one of them and

although he must have had hundreds, he could always lay his
hand immediately on any one that might come up in discussion.
(Once we sneakily replaced a treasure with a toy soldier from
Uniprix. I can still hear Julius' bellow of rage when, almost
forty feet away from the case in which the impostor had been
placed, he sensed that something was not quite right.)

Although he never learned the Japanese language, he became
an acknowledged expert in reading the signatures on these little
netsukes and deciding if they were "right." When he stayed in
our apartment on his visits to New York, a steady stream of
dealers and collectors came to consult with him, to sell to him,
to exchange with him and sometimes simply to seek his advice.
I remember one Japanese dealer, who spoke practically no English, soliciting his opinion on the genuineness of several pieces.
Julius knew every collector and dealer in Europe, and most in
the United States, and never left on a concert tour without taking a few selected *netsukes* with him—one as a talisman and
several for trading.

Of course, his playing came first. But there were moments
when he could bend his discipline a bit. Once Arlette, Naomi
and I accompanied him to a recital in Long Island. During the
intermission, a man came into the dressing room where the
four of us were sitting.

"Mr. Katchen," said the stranger, "I live nearby and was
wondering if you'd like to drop over for a drink after the concert."

"Mmmmmm," replied Julius, who, as a Parisian, had been
dreaming about pastrami at the exotic Carnegie Delicatessen.

"I have some *netsukes* you might like to see."

"Oh?" Antennae sprang up on Julius' forehead.

"In fact, I brought a photo of my prize."

Julius took it, glanced at it and began to sweat.

"It's not for sale, of course. I just wanted you to look at it."

"Mmmmm," said Julius, speculatively. "Yes, yes, we'd love
to come over after the concert."

He then played the *Carnaval* faster than I've ever heard it,
zoomed through a couple of encores and, without even chang-

ing his soaking shirt, dragged us off to follow his new friend home.

After we had been there for a few minutes, it became quite evident to us that Julius was deeply intrigued by the particular *netsuke* that was definitely not for sale.

"I'll get it from him yet," he assured us on the way back to Manhattan.

During the following two days, Julius laid siege to the hapless collector. He pleaded, he cajoled. He oozed charm. Offers of money were steadfastly refused, but cryptic and lengthy phone calls continued and eventually Julius resorted to a trade —one of the reasons he kept a batch of *netsukes* with him at all times. I think he gave up six or seven for the one he coveted. But, like the Royal Canadian Mounted Police, he got what he was after.

In the early sixties, Naomi and I bought a large, turn-of-the-century apartment a few blocks away from the smaller one that had become too cramped for us. Although the ceilings in our new place were not as high as those in the Katchens' Paris ballroom, they were pretty high and, except for a few lithographs from our old home that looked like postage stamps in their new surroundings, the walls were completely bare. Little clumps of spare Scandinavian furniture formed desolate oases in the desert of parquet floor. When Julius came to New York, he walked through the new apartment thoughtfully. He was very polite.

"I see that you're pretty well set up already," he said. "You just need a few things on the walls."

"Oh, sure," I remember replying, trying to imagine what we could possibly afford that would make a dent in that vast expanse of white. "Perhaps a few of the *Water Lilies* here, *Sunday on the Grand Jatte* there, and in the dining room, the Sistine ceiling, maybe?"

Julius pondered the matter seriously. "Have you considered Chinese paintings?" he inquired.

"You mean a big fat emperor smirking down at me? I've

seen some amusing ones, but how many of those things can you have?"

"Okay, okay. I see you don't know anything about Chinese paintings," said Julius crisply. "When you come to Paris I'll take you around to some of my dealers."

A few months later in Paris he kept his promise and introduced me to about a dozen Oriental art dealers. They were much the same dealers who trafficked in *netsukes*, so Julius was on intimate terms with them. Thus, when he brought me in as a novice, they showed much better things than they would have had I come alone. Probably the prices were lower as well, although, as there was no particular craze for Oriental art at that time, all prices were very low compared to what they later became. Buying an eighteenth-century Chinese scroll painting then was like buying a mink coat for the price of a bathrobe. So I was able to acquire a number of paintings, both Chinese and Japanese, simply because they pleased me, without having to worry about my lack of knowledge, or agonizing over the opinions of experts about how good they were.

This was fortunate, because in my ignorance I had stumbled into a thorny field—one might even describe it as a dragon pit. Oriental painting, especially Chinese painting, is one of the most difficult subjects in all areas of art. The problem of authenticity can often be insoluble, as it was considered an honor for one painter's work to be copied by later painters, signature and all. These copies were not considered forgeries but rather sincere homage to an old master. Thus, one might easily come across a seventeenth-century copy of a tenth-century painting in which the later painter had used paper and ink from the twelfth century. Then too, the seals of painters and collectors survived their owners' deaths and could be used perfectly well hundreds of years later. For all the hours I have spent reading and looking since the days Julius introduced me to this subject, my knowledge is still infinitesimal.

It has been amusing, instructive and somewhat comforting as an amateur to find that, unlike pianists, Oriental art experts are not a particularly close-knit brotherhood, sharing sympathetically their common sufferings. Although we pianists can often be very frank and sometimes even devastating with each other, we usually present a united front to the outside world. Not so, I have discovered, with Oriental art experts. On more than one occasion I have met, during a short period of time, two of the most distinguished experts in a particular segment of the field. Each has written oft-quoted volumes on the subject, has prepared bibliographies and is constantly solicited for opinions. When I am introduced to them, I feel like a passionate pianophile being introduced to Horowitz and Rubinstein.

A tattered Oriental scroll painting is unrolled.

"That's nice," I volunteer, boldly. "Yes," says the Horowitz. "It's a Tani Buncho." Later, the Rubinstein sees the painting, now identified as a Buncho. "Humph," he snorts. "If it *were* of that period I might guess that three artists could have done it, but Tani Buncho would definitely not be one of them. But that's all academic, because it's not of that period, and furthermore, it's Chinese, not Japanese."

This gives me hope.

My introduction to an involvement with Chinese and Japanese paintings, coming the way it did, may sound something like an arranged marriage. That is not precisely true. Although I had never studied or read or even thought much about the art of the Eastern world at the time Julius took me to his dealers, I had always gravitated toward it during museum visits, generally finding myself wandering in the rooms filled with scrolls, T'ang funerary ceramics or Indian sculpture. This attraction did not come from my parents, nor from anything I had learned in school, nor from anything else in my background. It was somehow an innate interest. Yet it does seem rather cold-blooded to decide to buy scroll paintings because the price is right and one has a lot of wall space to fill—particularly since the proper, Oriental way of enjoying scroll paintings is *not* to hang them in any permanent way, but to keep them rolled up and then, at an appropriate moment, unfurl one or two for serious viewing. This way they do not become stale to the eye by their constant presence. I must confess that I do keep most of them on the walls, Western fashion. And as sometimes happens in an arranged marriage, my love has blossomed slowly and steadily.

Julius haunted auction galleries in search of *netsukes* that he wanted and, in his zeal, over a period of years, drove up the prices of good ones from reasonable to outrageous. In spite of his incredible cleverness at bargaining, he would eventually pay almost anything for something he really wanted. He advised me to do the same. "You will only regret the things you didn't buy," he was fond of saying. He could discuss the intricacies of collecting and haggling endlessly and with such single-mindedness of purpose that nothing—not even the possibility of drowning—could deter him. I have a recollection of the four of us at the beach one summer. We are standing chest-deep in the water and Julius is lecturing us. He stands with his back to the waves and recounts his latest exploits with a tricky dealer. He describes the delicate negotiations in great detail and is winding up, "So he finally admitted to me that under no circumstances would he dream of going down to less than—" at which point a huge breaker comes up behind him, knocks him off his feet and inundates him. When the wave recedes, Julius calmly picks himself up, coughs, spits, blows his nose and continues, "three thousand dollars. Well, you can imagine what *I* told that bugger!" It was as if we had been sitting in a cafe. As I said, Julius always focused his concentration and left no room for extraneous disturbances.

That is why none of us could believe that such an extraneous disturbance as cancer could get the better of him. He fought it every inch of the way, and described his battle as if it were a fencing scene in an Errol Flynn movie. The last time I saw him he dramatically recounted how, the preceding month when he was in London for chemotherapy treatments, he spent his days in the hospital and his evenings playing a concert cycle of the complete piano music of Brahms—"with 'magic moments' galore." Surely anyone who can do that is invincible, he assured us. A short time later he was dead.

Although I have never been able to change my practice

habits and still waggle my fingers needlessly around for many hours each day, I like to think that Julius would agree that not all his admonitions to me have fallen on deaf ears. At least those enormous walls of our apartment are no longer bare. And whenever I sit in an auction gallery and the bidding for something I covet has gone above the estimate, above my limit and, in fact, above all reasonableness, I find that (in spite of any rational plans I may have had) my hand goes up for just one more bid. "You will only regret the things you didn't buy." Julius must be egging me on.

CHAPTER SIXTEEN

Stalking the Spotted Marilyn Monroe

THE CABLE FROM Manila had nothing to do with a concert. It said, simply, PLEASE SAVE EXTRA TIME FOR ARCHEOLOGICAL EXPEDITION. Save extra time? I would make a special trip almost anywhere for an archeological expedition. Surely, I thought, this was meant as a joke—my Philippine friends' facetious way of telling me that when I arrived in Manila to play the following week, they would be in town and would once again take me through the antique shops. Little did I know, then, what kind of shopping lay in store.

Past visits to the Philippines had whetted my acquisitive appetite. Spanish colonial art abounds, and during our first trip we shipped home crates of baroque candlesticks, inlaid furniture and little carved *santos*. Every antique shop had barrels of these wooden statuettes and, Jack Horner-like, we stuck in our thumbs and pulled out *santos* by the dozen, almost all of them attractive.

That was the first visit. On the second visit we met Leandro and Cecelia Locsin. I suppose that, for better or worse, they changed my life.

"No, Gary, you may *not* get that Martaban jar—the dragons are good, but the glaze is so eroded . . . The spout of that kendi has been replaced, see, over here you can tell . . . This bowl has an Indonesian repair—look, it's already turning yellow where the glaze has been refired . . . Ha, there's an interrrresting plate! I've never seen one quite like it, but Joey's asking far too much, the bandit. Naughty, naughty! I'll have a talk with him." Cecelia sits in the dark, scanning a ceramic jar with her black light—an ultraviolet beam which shows, somewhat like an X ray, what cracks and repairs lie hidden beneath its surface. As she analyzes the flaws and virtues of the pottery brought to her for study, approval or rejection, her low voice is thoughtful and businesslike. We are surely in the presence of a scientist. Then she finishes her examination, snaps the lights back on and—would it be too romantic to compare the face we see to a lotus flower in full bloom? Yes? Suffice it to say, then, that we are in the presence of a strikingly pretty woman with creamy skin and velvety dark eyes. She is dressed not in a scientist's coat but in a hostess' flowing silk caftan, and we are not in a laboratory but in the basement of the Locsins' extraordinary home in a suburb of Manila.

This basement (and what a humdrum word for such dramatically attractive quarters!) is a private museum, undoubtedly the most comprehensive of its kind. There are rooms upon rooms, the walls lined with lighted cabinets. Each one is filled with ceramics, most of them Chinese, most of them dating from the tenth to the sixteenth centuries and all of them found in the Philippines, many by the Locsins themselves.

Digging has always been a part of Leandro Locsin's work. But he is more frequently concerned with excavating for foundations than for artifacts: he's one of the leading architects of the day, and the most celebrated in the Philippines. Many of the new buildings in Manila and the smart suburb of Makati—concert halls, convention centers, office buildings, hotels, homes—bear the distinctively sculptural Locsin stamp. His continuing search for a distinctive Filipino idiom in his profession sharpened his awareness of the cultural vestiges of his country's colorful past, much of which still remained buried in the earth. (Riverine settlements had proliferated over layers rich in the material culture of the tenth to sixteenth centuries.) Invariably, these included huge quantities of Oriental trade ceramics, and after a heavy rain, pots popped out of the ground, sometimes, as he later wrote, "literally under people's kitchens." I well remember how, the first time we met Cecile and Lindy, he glowingly described the excitement of pinpointing an archeological site by tracing the source of some little celadon-green jars that were unquestionably twelfth- or thirteenth-century Chinese.

What were they doing in Manila?

From earliest times the Arabs and, later, the Chinese traded extensively throughout a huge area. Evidence in the form of shards is commonly found not only throughout Southeast and East Asia, but on the Indian subcontinent, in East Africa, in the Middle East and even in the place that was once called Fostat and is now Cairo. Many islands of the Philippine archipelago were ports of call along the most heavily traveled routes, and thus are especially rich in Chinese ceramics. These were buried by the local population with its dead, as was the custom before the Spanish colonial era.

In the Philippines, the earliest cultural level from which Chinese artifacts have been found is contemporaneous with the T'ang Dynasty (618–906) and the following Five Dynasties (906–60). It is only recently, however, that these artifacts have begun to be found in large number. At the time of which I am writing—the 1960s—most of the Chinese things being discovered dated from somewhat later periods, specifically, the Sung, Yüan and Ming dynasties.

The Sung Dynasty extended from 960 to 1279, and it was during the second part of that era that the massive South Chinese pottery trade began in earnest. Trading continued throughout the next, short Yüan Dynasty (1279–1368). Brief though it was, this Yüan Dynasty engendered a wealth of remarkable Chinese art. It also, incidentally, represented the first time that China was dominated by a foreign power—the Mongols—and is renowned in song and story as the epoch of Kublai Khan and the historic visit of Marco Polo.

(The timing of Marco Polo's journey was ironic. Here, finally, a European who passed a lengthy sojourn in China put down all his impressions—and they were of a country that, for the first time in its up-to-then 2,500-year recorded history, was under foreign domination. Nevertheless, the journals of his visit were immeasurably enlightening, and he is still credited with disseminating a great deal of information. When we were in Kabul we were treated to a local specialty called ashak. It was like ravioli, and I mentioned this to our host. "Naturally," he replied. "Marco Polo, passing through Afghanistan, enjoyed ashak and took some to China. On his way back he took another supply home to Italy. This should solve once and for all the riddle of where pasta originated: of course it was Afghanistan!")

The invading Mongols were finally removed in approximately 1368. This marked the formation of the Ming Dynasty, which continued until the seventeenth century (and overlapped the sixteenth-century arrival of the Spaniards in the Philippines). Three hundred years of Spanish colonization virtually obliterated the ancient Filipino life ways and customs, and trade with China gradually diminished in importance with the onset of the galleon trade.

In 1959, during excavations undertaken by Dr. Robert Fox of the Philippine National Museum in a place not too far from Manila called Catalagan, some artifacts were also found on land adjoining a quarry belonging to Cecile's family. The Locsins, who had been collecting art of one form or another since their marriage, requested a survey of the site by museum personnel, hoping to work out some kind of arrangement with the museum if the excavation proved fruitful.

Meanwhile, all hell had broken loose among the farmers and fishermen who lived along the coast near the museum's excavations. It didn't take long for them to realize that a piece of broken pottery would bring far more than whatever crops they had been growing, and they started hunting for gravesites. Having no idea of the artistic value or historic significance of the objects they found, the farmers hawked Ming plates by the side of the road as if they were ears of corn. As there were no fakes (yet) and the prices were minimal, practically anyone who could afford anything started to buy blindly. No thought was given to the irretrievable loss of scientific data as these ancient dishes and bowls disappeared, unrecorded, into the homes of the new collectors.

But who could worry about such boring details while Pot Fever raged? Even the Locsins, whose background and education had prepared them for a more dispassionate outlook, succumbed to the disease. The museum had not yet surveyed their property; others were already digging nearby; and so, chafing with impatience, they started to make their own excavations.

"You know, Gary," Lindy told me later, "we really didn't know what we were getting into! At the beginning it was almost a classic case of 'fools rush in.'" Cecile said, of their early excursions, "We'd look for a hill with a beautiful view and a spring or stream. That would be the most likely spot for an ancient burial ground. More often than not, the burials were oriented toward the east." The Locsins regaled us with tales of the innocence with which they approached their first excavations, and of the almost insurmountable difficulties that beset them. They were plagued by everything from poor weather and undrivable roads to the frustration of trying to organize and supervise diggers so that findings could be accurately recorded —and objects would not be spirited away behind their backs. Gradually, they seriously studied the methodology of systematic excavations and they slowly learned, through trial and error, how to form a disciplined and efficient excavation team. By the time we first met, in 1963, the Locsins were already acknowledged authorities on early Oriental trade ceramics. Before we left Manila that time, they showed us their growing collection and made us a present of three small jarlets of the Sung

Dynasty. I became fascinated, and started to read everything I could find about this subject.

The Locsins' cable reached me on the eve of my third visit, when I was finishing another tour of New Zealand. Getting to Manila that time was a saga in itself. The QANTAS plane that was supposed to go non-stop from Sydney ran into foul weather near Manila and circled the airport for a few hours. Eventually, the pilot announced that he had received permission to land at Clark Air Force Base, a huge United States installation a few hours' drive from Manila. When the plane landed we were herded into a large, barren room and told not to wander off because we were on American soil and could not legally enter the Philippines from there. We were advised that as soon as the weather improved and the plane was refueled we would proceed to the next destination, Hong Kong. The half-dozen Manila passengers would be put up in a hotel overnight and flown back to Manila in the morning. But I had a concert the next day in Manila, and so I was not at all happy about this roundabout arrangement.

I spoke to an American Air Force sergeant about my predicament. He called an officer who, in turn, called in a higher-ranking one. Then yet another was alerted and finally I found myself addressing the head of the whole Air Force base. This gentleman graciously offered to contact the governor of the Philippine province in which Clark Air Force Base was located. "I'll tell him that I've invited you to stay overnight at the base as my guest, and ask if he'll make an exception and allow you to enter the Philippines officially from here tomorrow morning, and then we can drive you to Manila." This was fine with me, but the QANTAS personnel, as always sticklers for rules, were apprehensive about any irregularity. (As things turned out, this was with good reason.) Several hours later the flight was ready to leave for Hong Kong, but the provincial governor had not yet been reached to approve my entry. Finally, all passengers except me boarded the plane. At that point the commander of the base told the QANTAS representative that he would personally assume responsibility for my not leaving U.S. territory until I had official Philippine permission to do so. A stewardess took my luggage tags and promised to arrange to have my bags sent back to Manila on the next morning's flight. I was then taken to the Officers' Mess for dinner.

"What did you say your name was again?" the commander asked me.

"Graffman."

"And you're from . . . ?"

"New York City."

He thought for a minute, and then excused himself. He returned shortly with a big grin and another officer in tow.

"This," he said proudly, "is Lieutenant Colonel Wexler. From Philadelphia. He'll be happy to look after you while you're our guest."

What a nice guy! He wanted to make sure that a displaced Jewish boy from the East Coast would feel at home on his base, and he knew just what to do.

"Come for breakfast tomorrow," smiled Lieutenant Colonel Wexler. "You shouldn't go to Manila on an empty stomach. We'll have lox and bagels!"

And sure enough, that's exactly what we had. The Wexlers explained that the stuff was flown in, frozen, of course. But before this airlift made such delicacies available, they had painstakingly instructed their cook how to make bagels. "You'd be surprised, Gary, how much they looked like bagels. But unfortunately," Mrs. Wexler explained, "they were approximately the size of automobile tires."

Some arrangements for my entry into the Philippines must have been made, because directly after breakfast I was driven to the nearby city of Angeles, where my passport was stamped. I was then driven to Manila, directly to the auditorium where I was to play that evening, and where I started to practice. After a few hours Cecile Locsin came to take me to their home, where I was to stay. The plane from Hong Kong, and thus my bags, had not yet arrived. However, in the Philippines formal attire can consist of black trousers and a *barong tagalog* (a loose, white, elegantly embroidered long-sleeved shirt that is worn tie-less and over the trousers), so I was able to borrow one as well as other necessities from my host. My rumpled traveling trousers were dark, so they were pressed and I was ready to play.

My unorthodox entry into the Philippines had repercussions, however. Although I was under the impression that all formalities had been taken care of when my passport was stamped in Angeles, the Philippine authorities did not agree. Apparently I needed permission from both Immigration and Customs, and my saviors at Clark Air Force Base had inadvertently asked for and received only one of these two. I don't remember which it was, but whoever didn't get a chance to stamp my passport felt slighted and made a fuss. The next day someone from QANTAS called and asked if he could borrow my passport. It was returned to me shortly thereafter with another stamp and no comment. But a few days later I saw a headline in the paper stating QANTAS FINED HEAVILY FOR ALLOWING PIANIST TO ENTER COUNTRY ILLEGALLY. I considered this modest revenge for past indignities suffered at the hands of QANTAS. Their idea of the "reasonable amount of reading material" then permitted in one's hand luggage for a twenty-four-hour journey wouldn't have gotten me off the ground, and I'll never forget the volcanic argument that erupted when they tried to charge excess baggage rates for my Sunday New York *Times*.

As soon as my concert was out of the way, the Locsins explained what they really meant by the cable they had sent me in New Zealand. Lindy began the story.

"A little while ago, in a small village about three hours' drive from here, there was a wedding at someone's home. One of the guests was Ferdy—you remember him, from the small shop on Mabini. Well, at the end of dinner, Ferdy noticed a greenish dish on which the fruit was served, and nearly choked. Although it was piled high with mangoes, he could clearly see that it was a Lung-ch'üan celadon, about thirteenth century. As soon as he could trust himself to speak normally, he said, 'What a nice dish.' 'Oh, you like it? We have lots like that,' said his host. 'Really?' asked Ferdy, breathing deeply. 'You know, there are tourists who come to my shop who might be interested in that sort of thing . . . where did you find them, anyway?' 'Oh, the kids dig around in the backyard and every now and then they come up with a few. They must have belonged to our grandparents.' 'Sure,' said Ferdy, somewhat relieved. 'By the way, I might be able to give you a few pesos for an especially nice plate of this sort.' "

Cecile continued, "Well, Ferdy had this source all to himself for a few weeks. But you know our sugar plantation? It's not far from this village, and one of the plantation guards has a girl friend who lives there. She told him what was going on, and since he knows how *inn*terrrested we are in these old pots" (she rolled her eyes expressively and gazed heavenward), "he told us what was going on. Needless to say, we wasted no time in getting over there. And Gary, it was just as we hoped: The village is next to an old gravesite. You know what that means!"

I felt my heart pounding.

"From our past experience, we had a pretty good idea of the way all of this would be laid out, and so we've been able to chart, more or less, where the digging must be located. The stuff that's coming out is unquestionably Southern Sung and Yüan."

My eyeglasses fogged over. My reading on this subject had included the scholarly volume the Locsins had just completed describing the excavations at Santa Ana they had undertaken a few years earlier. The book, called *Oriental Ceramics Found in the Philippines* (which has since become the standard text about artifacts of this type), detailed the various kinds of pottery which have been unearthed in this area. They were not all of Chinese origin. Some came from Siam (now Thailand) and Annam (now Vietnam) and dated from approximately the thirteenth through the fifteenth centuries. (Annam, by the way, means "the subjugated people of the South" in Chinese. During most periods, however, this was more wishful thinking than anything else on the part of the Chinese. But when Emperor Ch'ien Lung unleashed his campaign in the eighteenth

century, Annam was indeed badly battered. Nevertheless, some
letters, still extant, written by the Emperor's generals, complain
bitterly of the difficulty in making headway in Annam, and
describe the guerrilla-type warfare that was impossible to control. "Is it really worth the trouble and agony to continue?"
they asked their Emperor. *Plus ça change . . .*)

Cecile's voice roused me from my thoughts. "Shortly after
the digging in Laguna started, a few more gravesites were
found in the immediate area. Well, of course, the villagers have
now given up doing anything else except digging. They're at it
practically twenty-four hours a day!"

Lindy added, "Of course we tried to make them understand
how important it was to proceed with extreme caution and
neatness. You can imagine how enthusiastic they are, so we
had to make sure they understood that even a slightly chipped
pot loses a good deal of its value. Now that they realize this,
they're very, very careful indeed . . . no swinging around with
those picks. We also made sure that they put the entire contents of each grave in one distinct pile and not mix it up with
stuff from the neighboring graves—important for dating, of
course.

"In addition, we've stationed a few of our personnel about
the various sites to keep an eye on new developments. Cecile
gave them a crash course in potsmanship, so they can now
quite reliably tell the difference between, say, one of those common sixteenth-century blue-and-white dishes with the rock
design and the very early blue-and-whites which we think could
even be Sung, or in any case, fourteenth century." (A great
deal of heated controversy has simmered and boiled over the
exact period of these early blue-and-white ceramics, but calling
them "late thirteenth or early fourteenth century" and thus referring to the end of the Sung and the beginning of the Yüan
dynasties, seems safest; at least it avoids a duel, if not the
breakup of old friendships.) "Other stuff that's coming up is a
good deal of *ch'ing-pai*" (a white glaze with a bluish tinge),
"some spotted *ch'ing-pai*" (the same glaze with brownish spots
caused by drops of ferrous oxide on the glaze); "a lot of

celadons of varying shapes and shades, lead-glaze, gray glaze and creamish-white wares, and, of course, a great deal of brown-glazed potteries. In addition to all this Chinese pottery there are also Annamese and Siamese ceramics recovered from shallower graves. You can imagine how fascinating this is for us! So naturally, when we found out that you had some free time after your concert here, we were hoping you'd be able to stay for a while and come with us to the sites."

I nodded, speechless with excitement.

In the Locsins' magnificent living room, which is open to the garden and contains a little pondlike pool, were two beautiful Steinways. During this visit, however, I renounced them totally. My schedule was as follows: Up at daybreak. A quick check with Cecile, who had already been in communication with her representatives at the site via her radio-telephone (known locally as the "over-over"), and who would brief me on the latest reports.

"Last night they turned up a lot of the usual stuff, plus a couple of early blue-and-whites, one celadon dish of uncommonly good color, another one of rather unusual shape and, best of all, a spotted Marilyn Monroe!" (This was then the local name used to describe a type of spotted *ch'ing-pai* pouring vessel of a very curvaceous shape—actually, that of a gourd. It is bulbous on the top and bottom and has an extremely nipped-in waist.)

Very occasionally, we would hear the longed-for announcement that "We have seen one small square box, slightly chipped, of the 'secret color.'" This cryptic message referred to the relatively scarce ceramics with designs painted under the glaze in red made from copper oxide. Fourteenth-century craftsmen continued to find painting with copper oxide very difficult. The design on the pot often ended up looking more gray than red. But no matter—the "secret color" was rare indeed, and was just beginning to be discovered in that part of the world. Word of one would be enough to get us all into the car before breakfast.

Based on information from one of the personnel at the site,

Cecile would commit herself to buying any of these items, negotiating and transacting over the airwaves. The "over-over" was crucial because by now local dealers and collectors knew about the excavations and also journeyed there daily to buy what they could, giving rise to cutthroat machinations over the most desirable pieces. The digger or diggers who had turned them up normally held Cecile's pieces until we arrived.

When the "over-over" communication had been completed, we piled into a car which was part of a convoy of automobiles and jeeps filled with everything from lunch baskets to wads of cash. The diggers did not accept credit cards.

After a drive of almost three hours through fields and coconut groves, over bumpy and bumpier roads, we arrived at the excavation sites in the province known as Laguna. The ancient burial grounds covered three small villages, each embracing an area of fifteen to twenty-five acres. The personnel stationed there greeted us with the latest news. Then we generally paid a short visit to the local resident concerned, drank a Coke with him, and finally proceeded to the business at hand.

In front of each newly redug grave would be assembled the treasures excavated therefrom. These consisted of shards, damaged vessels, a few pieces in perfect condition and, rarely, a bit of jewelry like a blue- or green-glass bracelet. These diggers, who in normal times were local farmers, learned early in the game that if they sold individual pieces they would be left with the less desirable ones. So no matter what we wanted, we first had to purchase the entire contents of that particular grave (which explains why I have so many fourteenth-century ashtrays).

We would glance over everything with a most casual air (this took a good deal of practice), saunter around and note instantly that in one certain pile there was, say, a sixteenth-century blue-and-white dish—normally quite common—but in this case with an unusual design; in another, a *ch'ing-pai* pouring-vessel with spout and handle intact—flawless, in fact!; in a third one, a large lead-glazed vessel in which the amber color had hardly flaked off at all; and in the others, perhaps nothing of any importance. Then we would examine all the pieces, lavishing as much time and care on the ones in which we had absolutely no interest as on the ones we would kill for. The flaws, especially in the more desirable pots, would be pointed out to the diggers with a great deal of clucking and headshaking.

"Too bad about that little jar. It would have been nice, if only the ear weren't missing . . ." or, "If only the blue were a little better . . ." or, "If only the glaze weren't so eroded . . . what a pity, it's quite spoilt!" The Locsins already had superb examples of most of these things and were interested in buying only the absolutely top pieces. I, like a teenager who has just discovered girls, became quite promiscuous. I would whisper to Cecile, "I want that, and that, and *that*." If she agreed that what I had selected was worthy (for she would often say, "Oh, yes, it's interesting, but not at all that uncommon. I'm sure we'll get a better example as we go along"), she then negotiated on my behalf. These delicate maneuvers took place in Tagalog, the language of the local people, with occasional English words, such as "Marilyn Monroe," thrown in. Cecile would ask the price, recoil in horror, as if a cobra had struck, at whatever was said, and usually settled for a bit more than half of what had been asked, which at that time was quite reasonable.

(Things have changed considerably. When I was in the backwoods of Jogjakarta, near the temple complex of Prambanan, a few years ago, I wandered into a thatched-roofed hut where some of this type of ceramics were for sale, and asked the price of one. When told, I said, "But that's the same as it would be in London or New York!" "Not so," replied the native, as he pulled out from under a grass hat the catalogue of a recent Sotheby auction in London. "One just like it brought three thousand pounds last month. I'm asking 10 percent less, and no Value Added tax." But at the time of this Laguna excavation a good pot could be had for under $100.)

After a few hours on the site, we would all be invited to somebody's home, or to picnic under the coconut trees. Wicker hampers were unloaded from one of the cars, and we sat down to a repast worthy of being enjoyed in the French countryside.

Then more work until twilight, when we made the long drive back to Manila to bathe not only ourselves but, more important, our acquisitions.

For about a week I followed this existence of flitting from grave to grave. I became more knowledgeable, thanks to the Locsins' expert tutelage and on-the-job training. A few times during the week one or two other friends joined us for the day. What we did then was buy jointly whatever any of us wanted, dividing cost by number of buyers, as if splitting the bill in a Chinese restaurant. At night, after dinner, when the day's haul had been well cleaned so it could be properly examined and appreciated, the pieces were spread out neatly on a table. We then drew lots to determine who got first choice, second choice and so on, after which we selected, in order, the items we wanted. The fact that we all remained friends attests to the efficiency of this system.

In this manner I became the proud possessor of around two hundred ceramic pieces of different shapes, sizes, glazes and qualities; all dated from the twelfth to the sixteenth century, and almost all were Chinese. After obtaining clearance from the National Museum, I shipped home everything but about two dozen of the choicest—including a spotted Marilyn Monroe—which I carried back with me. Stopping in Paris, I exultantly showed these to Julius and some of his art dealer friends. The pieces were admired, but nobody—not even the specialists—knew anything about them. This was apparently one of the first occasions that Chinese ceramics of these particular types had ever been seen in the West. Nowadays, thanks greatly to the Locsins' book, their pioneering work in this field and their famous and ever increasing collection, this kind of ceramic ware, so beautiful in its simplicity, is well known and can be seen in many museums. It is becoming more and more appreciated.

Since that expedition I have never been able to resist any invitation to explore odd corners of Asia. I go ostensibly to give concerts, but am easily lured ever onward, by the promise of antiquity, to strange and mysterious places where no piano has ever been heard—or even seen. For form's sake, I may put up a little resistance sometimes.

"I really should be practicing," is what I say. But, "I really must see Borobudur," is what I do. Mad dogs and Graffmen go out in the midday sun. Naomi and I climb, crawl, slither and sweat our way through jungle trails and over mountain passes to countless ruins from Hadda to Angkor Thom.

In that part of the world, it is often only by playing in one city that I manage to make arrangements to visit monuments in another. A notable instance occurred a few years ago in Bangkok. I was giving a recital there, and I hasten to assure any reader who has heard of the infamous Bangkok performance of Myron Kropp that the piano (Steinway 364327) was, according to my Truth Box, nothing less than "excellent!"

(For the benefit of anyone too young to remember the international attention given Mr. Kropp's exploit, I should explain that a while ago there appeared in what seemed like every English-language newspaper a reprint of an article originally written for the Bangkok *Post* describing a local piano recital given by one Myron Kropp. The artist, frustrated by his instrument's ill-tempered behavior during the performance, was reported to have gradually demolished the damned thing—eventually going so far as to chop it apart with a fire ax. This tale of revenge warmed every pianist's heart and caused incredulous chuckles among millions of readers, who were finally informed that the original "review," exquisitely constructed by a Bangkok-based American journalist named Kenneth Langbell, was pure fantasy [as was Kropp], and had never been meant to be taken seriously. To this day, however, the mere mention of any pianist's giving a recital in Bangkok is greeted with whoops of laughter in certain circles.)

My thoughts in Bangkok at the time, though, were not directed toward the piano, but rather toward two little pinpoints on the map of Thailand named Sukhothai and Sawankhalok. The smallest of villages today, these pinpoints had been major temple cities from the thirteenth to the fifteenth centuries. Since they had been abandoned rather than destroyed (the action moved elsewhere, and the population followed), there was still, I understood, a great deal to see at these sites, but I had no idea how to arrange a visit. Almost any place in the interior of Thailand was virtually inaccessible to tourists at that time. Nevertheless, I was itching to visit these villages (and after doing so, I itched for different reasons).

Our problem was solved at a party after my recital. There, we were lucky enough to meet the Thai Minister of Fine Arts, and I wasted no time in confiding my desire. He was amazed that we had even heard of these places, much less wanted to visit them, but said that he would try to arrange something.

"A museum has just been established in a rebuilt former palace in Sukhothai," he told us, "and I'll wire the curator tomorrow to see what he can set up for you." (No phones in Sukhothai, of course.) And so, a couple of days later, without knowing what awaited us, we boarded the local form of milk train—a DC-3—for our trip into the interior. Naomi was not too fond of this type of aircraft, trustworthy though it is, because it reminded her of her first flight, from Los Angeles to New York, which made seventeen stops, at each one of which she threw up. Nevertheless, the advantage of flying low means that one can see terrain instead of clouds, and we had a very clear view of the peaceful Thailand countryside which reminded us, from the air, of central Florida. Little tufts of green treetops and scrubby brushes dotted the fields. Our destination was a town called Phitsanulok, the airport nearest the villages we wanted to see. There, assuming he had received the telegram and was in the mood to follow its instructions, the curator of this new museum would be awaiting us.

Sure enough, when we emerged from the plane we were approached rather tentatively by a shy young man (I don't know why he hesitated, since we were the only Westerners in sight), who asked the familiar, "You Graffman?" It was Bogotá all over again, only this fellow didn't even speak Yiddish. He ceremoniously ushered us into a jeep, and we jounced along non-roads through the lovely fields and paddies for a couple of hours. Finally we entered the village of New Sukhothai, at the outskirts of which was the former palace, now the museum. In the background we could make out the beginning of Old Sukhothai, with its temples and statues.

Behind the museum was a guest cottage where we were to stay. The accommodations were primitive, as expected. We were happily surprised, in fact, to see a bathroom with running water. We washed our sweaty faces and were further cooled as the water which flowed from the tap into the sink continued out of the basin not into a pipe, as there was none, but directly onto our feet.

In a few minutes we were ready to set forth to visit the Old City. In places like this it is wise to do one's sightseeing in the very early morning or very late afternoon and to spend the hottest part of the day as everyone else does—napping. But we had only two days, and there was a great deal to see. The humidity was overwhelming; we felt as though we were submerged in a bathtub of not-very-fresh tepid water. The poor curator was already exhausted from the hot and dusty ride to and from Phitsanulok, but we showed little mercy. We conceded enough to allow the jeep to take us from temple to temple, rather than walking, which we normally prefer; in this case it would have been like slogging through wet cement.

Soon we came face to face with rows upon rows of over-life-sized seated Buddha figures. There seemed to be hundreds of them, stretching off into the distance. Sukhothai-style Buddhas are unmistakable, with their impassive smiles, almost like sneers, and exaggeratedly broad shoulders. With this sight, there was no doubt as to where we were.

While our guide sprawled in the shade of a broad-shouldered Buddha and mopped his brow, we climbed to the summit of every temple and hill we could find. Once, on top of something high, we saw winding beneath us a colorful funeral procession and heard unforgettable sounds. The musicians or their forebears had, at some time in the distant past, been taught French military marches. These they now played on their indigenous wind and gong instruments, altering the Western melodies somewhat to fit their own musical modes. The result was a little like Malinin's Auckland friend playing wrong-note Schubert.

Our trip to Sawankhalok, the neighboring site, was mostly along the side of a wide river, the Yom. We thought the driver had gone completely mad when, at a certain point, he suddenly swerved the jeep directly into the river. But he knew the place that was not too deep (as did the local population, who, together with water buffaloes, were swimming, bathing and washing clothes all around us as we forded the river). The site of the Sawankhalok kilns was of special interest to us, as they had produced many of the ceramics we knew so well. As we walked through its vast area the ground crackled underfoot. We were tramping on millions of shards of old pots. "Millions" is not an exaggeration. From these kilns and the ones at Sukhothai, during the period that those two centers flourished, millions of bowls, pots, jars and dishes, mostly utilitarian, were shipped, first down the Yom River and then to sea, where they were sent throughout Southeast Asia. Many of the unbroken pieces are found in the Philippines, and that is how I first came to know of these old cities.

At sundown we dragged ourselves back to the guest quarters, where we once again washed our faces and, perforce, our feet. Then we walked in the soupy thick darkness to the town, which consisted of a few huts, illuminated mostly by kerosene lamps, and found the local restaurant—a big open kitchen. We ordered our dinner by the time-honored system of pointing at the woks in which various delicious-smelling but unidentifiable items were being stir-fried. All of this was washed down by good Thai beer. And so to bed. As is normal in "up-country" Thailand, sheets and blankets were not supplied. But the night was so hot and muggy we couldn't have cared less and slept through what must have been a dive-bombing attack by the crack Thai division of mosquitoes.

Naomi, however, was a bit restless. She kept mumbling something about "falling dragons." She had apparently convinced herself that the footing of the little reptiles crawling on the ceiling directly above our bed was not terribly secure. She had also convinced herself that they were dragons, and perhaps they were, if looked at with the eyes of a small insect or a wife. To me they were the local variety of salamander, quite harmless and, in fact, helpful, as they kept their territory relatively insect-free. I hate to think of what the mosquitoes would have done to us if the dragons hadn't kept at least a few of them at bay.

(Even Naomi will admit under pressure, though, that these Siamese dragons were far less distasteful than their cousins, the geckos of Kuala Lumpur. Those little beasts leave traces of what had once been their food all over walls and ceilings. In the house where we stayed in Kuala Lumpur, geckos nested behind the pictures, whence they would on certain passionate or otherwise-satisfying occasions emit shrieks or squawks. Our host in that house, a U. S. State Department attaché who had seen quite enough of Kuala Lumpur and was exceedingly short-tempered, would echo this shrill sound with a squawk of his own. "Goddam geckos!" he would roar. "Fornicating and defecating! That's all they do behind those pictures all day long! All day long! Those goddam geckos! Come outta there, you goddam bastards, I'm gonna get you!" And he would advance on the picture with a rolled-up newspaper, flailing wildly, punctuating his vicious but fruitless blows with anguished cries of "Fornicators! Defecators!" Luckily, he returned to Washington the following week. The house painters of Kuala Lumpur, incidentally, never bothered to remove these gecko traces, and there were many lumpy walls as a result.)

Next morning, our protective dragons scurried out of doors and we got back into the jeep for the bumpy return to the Phitsanulok airport. En route we were stopped and inspected by the local police chief, who had heard of our presence and made no attempt to conceal his puzzlement at seeing the likes of us in a bailiwick like his. He studied our passports and then us for what seemed like several minutes. Finally he inquired, "You go by fly?" Since, in the hierarchy of aircraft, the DC-3 is a rather small plane, I truthfully replied, "Yes," and he waved us on.

CHAPTER SEVENTEEN

Survival

IT HAS BEEN observed that the higher one climbs on the ladder of life, the lighter the hand luggage one takes along. Captains of industry do not carry bulging briefcases. I will never be mistaken for a captain of industry. This is largely, if not entirely, due to a volume approximately the size and weight of the Manhattan telephone directory that must be at my side at all times while traveling. It is known as the Official Airline Guide, and lists every flight to and from every airport in North America (a companion volume, even heftier, taking care of the rest of the world, down to the flylike DC-3s that buzz around Phitsanulok). No matter that the information is not always correct. At least it gives one a point of departure, so to speak, for the possibilities that exist, which is considerably more than one can find out at an airline counter.

My wife, who has never completely forgotten the days when every conceivable item accompanying an air traveler was put on a scale (and she, therefore, slogged around the world with toothpaste tubes and the like jammed into her coat pockets), often chides me for stuffing my briefcase with this ballast.

"For Godsakes, we're only going to *Buffalo!*" she'll groan. "Just to *Buffalo* and *back!* How many ways are there to get from *Buffalo* to *La Guardia*, for Godsakes?"

So I obligingly leave the OAG at home, and that's the time we find ourselves socked in somewhere in Canada because of a snowstorm when, after the Buffalo concert, I have been unexpectedly and urgently summoned to Dallas.

At home in New York, my redoubtable travel agent and his formidable staff organize itineraries with tender care, ingenuity and—when necessary—a touch of insanity. Where almost anyone else would say, "It can't be done," when presented with a list that includes several cities even Rand McNally has ignored, these hard-bitten professionals merely cry, "Aha—hittin' the biggies again!" and set forth with a will. John Zorek, boss of the establishment, knows the answers to every question about travel except why anyone would ever want to go anywhere. (On the occasions I've confessed to him the desire to make a trip for holiday purposes, he has favored me with a look of pure horror.)

In spite of all these thoughtful preparations, schedule changes en route are almost always necessary for one reason or another, and before I carried my own OAG I had to rely on airlines personnel for this information. I soon learned never to trust even the most charming airlines reservation clerk for anything. With the best will in the world, even the brightest of them seems only to comprehend the activities of that particular airline which employs her—limiting the traveler's options somewhat. Eight major airlines ply the skies between London and New York; one would never suspect this in talking to an agent of any one of them.

To confuse the passenger further, some airlines even have their own bowdlerized versions of the OAG. United Airlines, in its rendering, for example, will list Air Canada and American Airlines flights between New York and Toronto, since they don't fly that route. The innocent voyager will then check on other itineraries listed in that guide and find that only United now flies between New York and Los Angeles. Its competitors have, apparently, given up. I remember once being informed by a United clerk somewhere on tour that the only possible way to get from New York to Calgary was via Denver. That was the only possible way listed in United's directory. The clerk seemed genuinely surprised when I suggested that one of several quicker and cheaper ways was via Toronto. But then again, United goes to Denver.

Other necessary information included in the OAG concerns equipment used on the various flights. This makes it possible for me to avoid a DC-8 in favor of a 707, which I do whenever I can because DC-8s are equipped with abominable reading lights and 707s with fine ones, making the difference between a few hours passed pleasantly with a good book, and a miserable headache. (Speaking of headaches, I want to mention for the edification of anyone who cares and is not aware that it is illegal—in the United States, at least—for piped-in music to be played over the loudspeaker once a plane is aloft. If someone forgets to switch it off when the plane becomes airborne, to achieve instant relief the traveler has only to remind the stewardess. This does not, unfortunately, apply to restaurants and elevators. We were once told that Bruno Walter flatly refused to remain anyplace where he could hear piped-in music. If, sitting in a restaurant, he became conscious of soft, soothing strains emanating from an undetermined spot, he simply got up and left. This was when the concept of Forbidden Silence was first introduced in, I guess, the early 1950s, and I suppose it was fortunate for Dr. Walter that the span of his life did not overlap Muzak by many years. On the other hand, I am told that Muzak is good for cows.) Of the wide-bodied jets, I would choose the 747 over the DC-10 or L-1011 because the upstairs lounge offers a chance to move around, very welcome on a long flight. (Changing planes in Chicago, if one has to change planes, can also be revivifying because the layout of the O'Hare Dog Run, as we have nicknamed the airport, permits one to walk briskly from one end to the other and back again—a distance of about a mile. Amazing how much better one feels after the O'Hare Dog Run!) Since the OAG informs me of *all* the airlines flying a given route, I know all my options. Regrettably, though, services and amenities decrease daily, and it is now all too possible to find upstairs lounges given over to additional seating, burned-out light bulbs (seemingly irreplaceable in the air) on 747s, and cardboard food served on even those airlines which were once flying pleasure domes.

But without the OAG one can only throw oneself upon the mercy of whoever happens to be across the counter or at the other end of the telephone. Engraved in my memory is the recollection of a night when I needed to know how or if I could make a connection at an odd hour from somewhere in the Middle West to London. That was in the pre-jet era, when travel to Europe from the United States was not as routine as it later became. I called all the obvious airlines, and then began to phone more unexpected ones, hoping to find a schedule that jibed with mine. Finally I got El Al. When I asked the usual question, the reply came instantly (in a rather offended tone): "So, vy you're only going to London?" Like an orchestra, each airline has its own personality.

On another occasion, my problem was in leaving London. I was due in Frankfurt, a simple non-stop trip under ordinary circumstances. But that morning there had been a snowstorm. We were already buckled into our seats in the Lufthansa plane when the snowstorm escalated into a blizzard. We were served lunch in our seats as we watched the airport disappear under a blanket of white. After our meal, we were told to leave the plane (still on the ground, I am happy to add), as the flight to Frankfurt had been canceled. Back at the terminal the passengers clustered around the airline information desk to see if there was any other way of making the journey.

"Well," we were told, "in about forty minutes there's a Misrair flight to Cairo" (Misrair was the name of one of the Middle Eastern airlines of those days, the one that employed an advertising slogan that went something like, "None faster, none smoother, none safer," which I actually saw printed on a poster in some desert airport as "Non fast, non smooth, non safe.") "If you'll check at the Misrair desk, there may be room."

"What has that to do with us?" I asked reasonably.

"The flight stops in Frankfurt on the way."

"Marvelous!" I exclaimed. Then, warily, "How come they have a flight, and yours is canceled?"

"They operate under . . . ahhhh . . . different regulations."

Undaunted, all the good burghers of Frankfurt plus miscellaneous travelers such as we proceeded dutifully to the Misrair counter. As we walked, we heard status reports over the public address system. "TWA regrets to announce the cancellation of its flight to New York." "BEA flight from Amsterdam diverted to Manchester." Or, if one wanted to look at the bright side: "Air India announces its Maharajah Flight to Bombay, now boarding . . ."

Misrair had room for all of us, and at the appropriate time we boarded the aircraft—a Comet, as I recall. It was awfully cold inside. We soon saw why. Both emergency exit doors leading to the wings had been removed, and a workman in coveralls, standing on one of the wings, was sweeping off the snow with a big push broom. This human de-icer wasn't making much headway, as the snow was coming down too fast, but he did his best, and after a while he came back inside and replaced one of the doors. It closed with a click, and then he went out to push the snow around on the other wing. When he decided he'd done enough, he returned to the cabin and replaced the second door, which didn't close with a click. He tried several times, but nothing seemed to be happening. He hit it with some force, causing it to fall inward into the cabin. He then returned to the first door, removed it, put it back, heard the click, and once again tried to do the same to the other door, which steadfastly refused to make any comforting sound whatsoever. The fellow then gave it a kick (still no click, but on the other hand it didn't fall in), shrugged his shoulders and left the plane. We did arrive in Frankfurt without incident, but I remember wondering at what point a performer has the right to decide that the show doesn't *have* to go on.

Although even the OAG wouldn't have helped me to get to Frankfurt on that occasion (when, obviously, I was subject to the will of Allah), after a few more years of touring it became apparent that on the road the key to survival—if not total happiness—was self-sufficiency. One of the lessons we learned, painfully, was never to depend upon anybody for anything. Eventually, we set up guidelines for safety and comfort which, with refinements necessitated by the ever increasing decrease in service, are still in effect.

The first rule, in any city, is to try to avoid relying on any means of transportation other than foot. I feel most secure when my hotel is within sight of the auditorium where I'll be playing. Awful things can happen otherwise. In Chicago, for example, there are frequent meteorological disturbances—blizzards, mostly—during which all taxis mysteriously but definitively vanish. I can easily mush the two blocks to Orchestra Hall from the Palmer House in any kind of weather, but if I were staying at one of the more favored, and undeniably more charming, hotels farther away, I could be in deep trouble as well as snow. Even if I made it to the hall on time, it would be a nerve-fraying experience, and I'd rather have a frozen nose than a case of the jitters.

Another protective device for the well-being of the traveling performer is a nearby supermarket. Over and above the fact that most hotel and restaurant food ranges from mediocre to downright inedible looms the schedule factor. Saving time is essential. Sitting in a restaurant can be forever. Room service can be even longer (although I've discovered that a phone call to the kitchen announcing that I'm leaving my room in exactly five minutes can bring a long-delayed hamburger instantly). More often than not, I must dine at hours that many restaurant managers consider odd or impossible: either very early, before getting ready for the concert, when I'm told, "Oh, no, sir, we don't start to serve before six," or very late, after the concert is over, when I hear, "Oh, no, sir, the kitchen closed at nine-thirty." Once again, self-reliance—this time on one's ability to forage—is the answer. Naomi has sealed in her brain the locations of strategic supermarkets and food shoppes the world over. Like a bird dog, she can unerringly point her nose—even after a lapse of several years and a complete change of terrain, thanks to urban blight and/or redevelopment—through rubble, red-light districts, college campuses, Indian bazaars and endless blocks of auto-repair shops to the twenty-four-hour We-Never-Close deli with the barbecued chickens. (She can also unfailingly lead me to the town's other Mecca, which she refers to as the Dirty Book Store, where, among the Dirty Books, it is occasionally possible to negotiate for a New York *Times*.) Whatever comestibles we can find locally are served with material from our Food Survival Kit, which, like the Official Airline Guide, accompanies us everywhere and consists of the following:

> Immersion heater (heavy-duty, as the little ones from the five-and-ten don't last and are also very poorly balanced, requiring constant attention);
>
> Extension cord (electric outlets are very often concealed in strange and ingeniously inconvenient places);
>
> Teapot (not an absolute necessity, but comforting to have);
>
> Teabags, or tea and tea-infuser;
>
> Instant coffee (can be far better than 99 percent of the coffee served in hotels or restaurants anywhere in the world. It can also disguise the taste of hotel-restaurant coffee, as we learned from Mrs. Eugene Ormandy. Once, in Ames, Iowa, we saw her take a little jar from her purse and spoon a bit of the contents into the cup of brownish dishwater she'd just been served. "Now," she explained, "it is possible to drink this stuff");
>
> Cups or mugs (particularly useful nowadays when some hotels have taken to providing only little plastic throw-away glasses, unusable for hot beverages or even for holding toothbrushes);

Little bowls for whatever we've found to eat;

Sharp knives, spoons and forks;

Can opener with every possible attachment;

Corkscrew. (I cannot overstate the importance of this. Once Naomi forgot to take one, or decided it wasn't necessary. She brought along instead, on that trip, a split of very good champagne for a birthday celebration in Fort Collins, Colorado. When I tried to open the champagne, a freakish thing happened: the knob of the cork broke off. Nobody in the motel or nearby diner had a corkscrew. Finally, the manager of the diner, a college boy with a handlebar moustache, a sense of humor and a warm heart, risked his life by banging the bottle on the floor and attacking the cork with a screwdriver. Eventually he pried it out safely [and the champagne was fine], but one cannot always count on finding such a noble soul to come to the rescue);

Vegetable peeler;

Plastic orange juicer (aside from one happy week in Syracuse, New York, in April 1974, when I was able to avail myself of the Dinkler Motor Inn's truly freshly squeezed orange juice, it is amazing how, even in Florida and California, almost all hotel and restaurant juice is frozen, canned or, even worse, "reconstituted"). The juicer is also handy to make fresh lemon or lime juice to add to rum, vodka, bourbon, cachaça, pulque or whatever your pleasure;

Pepper mill and, in little pill vials, salt, sugar, maybe a dried herb or two.

Of course, it is necessary and even desirable to go to a restaurant every now and then, if only to assure oneself that an all-yogurt diet is, in the end, preferable to freshly thawed plastic. Happily, many cities still boast some splendid eating establishments; and in any case, almost any Chinese restaurant, even the most nondescript, does not sink below a decent level. At least the vegetables aren't overcooked. Nowadays there are a goodly number of Chinese restaurants to choose from almost everywhere. When I first started touring, most of these (in the United States, anyway) featured what was called "Chinese and American Cuisine." The menu was divided into dishes designed to please the two ethnic groups, with chow mein heading one side and breaded veal cutlet heading the other. I entered one of these places somewhere in Utah once, and when the waitress came around I told her of my choice: chicken chow mein. She thumped me heartily on the back and cried encouragingly, "Good for you!"

In addition to the Food Survival Kit, it is also essential to carry a few items for the purpose of making hotel rooms habitable. Life on tour has gradually become a game in which the object is to outwit hotel managements, whose goal is no longer to welcome guests but rather to punish them. Even once-splendid old hostelries, having succumbed to "modernization," are virtual disaster areas. Normal furniture has given way to those all-of-a-piece Formica abominations (in the more elegant rooms, Louis XV-style Formica abominations, to be sure) which pretend to be a desk, chest of drawers, dresser, lampstand, luggage rack and repository for the Super-Monarch QuadroStereo Living, Breathing, Fire-Eating Color TV set and succeed only in being too heavy to push even one inch in order to locate, somewhere behind this monster, the cleverly concealed electric outlet.

I sometimes wonder what makes a hotel management catering to clients who pay considerable sums for the privilege of staying in so-called deluxe establishments assume that these people don't have their own clothes hangers in their own closets at home, or their own bedside lamps on their own bedside tables. As if it isn't enough to subject us to the indignity of struggling with those devilishly inconvenient, if pilfer-proof, hangers, many hotels have taken to bolting down the bedside lamps as well. It wouldn't be so bad if only the lamps were bolted down in a place where the light they shed could illuminate something other than the bedside table they are bolted to.

Unfortunately, however, some compulsively precise interior decorator has ordered them to be secured to the exact center of the bedside table, which means that there is no way any glow from even the brightest bulb can reach a page of a book held in a hand attached to a body which is either lying in the bed or seated nearby.

To minimize these and other discomforts inherent in the modern hotel room, we bring the following:

Folding hangers and trouser hangers;

Two 100-watt bulbs (even the best hotels now rarely provide a wattage higher than 40, or at most, 60);

Extension cord (from Food Survival Kit);

Flat sink stopper (for leaky drains in sinks and tubs—mostly the newer ones, of course);

Soft cloth shoe cleaner (when provided nowadays, they are usually made of scratchy paper);

Writing paper and envelopes (increasingly hard to come by. It is usually necessary to beg a few pieces from the maid, if and when she can be located);

Steamer for freshening clothing (after arriving, wrinkled and crumpled, in a first-class hotel on a Friday evening, only to be confronted with a neat little sign on that all-in-one piece of furniture, saying: "Be sure to try our INSTANT VALET SERVICE, no service on weekends").

For travel outside North America, it is necessary to have, in addition to the items mentioned above:

Immersion heater for 220 volts;

Heavy-duty extension cord (safer for use with 220 volts);

Miniature voltage converter, if electrical appliances require it;

Adapter plugs of every imaginable type. (Don't believe any of the ads for adapter kits. Although two sizes of round prongs will suffice for most European countries, electrical wizards of the British Empire or former

parts of it have devised all sorts of variations. In some
parts of the United Kingdom the electric receptacles
contain three round holes; others have two holes and
one horizontal slit; still others, two slanting slits and
one hole. Sooner or later, one will need a plug with
any combination or arrangement of prongs, round and
flat, to fit these assorted holes and slits, that may or
may not be conceivable to the human mind. It is necessary to pack almost a suitcaseful of these adapters
to stand a fifty-fifty chance that one of them will work.
For this reason, there are two additional adapter plugs
that we never travel without. These are for lamp
sockets. In cases of dire need one can remove a lamp
bulb and substitute an adapter for one's appliance, although this can be rather a nuisance if there is only
one lamp in the room. Two kinds of adapters are essential for lamp sockets, because two types of light
bulbs are used outside of North America. In addition
to the familiar screw type, there is also something
with the sinister name of "bayonet." In order for the
bayonet bulb or adapter to work, one must plunge the
object fearlessly into the empty socket and then twist
it until a little projection at its bottom catches in a
groove in the socket. It is very broadening to be a
touring pianist.)

All of this reminds me of the evening we spent in Kuala
Lumpur at the home of the State Department attaché—the
one who had it in for geckos. He was not in very good humor
at that time, as described earlier, and he attacked the local electrical system with the same vehemence with which he swatted
the geckos. At one point during the evening he tried to move a
lamp to another room and got so snarled up in pieces of equipment—adapters, transformers, extension cords and the like—
that *he* blew up, screaming at the top of his lungs, "*Two-
twenty volts, I HATE you!*"

A similar experience of being entangled, Laocoön-like, in

electrical serpents of our own devising befell us recently at the Peshawar Intercontinental Hotel, where our room, although fancily decorated and priced, had no lighting facilities that permitted two people to read simultaneously. There *were* two lamps—neither of them near furniture that one could sit or lie on. And of course there were no electrical receptacles anywhere near where the lamps *should* have been. A long evening stretched out before us—it got dark awfully early in Peshawar —and we were determined to have a good read. At first glance, the situation looked hopeless. But we hauled out our Survival Kit and, by composing a Rube Goldberg-like arrangement of incredible complexity, we were, after several tries, able to drape the equipment around the room so that the cord from a lamp, placed where we could sit nearby, would—hallelujah!—just reach an electric receptacle. After engaging in contortions that would have done a master fakir proud to plug the snakelike contraption into the receptacle (secreted as usual behind an immovable piece of furniture—in this case, the bed), we managed, sweating and panting, to connect the confounded thing. It worked! But then we made our fatal error. Drunk with power, we decided that the arrangement would be yet more convenient if the lamp were on the *other* side of the bed. To move the lamp, though, we had first to remove the plug from the electric receptacle into which we had so laboriously placed it. I performed this operation delicately, being extra careful not to exert any real force. So ingeniously had the electric outlet been installed, however, that as the plug was pulled, with it came not only the entire receptacle but a veritable jungle of wires; mice; a chunk of wall; and God knows what else, since by then the room had been plunged into irrevocably total darkness. We gave up and went to sleep.

Every morning that I am on tour brings with it another challenge to survival. It is not enough to carry the Official Airline Guide, kitchen paraphernalia for an army of cooks and electrical equipment sufficient to illuminate a catacomb. I also need a piano to practice on. Without one, all is lost; and this is one department where, unfortunately, it is not possible to be self-sufficient. A pianist is just about the only kind of touring animal who does not carry his own instrument as a matter of course, but his need to work during the day for several hours is not universally understood.

"You mean you also want to practice on the day of your *concert?*" This was a question I used to hear frequently. In each city my hosts seemed to feel that what I really needed was a lengthy lunch at the club, sightseeing and a nap. Since almost every day culminated in a performance, such a routine would soon have resulted in great embarrassment. A tour involves playing much more repertoire than is heard in any one place: the concerto I play tonight in Detroit is different from the one I play three days later in Buenos Aires, and the recital programs for Düsseldorf next week and Iowa City the week after have to be practiced as well. Nowadays, my practicing requests are reasonably well fulfilled in most parts of the world. Even in Latin America, where, as noted, schedules are often written on the wind, I have managed to convince most of the local managers of my seriousness with regard to this subject. But in Japan I have found it impossible to get the concept across. This has nothing to do with the language barrier. There is simply an unbridgeable cultural gap: one comes to Japan to perform. Therefore, one must have prepared for these performances, and if one has prepared properly for these perfomances, one does not need additional preparation. To get into the auditoriums in Japan other than for rehearsals and concerts is usually not possible, and were it not for the generosity of the Steinway—and sometimes the Yamaha—dealers in sending little uprights to the hotel rooms, I don't know what I would do.

Although I am grateful for almost any kind of practice piano, I need to work at least a few hours on the instrument I'll be using at the performance as well. The more I can plumb its secrets—and make my peace with it—before the concert, the better the chances for a good performance. Again, the pianist is at a disadvantage here compared to his fellow performers. Even if he is lucky enough to have his own familiar piano shipped around—increasingly rare these days—that doesn't mean that it can always be at his disposal for practicing. Concert pianos are generally kept just offstage until required onstage; and as most auditoriums are used for a variety of rehearsals and performances, what this often means, for the pianist, is seeing but not touching.

Stagehands can present further problems. In Washington once, when the Kennedy Center was new, I'd finished a rehearsal with the National Symphony and then, as is my habit, stayed around on the empty stage for about fifteen minutes going over the cadenzas to the concerto (which are not customarily played at orchestral rehearsals). A few weeks later I learned to my mortification that the National Symphony's management had received a bill from the stagehands for the time that they "had" to hang around while I was on the stage. (The National Symphony's management, by the way, was far too polite to call my attention to this expense. I read about it in, of all places, a *Wall Street Journal* article about extortionate contracts with stagehands' unions.) A rather extreme case, it is true; but these days I must ascertain beforehand that my sitting alone for fifteen minutes on a darkened stage will not result in six men's receiving an hour's overtime pay.

In addition to sending out advance pleas and warnings about my practicing needs, I try to arrive at my destination the night before my concert or rehearsal. When I first started to give concerts, this was standard procedure for everyone. Perhaps because there were fewer concerts, I think performers took each concert more seriously in those days than it is customary to do now. That was partly because it simply took longer to get places. Since plane schedules were even less reliable than they are today, few serious artists would have dreamt of planning to arrive in a town on the day of a concert. Nowadays it is common practice (not only accepted, but expected) for an artist to fly all the way across the continent—sometimes even across oceans—and perform the same night. I am looked upon as an old fogey because I prefer, still, to arrive the night before. My secret reason is that traveling late in the day or evening (assuming one has a free day) saves time: I can get a full day's practicing accomplished before leaving whatever city I'm in, and another full day's work done in the city I'm going to, instead of spending prime time in the air.

On the positive side, no matter how long the distance between concert cities, I am never without a piano of some kind, somewhere, for more than twenty-four hours. This is a vast improvement over the golden era of surface transportation, when a pianist could be stuck for days without a piano. He often carried as an indispensable addition to the inevitable wardrobe trunk a long, thin case in which reposed a silent keyboard. I don't know if they still exist—I never used one, and haven't seen one for years—but this contraption could be set up on a table or any kind of flat surface, enabling idle fingers to get some exercise, at least, while the Twentieth Century Limited chugged over the Great Plains. The European-based virtuoso Shura Cherkassky played in the United States often during the great train era, and was never without his silent keyboard for the four-day trip between coasts. Once he was practicing on it in his compartment. It was stuffy in the room, so he left the door open. Two young girls walked by and he noticed that they were staring at him. Five minutes later, they marched back in the other direction and peered into his compartment again. Not long after that, they paraded past once more, ogling Shura as he trilled and thundered his silent way through the Tchaikovsky B-flat minor Concerto. The fourth time they peeked in, he stopped, looked up and asked, "Girls, girls, what's the matter?" The two young ladies gasped. "Ooooh, see, he *can* talk!" one of them said to the other. "Of course I can talk," replied Shura indignantly. "What do you mean by that?" Explained the girls, now dissolved in giggles, "Well, we were sure you were deaf and dumb!"

Shura, by the way, memorized ship and train timetables the way I study my OAG. He can still recite schedules that existed before the Second World War, and if one cares to know how it might have been possible to get from Yokohama to Rotterdam in February 1936, he could, I am sure, instantly advise on what day of the month which line was sailing. Another OAG

addict is Erich Leinsdorf. The first time we met, we quizzed
each other on the shortest way to fly, say, from Cochabamba to
Abu Dhabi. These are very important things to know. I cannot
impress enough upon the reader the feeling of security such information imparts to a constant traveler. It gives one the moral
fiber and confidence to assert oneself, as I did a few years ago
while waiting for a plane at the Philadelphia airport. Emerging
from the flight that had just landed was one quarter of the
Guarneri Quartet. (Guarneris travel separately whenever possible, abiding by a motto that says, "The Quartet That Plays Together Travels Apart." They can rarely be observed as a foursome except onstage. This is undoubtedly one of *their* secrets
of surviving on tour.) Anyway, I saw Michael Tree coming up
the ramp.

"Hi, Gary!" he greeted me. "What were you doing here in
Washington?"

"Michael," I replied, "this is Philadelphia."

"*Philadelphia?* Impossible. It can't be." He consulted his
watch. "Isn't today Wednesday?"

I consulted my OAG. "No, Michael," I answered
confidently, "it happens to be Tuesday."

"Oh, well, then," he acknowledged, "in that case I guess it *is*
Philadelphia, after all. So tell me, what were you doing here in
Philadelphia?"

CHAPTER EIGHTEEN

Explosion
in Mississippi

Jackson, Mississippi
February 4, 1964

Mr. Gary Graffman
% Columbia Artists Management
New York, New York

Dear Mr. Graffman,

We are looking forward to your appearance in Jackson, Mississippi. As a columnist for the Sunday Edition of the Jackson papers I would be very interested in interviewing you. The name of the column is "Little Things of Value." It deals with the cultural education of young children.

Having four children of my own, it has been my experience that the young child is most responsive to cultural stimulation. I try to encourage young parents to open all avenues of education to their children. With a wide cultural background they have a chance to decide for themselves

what they like or don't like. They don't just inherit the
tastes of their parents.

If artists, like yourself, will speak out encouraging this, it
could have a tremendous impact on our cultural
understanding . . .

If you can find time during your stay here . . . I will
certainly appreciate it.

> Yours truly,
> Mrs. William Scott

I would like to have met and chatted with Mrs. Scott. Her
ideas, as expressed in that letter, seemed right on target. Unfortunately, however, I never did make it to Jackson that year,
thanks to the efforts of another correspondent from that area.
His name was Austin C. Moore, III, and he wanted nothing
more than to have me stay away. Mr. Moore had started writing to me a couple of months earlier, and although the subject
concerning him was of a different nature than that of the cultural education of young children, his message carried the identical refrain: "If artists, like yourself, will speak out . . . it
could have a tremendous impact."

I would never presume even to hint that an ideal level of
civil rights for all human beings in the United States has been
reached at this stage of our history. Nevertheless, I believe it is
accurate to say that nobody who was born after the 1954
Supreme Court desegregation decision can have any real concept of the imbecility, cruelty and irrationality that abounded
in this country at that time concerning a certain segment of
the population, then known in polite society as "Negro." Although by February 1964 the decision had been law for almost
ten years, its effect on certain portions of the country had as
much reality as does the Soviet constitution's on life in the
U.S.S.R. True, there were sporadic incidents of desegregation,
but the basic feeling, especially in the Deep South, was epit-
omized by the sight of various governors standing at entrances
to schools and colleges, saying, "Never!" Bombings, shootings,
murders, intimidations and humiliations in most cases went un-
punished; the law-enforcement agencies were themselves often

the perpetrators. Today, rereading statements and speeches of supposedly well-educated adults who held important positions in the community, one is tempted to believe them scripts for bad melodrama, so demagogic and specious is the verbiage. Someone not alive in those days might have difficulty imagining that real people actually said such things.

Most public gatherings in the South at that time—especially in Mississippi—were still segregated. This was done in one of two ways. Blacks were excluded entirely or, in some places, were allowed only in a designated area of the auditorium, usually the balcony (very often, as it happens, the best place to hear music, although this was not the reason they were instructed to sit there). This was a fact of life in the United States, and any artist who performed in the South performed for segregated audiences, no matter how hard he may have tried to convince himself that this was not so. (When the confrontation I am about to describe finally came, a spokesman for the Hurok office said that his organization had tried to avoid booking artists in segregated halls for the past ten years. Nonsense. The only way to have done so would have been to have had the artists avoid the South—with very few exceptions, such as Atlanta and New Orleans—entirely.)

Austin Moore's first letter to me was an impassioned one. A student at Tougaloo College, a black school outside of Jackson, he was active in the Student Non-Violent Coordinating Committee (known as SNCC and pronounced "snick"). This civil rights movement was composed of a group of college-age young people, most of whom felt that the other organizations, especially the NAACP, had tried long enough, and fruitlessly, to operate within the system. Such a movement often manifests itself during the last stages of a hitherto gradual evolution, with the aim of speeding up the inevitable. SNCC, understandably, wanted nothing less than immediate action.

Mr. Moore wrote to me in behalf of SNCC about my scheduled recital, at the end of February, in Jackson's Municipal Auditorium as part of the Community Concerts series. He implored me to consider participating in a boycott that SNCC had instigated. Several lecturers and television entertainers had already been prevailed upon to cancel their scheduled appearances in Jackson, and he was hoping that after I had been informed of the situation I would follow suit.

His letter next described an incident at an earlier concert on the same Community series that was to present my recital. An English exchange student from Yale and a black student from Tougaloo College were standing together in line to enter the auditorium for the Community series' concert by the Royal Philharmonic of London. They had tickets (provided, of course, by sympathetic subscribers). Nevertheless, they were barred from the concert and, upon protesting, were arrested and jailed overnight. In this instance the usual problem of who should or should not be allowed to enter an auditorium was exacerbated, or brought into sharper focus, by the operating system of Community Concerts. A Community Concerts series subscription (in any city, North or South) is theoretically nontransferable and therefore not unlike membership in a private club. Although the Organized Audience concept was devised to give anyone who liked music an opportunity to hear it as long as he was willing to buy a series subscription, in this case the "private club" aspect was emphasized to explain how it was possible to exclude even people with tickets. On the other hand, the Jackson Community concerts were not held in a private clubhouse, a private home or even in a privately owned theater, but in the Municipal Auditorium, built by Jackson taxpayers—blacks *not* excluded. Austin Moore and the Tougaloo College SNCC were trying to arrange an effective boycott of Jackson by visitors in the public eye.

Mr. Moore's letter fell on fertile soil. Not for nothing did my grandfather instill in me a sense of political awareness. He encouraged me, on our long walks and talks down West End Avenue, to be outspoken in my opinions of political and social behavior, and I followed his advice—sometimes to an extreme degree. Like most of my colleagues, I felt very strongly about social injustice. Nevertheless—and also in common with just about every other performer on the concert circuit—I'd play in the South whenever invited. I even toured South Africa in 1961. There, by the way, practically all the people I had contact with (unlike many of the concert sponsors I met in Southern parts of the United States) were in the forefront of the unsuccessful attempt to steer that unfortunate country into a different path.

If the issue of human rights determines whether or not one will play in a particular country, then there would be very few places to play. Nevertheless, I do feel that one has a special moral responsibility to one's own country. Most of us who take stands do so, I believe, selectively—according to which issues we are most strongly concerned with and where we can be most effective. The effectiveness, however, depends to a great extent upon one's station in life.

Until I heard from Austin Moore it had never occurred to me that I could take an effective stand against segregated audiences. Indeed, this was why I and, I assume, most of my colleagues had been playing in the South all along. If any one of us OYAPs had made a grand gesture and announced, "This has got to stop! I refuse to play in such places," instructing our managers not to book us in all but a few cities south of the Mason-Dixon line (which, as they reminded us, begins as far north as the southern border of Pennsylvania), others would have played; we wouldn't have been missed; the world would have gone on turning. Now, for the first time, I was being told that my protest might make an impact.

Instinctively, temperamentally and emotionally I was ready. But to proceed as requested was not a course to be followed lightly. I had a contractual obligation to perform at the Jackson Municipal Auditorium under the auspices of the Jackson Community Concerts series on February 27, 1964. If I canceled the recital, claiming to be indisposed, nothing would be achieved. And if I announced that I would not play because I was supporting the boycott, I'd be violating the terms of my legal and binding contract. I pondered and discussed and asked the advice of my managers, whose general reaction seemed to be, "Cool it! Don't let yourself be used. Nothing will come of the whole thing, anyway." One of them informed me that the balcony of an auditorium in (I think) Birmingham had recently been opened to blacks. "And do you know what? Only nine of them came to the concert. So they really don't care about good music, anyway!" Meanwhile, more letters came from Austin Moore telling of the continuing success of the boycott and making it increasingly clear that a "business as usual" appearance by me could well impede the gathering momentum.

Finally, a fiendish solution came to mind: one that both appealed to my theatrical instincts and was a morally acceptable compromise. I would play the recital, and then publicly—as publicly as possible, from the great stage of the Jackson Municipal Auditorium!—I would donate my fee to SNCC or to any organization it designated. The opportunity to turn over white Jackson money to a black Jackson organization enchanted me. Before making a final decision, however, I sought advice from civil rights leaders whom I respected. Through a chain of mutual friends, starting with Ken McCormick, who knows just about everybody, both Martin Luther King and Roy Wilkins were contacted. Their attitude was surprisingly conservative. My willingness to help was appreciated; still, they felt that I might be jeopardizing myself to an extent greater than anything that my co-operation might accomplish.

I then phoned Austin Moore and told him of the advice I'd been given. He replied, in an anguished voice that stays with me still, "Dr. King . . . Roy Wilkins . . . they have no idea of what's actually going on down here, or how bad things are. And they don't have a clue to how we're beginning to make a dent, or what a commotion these cancellations we've already had are causing." He began to describe the effects of the boycott, but our phone connection got progressively worse, and eventually almost all I could hear was a rasping buzz. "Something's wrong with the line," I finally said. "Hang up and I'll phone you back." "Oh, don't bother," replied Mr. Moore, matter-of-factly. "That noise is just the phone tap. The police tap all our calls here, and I'm quite used to it." I delivered myself of a few deletable expletives, which I'm sure shocked Austin

Moore more than anyone who might have been tapping the
phone, and apprised him of my scheme to play the concert and
donate my fee publicly afterward. He replied, through an ever
increasing orchestration of electronic blips, "We'll appreciate
anything you can do. Really. But believe me, it will have far
more impact if you cancel your appearance here."

Early in February, three stars of "Bonanza," one of the most
popular television shows in Jackson, were scheduled to give several performances in the local coliseum at a trade show depict-
ing "100 Years of Progress . . . in Mississippi." Just before the
event, one of them, Dan Blocker, telegraphed that he had
"long since been in sympathy with the Negro struggle for total
citizenship, therefore I would find an appearance of any sort
before a segregated house completely incompatible with my
moral concepts—indeed, repugnant."

Two days later, the mayor of Jackson, Allen Thompson, himself made a television appearance. The purpose: to suggest that
local viewers retaliate by turning off "Bonanza." " 'Bonanza'
will never come through the air into my house again!" he cried,
and asked, "Who buys these automobiles in Mississippi?"
("Bonanza" was sponsored by a car manufacturer.) "You
know, the South is where cars will be sold in tremendous numbers." Austin Moore sent me a clipping from the Jackson *Daily
News*. On the front page a large headline stated, MAYOR URGES
WHITE BOYCOTT. The story quoted Mayor Thompson as propos-
ing a "selective viewing" of television programs and "selective
buying" of the sponsors' products. He outlined his philosophy
succinctly, explaining, "We want business, industry and people
to come into Jackson, but only if they like what we are doing
and the way we live." For me this was clearly a formal invitation to stay away.

"I completely understand your point of view, Gary," said one
of my managers, looking for all the world as if he were about to
burst into tears. (I'd told him that it was becoming increasingly difficult for me to consider fulfilling my contract in Jackson.) "But honestly, I'd feel a great deal better about the
whole thing if the NAACP, rather than SNCC, asked you to

cancel." I promptly returned to the office of Jack Greenberg, head of the NAACP's Legal Defense Fund, another of the people I'd been consulting, and asked him to find out once and for all from the NAACP in Jackson what *they* would like me to do. In fairness to those who felt that SNCC's tactics were too militant, I agreed to accept the Jackson NAACP's decision.

A few hours later the reply came back from Charles Evers, then field secretary of the NAACP in Mississippi. "We'd be most grateful for anything you want to do," he said. "But since you ask us, the act that would be of greatest help to us, and that would have the greatest impact, would be cancellation." That was it.

One of the advantages (perhaps the only advantage) of being associated with a giant concert agency is that the artist works with a team of managers. Several people were more or less responsible for different facets of my business affairs and welfare. Like a group of medical specialists, there was the equivalent of an internist (bookings); the ear, nose and throat man (financial accounting); the neurologist (programs); the plastic surgeon (public relations); and the psychiatrist (all other problems). At this point, I decided to consult the latter. He was the manager I felt closest to, the one who had always considered the long-range effects of any decision, the one who was least swayed by immediate gain or loss, the one who weighed logically all aspects of a situation, and, not the least of it, the one who kept his head when all about him were losing theirs.

Our interview surprised me. He knew, from earlier conversations, that I'd been getting these letters from Tougaloo, but since I hadn't made up my own mind as to what I thought I should do, I hadn't kept him apprised of the daily buildup. Now I gave him all the details. I think the first thing he said when I had finished was something like, "I gather you are telling me what you are going to do, and not asking for my opinion of what you *should* do." I told him that was true, but that I had given the matter a tremendous amount of thought before reaching this decision. I didn't say what I had hoped—had, in fact, assumed: that, once everything had been explained, once he had been made aware of the actual situation, he would give me and my actions his firm, even enthusiastic, support. He did not. That he was less sympathetic than I had expected could, in part, have been due to his broad overview of the situation. I think he honestly believed that any swashbuckling altruism on my part would create a good deal more annoyance for all of us than lasting benefit for the cause I now so passionately espoused. But this feeling (if I interpret correctly) was possible because, unlike me, he had not been besieged by an almost daily bombardment of information, pleas and tales of horror. How could my vivid description of what was taking place not have convinced him? It was as if a soundproof glass wall had slid down between us. I talked myself hoarse; he only asked, "And what about your legal and binding contract?"

"I'm not a lawyer," I remember replying, "and neither are you. But you know that the concert is to be held in the Municipal Auditorium, which, according to the Attorney General, is breaking a federal law by permitting any segregated event to take place there. Furthermore, the mayor of Jackson invited me to stay away," I finished, somewhat facetiously.

He became visibly upset, trying to figure out a way to keep the situation contained. He was silent for a while, and finally suggested, "You know, we could arrange to have you flown to a neighboring airport. They won't know which one. We could have a car pick you up, drive you to the hall and immediately after the concert take you back to a different airport."

I began to lose my temper. "You mean that you feel all we should do is try to avoid a confrontation with pickets? Hasn't anything I've said gotten through to you? None of this makes any sense!" I flared. "Don't you see that there's just no alternative to canceling now?"

He, who normally spoke eloquently and convincingly of anything he believed in, did not make a very good case in rebuttal. He tried to calm me down, and when he saw that this was impossible, sighed resignedly. "Isn't being 'indisposed' the simplest way, then?"

This was truly the last thing in the world I expected to hear. I wonder, now, if he just let those words roll out so that he could tell his Board of Directors that he wore the corporation hat at this encounter. (I trust this was the case, as our conversation that day was by no means typical of our many encounters over the years.) But at that moment, I realized that my management, as a corporation, was not going to back me in this situation. Ever since I first read a managerial contract—the one that Hurok sent me when I was seventeen—and saw that it specified "Artist engages Manager . . ." I'd been conscious that in real life things seemed to work just the opposite. I determined to make sure that no double-crossing would take place in this instance, at least. I was not embarrassed by the situation in the slightest. Since it is very seldom—if ever—that one can do something one believes in with some realistic hope that it will have positive results, I was going to make the most of this. Let the chips fall where they may.

"So I'll write you a formal letter telling you that I'm going to cancel the concert, and I shall give the reason for so doing in the letter. And just to make sure that nobody thinks I'm 'indisposed,' I'll send a copy to SNCC at Tougaloo."

His last words to me were, "Remember, you have a contract."

I went home and called my lawyer.

Four days later, after much drafting and redrafting (and hardly any piano practicing) the first formal document went forth to my managers. It was a long letter (my letters usually are) and the gist of it was that "because of SNCC's work in the entertainment field during the past few months I would find myself for the first time actively supporting this barbaric philosophy of segregation just by playing a concert . . . and equally, for the first time, possibly producing results by taking a positive stand." I quoted the Jackson mayor's comment about not being welcome there unless I agreed with their philosophies, and wound up, "I feel that his statement has put me in the position of endorsing the political philosophy of the State of Mississippi or at least the city of Jackson, merely by voluntarily setting foot in it. Not even the Soviet-dominated countries of Eastern Europe go this far." I then left for California on the first leg of the tour that was to have included Jackson.

Lawyers never sleep. The following week, while I was sunning myself by the pool at the Hollywood-Roosevelt with, like a local mogul, a telephone by my tanning oil, back in New York all sorts of legalistic machinery churned along to guarantee that nobody could possibly think I was unwell when I bypassed Jackson. A telegram over my signature to Mayor Thompson as well as to the local Community Concerts association asked if I would be required, by local ordinance or policies, to appear before a segregated audience. The mayor didn't reply, but the Jackson Music Association gave an unequivocal response, describing itself as "A PRIVATE MEMBERSHIP ORGANIZATION WITH THE PURPOSE OF PROVIDING GOOD MUSIC FOR ITS OWN MEMBERS EXCLUSIVELY. THE ASSOCIATION RESERVES THE RIGHT TO CONTROL ITS OWN MEMBERSHIP POLICIES, PROGRAMS AND PARTICIPANTS . . . IF YOU HAVE ANY PROBLEMS . . . WE RESPECTFULLY REQUEST THAT YOU MAKE THE REQUIRED ARRANGEMENTS WITH YOUR CONTRACTUAL AGENCY."

This paved the way for another official letter to be sent to Columbia Artists Management, my contractual agency, explaining that under the circumstances I was following the instructions of the Jackson Music Association and requesting to be relieved of my commitment to this performance. The lawyers concocted a mouthful (even for me) which read, in part, ". . . in the past I have played before segregated audiences, but I did not do so by preference . . . I have not heretofore regarded myself as being in a position either to make a positive contribution to the civil rights movement by declining to appear, or to harm the civil rights movement by agreeing to appear. With all the recent developments in the achievement of meaningful civil liberties, and particularly in light of the civil rights legislation now in process of enactment by Congress, I feel more keenly than ever that it is my duty to be responsive to a situation like the one confronting me . . . the Jackson

Music Association has suggested that if I wished to cancel my appearance I should make such arrangements with you. Under these circumstances, therefore, I request that you relieve me of my commitment . . ."

By then, of course, this came as no surprise to my managers, who were already expressing great concern to my wife and attorneys (I was still basking in the California sunshine) about the grave consequences I would have to face after my fleeting moment of glory. Hattie Pearl Lea was not the least of these. A longtime representative of Community Concerts who booked engagements in the territory that I was now insulting, she lived in Jackson, where, among other things, she was very active in politics. Hattie Pearl was not at all happy. "It might not be amiss," Naomi was told, "when all of this blows over, to drop Hattie Pearl a note of apology for the inconvenience and embarrassment Gary has caused her. He can say something to the effect that he realizes how difficult he's made things for her, but it was a matter of conscience and various pressures, and he had no alternative. Perhaps this will help smooth things over because," it was further explained, "Southerners set such store on courtesy."

(I do not intend to give the impression, in reproducing these conversations, that I have total recall. Most of the foregoing and following quotations have been gleaned from copious daily notes and memoranda that I made at the time, at the behest of my lawyers. Why I piled the stuff into a carton and saved it all these years, only my unconscious mind knows. But the fact remains that I did, and when I started to write this memoir, Naomi dragged the dusty box down from its resting place on top of the highest closet shelf.)

On Tuesday, February 25, instead of proceeding to Jackson after my Tulsa concert, I returned to New York. Awaiting me was an urgent message to phone my colleague David Bar-Illan the instant I came home.

"What the hell is going on, and how do you feel?" was the way he greeted me.

"I feel fine, but what are you referring to?" I asked, unconvincingly.

"So you're not sick."

"Not yet."

"I had a feeling there was something suspicious," he said. "I got a call asking if I would play your date in Jackson . . . but from the way I was asked, I got the feeling it wasn't just a normal cancellation." (Almost everybody gets sick at one time or another, especially in February.) "And when I asked what was wrong with you I got a vague story about its being something political. So, what's up?"

I told him.

"Boy," he said. "They certainly didn't give me all the facts. I had no idea what a hornet's nest they were planning to send me into. I'm glad I spoke to you before I decided what to do. Of course I won't go, either. And I'll call my friend James Farmer" (of CORE, another major black organization at that time) "and tell him what's going on." Then David continued, "But listen, Gary. The person from Community who called me said some peculiar things about you—that you'd gone off the deep end—that you'd received a letter from some student group and had decided not to play as a publicity gimmick."

"Who the hell told you that?"

David mentioned a name. I hardly knew who he was talking about—an employee of the Community Concerts division of Columbia (I don't remember exactly in what job)—but in the normal course of business our paths rarely crossed. Any dealings that office had with my bookings were channeled via my managers. Trembling with rage, I phoned them and demanded an explanation.

"Come in first thing in the morning," I was told.

After a restless night of being chased by Hattie Pearl Lea on a broomstick, I was awakened early by the telephone. It was Henry Raymont, a music-loving reporter for the *Times* who was then a casual acquaintance of ours. Henry, born in Königsberg and raised in Buenos Aires, has a remarkable gift of mimicry and very rarely spoke on the phone in his normal voice. Sometimes he was a Russian prince; on other occasions, an aged Hungarian musicologist; at times he turned into a Viennese professor, dripping *Schlag*; and every now and then, he became Che Guevara. So when he addressed me that morning in plain New York *Times* English, I knew I was in for it.

"Tell me about Jackson," he commanded.

"What do you know, and from whom?" I hedged.

"A reporter does not divulge his sources, and I don't know as much as I want to know. So tell me about Jackson," he insisted.

I'd been stewing ever since learning from David Bar-Illan that Columbia was in no way trying to protect me on this occasion—in fact, quite the opposite, it seemed. During the sleepless night this perfidy had ballooned in my mind to zeppelin-like proportions which, as it turned out a short time later, were in no way exaggerated. Up until that moment I had assiduously followed my lawyers' instructions to maintain utmost discretion precisely to avoid notoriety for my part in the affair. But now I gave Henry a much more emotional and angry résumé than I might have, had the Community employee spoken more circumspectly.

I then got up, got dressed and, wrapping myself in a thundercloud, marched portentously across the street to the Columbia Artists Management building, where I was hailed like a patient on leave from a mental hospital. "You were very excited last night," I was informed.

"I am still very excited," I snarled. "I feel I've been misrepresented by an employee of this corporation. Even if this were not the case—even if he were not slandering me, which he was —it seems to me that since I employ you as my agent, manager, impresario or what-have-you, you are obligated to defend me, no matter what your personal feelings may be."

"I agree," said my manager. "But I can't exercise thought control on the staff."

I gave one final try. "I know it's none of my business. But it does seem to me that if Columbia—the biggest corporation in music management—took a stand on this issue right now, other managements would have to follow suit, and the whole situation would resolve itself after perhaps a few messy months."

My manager said he felt that it should be up to the individual artist to make up his own mind as to how to handle the situation.

I returned home still seething.

Meanwhile, with increasing desperation as the clock ticked on, Columbia Artists Management employees were phoning every pianist who could be reached in an attempt to find someone to play in Jackson the following evening. By then, however, the remarkably efficient Pianists' Grapevine had done its work and nobody would agree to go. Help came at the eleventh hour from somewhere in Missouri. Hans Richter-Haaser, a German pianist on tour there, was not hooked into the Grapevine, and when he was asked to substitute he naturally assumed that the reason for the cancellation was sickness. He agreed to go to Jackson to save the day.

The next morning, all hell broke loose. Spread over three columns in the *Times* was Henry Raymont's story describing the whole affair to date. It might not have been as detailed or prominent if I had exercised discretion in talking with him. Since I didn't do so purely because I felt I was being mistreated, I found partial satisfaction in knowing that my management's cavalier behavior had backfired, to a certain extent, at least.

That afternoon, a few hours before the recital, Richter-Haaser arrived in Jackson, all innocence. When the situation was explained to him and he was asked why he still agreed to substitute for me after so many others had refused, he judiciously told the press that "as a foreigner" he saw no relationship between music and the race issue. "I think it was best that I came," he said. And so the concert did take place as scheduled. But that was by no means the end of the Jackson Affair. In a way, it was really the beginning.

Like a bull moose sniffing out a distant lady friend and stopping at nothing to track her down, Henry Raymont was hot on

the trail of what he sensed might be a good story. He began to
phone musicians, many of whom he knew and some of whom
he did not, to ask what their stand was on this matter. During
the next few weeks, every other day or so, major articles appeared in the *Times* repeating the Jackson story and adding information as one after another artist announced that he would
no longer perform for segregated audiences. Concurrently, the
NAACP circulated a plea addressed to virtually every artist
under United States management requesting that they ask
their agents in future to desist from accepting engagements for
them in segregated auditoriums. Although a few of the musicians subscribed to the theory that this was a matter of individual concern, most replied in the affirmative, and each *Times*
story carried long and longer lists of those who had joined the
boycott. It was almost as if everyone had been waiting for
something like this to happen so he could jump in. Inflamma-
tory headlines heated the issue further: ARTISTS' ANGER AT SEG-
REGATION OF SOUTHERN AUDIENCES RISING was one; RUBINSTEIN
SAYS ARTISTS BELONG IN CAMPAIGNS AGAINST PREJUDICE; PRAISES
MUSICIANS WHO BAR APPEARANCES BEFORE SEGREGATED GROUPS
followed a few days later; two days after that, we read with our
breakfast coffee that THREE MUSICIANS BACK CIVIL RIGHTS PLAN;
DRIVE FAVORED BY HOROWITZ, BERNSTEIN AND LEINSDORF. Needless to say, these articles were reprinted, paraphrased and/or
embellished by many other publications throughout the country with the result that this subject did not escape notice.

So far, then, Austin C. Moore had not been proved completely wrong. Although there were no tangible results yet—
after all, the Community concert on February 27 did take place
as scheduled—something was happening. A dinosaur was awak-
ening, yawning, stretching and shaking himself (and splatter-
ing mud on everything in sight). As with any social change, a
certain amount of inconvenience was visited upon those most
directly concerned.

I don't believe that anyone who worked for a New York concert management firm wished for anything less than equal
rights under the law for everyone. Yet it became increasingly

evident that Columbia Artists Management wished the whole thing would just go away. This is quite understandable. The headaches involved in dealing with such a prickly and unprecedented situation were monumental and time-consuming—not exactly what was needed in the middle of a hectic concert season. Still, did they really have to blame *me* for everything? I began to realize the extent of my abandonment by my (theoretical) employees when, in the course of one week, both Horowitz and Szell offered to lend me money. "Ho, ho!" thundered Szell jovially on the phone, after describing in minute detail the crimes with which I'd been charged. "You're lucky I knew the real story, or I'd never have anything to do with you again . . . Now, about that Chinese restaurant on 102nd Street—do you promise that they have the very best dumplings?" Rumors and accusations about my masterminding of the Jackson Plot swirled around my head, upon which rested (depending on who looked at it) either an angelic halo or the horns of Satan. Would that I were so powerful! Nevertheless, having burned my bridges, it cannot be said in all honesty that I was not amused.

The final concert of the Jackson Music Association's series for the season was to be a recital on April 9 by Birgit Nilsson. Six days earlier, a headline in the *Times* blazed, CANCEL CONCERT, MISS NILSSON TOLD. CIVIL RIGHTS LEADERS APPEAL ON MISSISSIPPI DATE. At this point (since Mme. Nilsson was not an easily replaceable commodity—and besides, by then not even the most socially unaware and apolitical artist would be caught dead performing in Jackson) Columbia opened a dialogue with the NAACP, and a subsequent *Times* article announced that an arrangement had been made for her to sing and donate her fee "to an integrated charity designated by the NAACP." Somewhere I remember reading that this charity was to involve "integrated orphans." Charles Evers promptly made it clear that there was "no such animal" as "an integrated charity" (orphan or otherwise) in Mississippi. So the next day we were told that BIRGIT NILSSON SERIOUSLY WEIGHS CANCELLATION OF SOUTHERN CONCERT; and finally, three days before her scheduled appearance, MISS NILSSON BARS JACKSON CONCERT; SOPRANO SAYS SHE WILL NOT SING IN SEGREGATED HALLS.

To the best of my recollection, however, the Jackson Music Association did present a vocal recital on April 9, 1964, although not in the Municipal Auditorium. The performance took place (as was fitting for a private club) in the music room of somebody's mansion. A local singer did the honors, and for all I know, it may have been a splendid event. After all, Leontyne Price comes from Mississippi. Charles Evers was delighted about the whole thing. "If the white folks want to have a musicale in someone's home and invite their friends, that's fine with me," said he. Thus ended the Jackson concert series for 1963–64.

Shortly thereafter, Columbia Artists and I parted company, and nobody cried.

CHAPTER NINETEEN

A Cozy Little Table
in a Quiet
PECTOPAH

EVEN IN SIBERIA the dawn can be rosy-fingered, especially at 30,000 feet. The pink streaks that lit the sky like flares appeared on the horizon not a moment too soon. Immobilized like a pretzel in that cramped plane seat for five hours of darkness, I'd had far more time for reflection than I really wanted. Vengerova and her splintered chairs, Ruth O'Neill and her nickels, poor old gouged-out 199, Australian cockroaches, Mayor Thompson of Jackson—and now what? I mused, as we finally began the descent to Novosibirsk. The endless night had ended at last, and I writhed gingerly, trying to awaken numbed extremities in order to be able to move when the plane landed.

Those roly-poly Russian grandmothers, bolstered on either side of me like squashy, over-life-sized stuffed dolls, had snored and grunted the night through, which was amazing, considering the terror that had gripped them when the plane left Moscow. Neither of them had flown before, and they were not shy at expressing their innermost feelings about what would happen when—if—the plane became airborne. Let nobody say that religion is dead in the Soviet Union. Such prayers and signs of the cross would have been excessive even in the Vatican.

And the churches here were always full; Marina had taken us to some splendid ones on this trip—no shortage of candles or incense, either. Whenever I asked her about religion in her country, though, she (who was reading *Gentleman's Agreement*) asked me about anti-Semitism in mine. But this was done teasingly, almost in the nature of a joke. We had developed a protectively flippant way of speaking about any matters that might become serious in order to avoid what we all knew could so easily happen (and had, as we'd heard, in certain instances): a continual political squabble, accomplishing nothing except the fraying of nerves. Naomi and I had learned from our earliest days of touring with a stranger-as-nanny, in Australia, that the easiest—possibly the only—way to survive the constant forced intimacy was to keep everything lighthearted. Stay cool. Grin and bear it. Laugh, and the world etc. Above all, don't lose the temper. And if only I had followed my own advice the night before, I wouldn't have been deserted by my traveling companions, left to squirm away the flight in solitary misery—while they were being elbowed by God-knows-what other passengers wherever they were sitting. (Naomi later reported that she had secretly been looking forward to this all-night flight, having saved a mildly pornographic paperback to see her through. She had just settled herself in her seat and cracked the book open with a satisfied sigh when her neighbor, who looked to her like a Russian farmer, leaned over and intro-

duced himself as Professor Jenkins from the University of
Texas on his way to an educational conference in Novosibirsk.
She claims I was far better off with my barricade of
babushkas.)

We were lucky to have had Marina assigned to us by Gosconcert, the Soviet government agency that arranges concert
tours. A foreign artist couldn't possibly get along without a
perevodchitsa, an interpreter (which was the nanny's official
title, no matter what her true function might have been). Even
if one spoke the language perfectly, simply untangling the webs
of red tape woven over and under the thread of daily life would
take the better part of one's waking hours.

Marina was most attractive: a slim, young blonde, capable
and bright, whose English, slightly British-accented, was remarkably fine. The only word we ever heard her say that betrayed
her Russian origin was "onion," which for some reason she pronounced *OH-nee-ohn*—and which, in a Hitchcock film, would
have given the whole show away. In real life, one would have
never known that she was Soviet from the way she spoke—or
from the way she dressed, either. As an English-speaking employee of the Ministry of Culture she occasionally traveled
abroad, translating for such large groups as orchestras and
ballet companies, and she managed to buy most of her clothes
in the West. When we first met her, at the height of the mini-
skirt era, she was Carnaby Street incarnate.

Once, a year or so after our first tour of the Soviet Union,
she made her first visit to New York, as *perevodchitsa* for a
Moscow orchestra, and we were at home when she phoned.
She'd just arrived in the hotel, and when we started to speak
she was laughing so hard that she could barely make herself understood.

"I've just unpacked," she gasped between hiccups of laughter, "and you won't believe what my mother put in my suitcase!" She explained that the trip had been a last-minute one
for her. When she received the call to return to Moscow for
immediate departure with the orchestra, she was with an American group in Tashkent. She had phoned and asked her

mother, with whom she lived, to pack a bag for her for a month-long tour and have it sent to the airport. The bag was waiting for her as requested and, as it hadn't been opened either by the Soviet or U. S. Customs, this was the first chance she had had to examine what her mother felt she would need. "Plenty of clothes," she said, "and the usual stuff like that. But here are several bars of soap . . . cookies . . . tea . . . canned sardines . . . and three rolls of toilet paper!" (Exactly what we had taken to Moscow.)

Marina's only weakness was that she didn't especially like to drink. But one doesn't have to like vodka to be Russian, as has been brought home to me on several occasions, the most notable of which occurred not long ago when Lazar Berman made his first appearance in New York. Up to the time of that visit he was completely unknown in our city; and imagining how depressed he would be after making his debut in a half-filled hall, we had invited him and a few Russian-speaking friends of ours to come to our home for supper afterward. By the time this concert took place, however, Berman was the sensation of the season, and our intimate gathering had become a gargantuan happening complete with a delegation from the Soviet Embassy and a photographer from *People* magazine. During the preceding days instructions as to what would and would not be appreciated by the guest of honor were passed along to us by Berman's manager, our longtime friend Jacques Leiser, who had been nanny-ing the artist on tour in the Midwest and had observed his foibles.

"Maestro doesn't drink," Jacques informed us. "Just a lot of fruit juice. He loves grapefruit juice. But no booze for him." We stocked the refrigerator with all kinds of fruit juice as instructed, and when Maestro arrived, he asked for, and downed, a most impressive quantity of "Skawtch." But Marina didn't even like Skawtch, although on one occasion, in Minsk, she obligingly joined us for a rum festival.

In Minsk, the Philharmonic Hall was about a mile away from the hotel. During our four-day stay there, I walked back and forth most of the time. It was a pleasant, although rather curious, stroll, as Minsk is a strange-looking city—certainly far different from what we expected. It had been leveled during the war, and the town planners had had an opportunity to start from scratch. The fantasy that sprang forth from their drawing boards can only be described as Heroic-Ptolemaic-Greco-Roman-Art-Deco. On the main street, between the hotel and the auditorium, one passed before an unbroken line of imposing, columned, stone facades, each building looking as if it housed, at the very least, an embassy of a Mediterranean nation during Classical times. But no: the ground floor of most of these dramatic edifices was occupied by nothing more than the usual drab little shops—a watchmaker, a pharmacy, a government food store offering a few cans of Bulgarian preserves. What gave the place its bizarre quality, however, was the fact that every building had a twin facing it directly across the street like a mirror image. Minsk marched two by two.

One afternoon, about halfway back to the hotel, at the intersection where twin pink sandstone Grant's Tombs and twin gray granite Lincoln Memorials regarded each other solemnly, I noticed a crowd gathering in a neat line next to a large van. As one tends to do in Russia, I immediately joined the line to see what was at the end of it. Crates were being removed from the van, and after a while, lemons appeared—three for a ruble. By the time we'd reached Minsk on that tour, we had learned to buy fresh fruit whenever we saw it. Furthermore, we had foresightedly bought a bottle of rum at Orly when our plane made a brief stop there en route to Moscow. This was the moment, I decided. I'd squeeze the lemons into the rum, add some Bulgarian preserves and *voilà*: the Minsk Trader Vic's. So I bought the lemons and sauntered toward the hotel, music in one hand, unwrapped fruit in the other. After a while I began to have the feeling that I was being followed (the only time, by the way, I had that feeling in Russia). The footsteps got closer, I heard heavy breathing and finally I was overtaken by a most attractive young lady.

"Excuse me, sir," she said. "I'm terribly sorry to bother you."

"You're not bothering me at all," I leered, realizing at last

how wonderful it was to be able to speak Russian. "Not . . . at
. . . all, my dear. Just tell me what I can do for you?"

"Would you tell me, sir, please . . ."

"Yes? Yes?"

"Where did you get those lemons?"

I was on the verge of asking her to join us for mai tais at the
hotel, but decided it would make for too many complications.

Considering how many hours each day we spent sitting in
hotel restaurants the length and breadth of the Soviet Union,
it was undoubtedly far better for our livers that Marina didn't
care for alcohol. Her primness in this matter kept us in line.
Otherwise we probably would have been in a constant stupor.
As is well known, restaurant service moves (or moved, when we
were there) with the speed of a glacier. "*Seichas!*" was what
the waitress said if you caught her eye. It translates as "Right
away!" but actually means in that context either "*mañana*" or
"*jamais.*" The object of the game was to see who could outwait
whom. Would the waitress ever come over to consult with the
customer (or victim), and would some food (not that which
was ordered, certainly) ever get served, or would the customer/
victim just give up and leave without eating, his only reward a
big farewell smile from the waitress, who had thus successfully
avoided, or at least postponed for a little while longer, confrontation with the kitchen help? Thanks to Marina's perseverance
we managed, most of the time, to overcome. She was somehow
able to make "arrangements" which enabled us to have at least
one meal a day: a good dinner after the concert. This was no
small accomplishment, particularly on weekends, when every
restaurant—and there weren't all that many—was jammed from
opening to closing. Marina would have a little talk with the
dining room manager early in the day, and things usually
worked out surprisingly well.

Getting into the restaurant was often the most difficult part.
Doormen were employed, it seemed, for the sole purpose of
keeping would-be patrons out. I'll never forget the sight of the
doorman, or bouncer, at the hotel restaurant in Kishinev. He
was very tiny and dressed in a uniform reminiscent of the

Philip Morris cigarette bellboy, Johnny, complete to the pillbox cap. He wore also the expression of a poodle threatening to devour a rhinoceros. He would open the door just wide enough for us to see his fangs and hear his snarl, give a sweeping, freezing glance at the supplicating hordes pressing against the restaurant's entrance, growl something like "Go away!" and slam the door shut for another ten minutes or so (with himself inside), after which he would peek out again and repeat this performance. I think Marina was prepared to sacrifice a foot to get close enough just to beg him to summon the dining room manager, who would vouch that special arrangements had been made for us. When she finally reached him, after a few minutes of the obligatory threats and curses on each side, he, snarling all the while, sullenly opened the door just wide enough for us to sidle in. That we were not attacked then and there by those less fortunate was purely because, as foreigners, we were treated always (except by restaurant doormen) with great deference.

Unlike the citizens of many other countries (if I may be permitted to generalize, France particularly comes to mind), the Russians seemed sincerely anxious to show hospitality to strangers—to Americans, anyway. Most frequently the only hospitality they could offer was a place at the head of the line. Since everything I can think of involved a line, we were actually spared considerable anguish by this gesture.

Once inside the restaurant, the waiting game began again. In the evenings, this irritation could be alleviated or exacerbated by sweet music. After dark, all restaurants turned into nightclubs. There was always a little stage at one end of the dining room, and at about eight-thirty or so a seedy-looking group would shamble up, a variety of instruments in hand, and proceed to tootle or saw or croon or shout while most of the patrons danced to their tunes. Everyone seemed to love dancing. Stolid citizens became positively giddy, and as the night wore on the noise level increased.

The music ranged from atrocious to wonderful. To be on the safe side, Marina, when she made the "arrangements," would ask for a table as far away from the bandstand as possible. Only

once did we regret this—in Odessa. After our first night at the
hotel restaurant there, we were so mesmerized by the trio that
we began to creep nearer and nearer to the stage. The ensemble consisted of a violinist, a clarinetist and a percussion player.
They were nothing less than spectacular. We were told that
the violinist had been a classmate of Oistrakh's and that, as a
conservatory student, he'd been considered on a par, but excessive nervousness made it impossible for him to play without
music. So here he was. He seemed content, and he was greatly
beloved by the regulars, it was clear. The percussion player I
can only describe as Peter Sellers turning himself into a one-
man band. One of his habits was to follow with his eyes—with
his whole body—the sound of a cymbal crash as it wafted toward
the ceiling. Soon we all did the same. He was irresistible. And
so was the Pied Piper of a clarinetist. Whenever he swung into
a hora, the entire dining room arose *en masse* to dance it,
to our astonishment, and to their obvious, stamping delight. In
Odessa we almost enjoyed waiting for our dinner.

The fact that I understood the language and spoke it
fluently, if ungrammatically, seemed to charm everyone. My
quaint, pre-Revolutionary way of expressing myself engendered
considerable amusement. But "Prithee, kind sir, wouldst thou
direct me to that small room even the Tsar has to visit?" is as
easily understood as, "Hey, buddy, where's the can?" and although my language was neither as flowery as the former nor as
up-to-date (or down-to-earth) as the latter, it nevertheless
sounded odd enough to elicit much merriment. Ladies wanted
to mother me—indescribably helpful in restaurants, where the
waitresses, usually of—or past—a certain age, tenderly squir-
reled away several large dollops of caviar for our post-concert
supper.

Contrary to legend, it was not always easy to get caviar. And
this had nothing to do with money. I had rubles to burn. Any
Western artist who visited the Soviet Union did. We were paid
a certain amount in hard currency. Not very much—nothing
like the large sums Americans paid Soviet artists, even those
relatively unknown, coming to the United States for the first

time. The Soviet artists never saw most of these fees; instead, their government usually paid them approximately what they would have received for playing in the Soviet Union, plus enough hard currency to take care of hotel bills, food and other such necessities. (The Soviets justify this by pointing out that all of their talented artists are, from the very beginning of their education, given the opportunity to study, free of charge, with the greatest teachers; are given instruments to practice on; and are housed, clothed, fed and kept free of any financial worries. Even those artists who do not attain the highest success are looked after by their government, the only catch here being that the government determines where the artist makes his living. Thus, a perfectly good pianist, say, who studied in Moscow and might prefer to continue living and teaching in Moscow, even without the opportunity of pursuing an active concert career, might be assigned a position on the faculty in a conservatory of some remote city. His acceptance is normally as automatic as that of an officer in the armed forces assigned to a new post. Thus, the "successful" artists—the ones who tour abroad —pay back their debts to the State not only by teaching [Richter, I believe, was at that time the only one exempted from this task] but principally by having most of their foreign earnings paid directly to the organization that subsidized their education, thus becoming the instruments through which their government acquires some hard currency.)

Every now and then the most prominent and sought-after Soviet artists are given permission to use some of the hard currency they've earned to buy something nice—like a Maserati. There is an apartment building in Moscow primarily inhabited by top-notch musicians and other hard-currency-producing citizens, and the garage there looks just like its counterpart on Wilshire Boulevard. When Emil Gilels first visited New York in 1955, he became the first Soviet artist to hit West Fifty-seventh Street since the Second World War, and as such was an extra-musical curiosity. People stared and pointed, and Naomi tailed him now and then just to see how he spent his time. She was not, and never has been, associated with the CIA. But remember, we hadn't, until then, seen a live Russian—from Soviet Russia—on the loose.

"He went into Rappaport's toy store and came out with a stuffed Snoopy!" . . . "He went to the Carnegie Delicatessen and ordered blintzes!" . . . "I saw him buying packages and *packages* of jockey shorts in the five-and-ten!" She issued these fascinating bulletins periodically. Fritz Steinway, who then worked for the family piano company, was able to report a purchase on a far more exalted level. "Would you believe he paid for it in *cash?*" Fritz asked, describing Gilels' selection of a concert grand to be shipped home to Moscow. "He just kept peeling those hundred-dollar bills out of his pocket, endlessly . . ."

But American artists didn't go to the Soviet Union to make money. When the first cultural exchanges began after the Cold War, everyone was as interested in seeing the place at least once as we now are in seeing China. It was exotic, mysterious; the audiences were said to be extremely knowledgeable and fantastically enthusiastic (a great persuader for performers); and, as a goodly number of American musicians had Russian antecedents, many of us were eager to visit our ancestral homeland. So we accepted a token amount of dollars and an even smaller amount of rubles—which, nevertheless, we had great difficulty in disposing of. The rubles, of course, were worthless outside of the Soviet Union, and this was just as well because it was illegal to take them out. Since, under the terms of our contracts with Gosconcert our hotel and transportation expenses were paid for, and since the Soviet Union was not noted for its consumer goods (anything worthwhile prepared for export, like first-quality furs, needing hard currency for purchase), we had, as I said before, rubles to burn. Literally. A colleague who preceded me through that exasperating maze of frustration and bureaucracy efficiently disposed of his left-over rubles—and his pent-up rage—just before his departure by publicly setting them on fire. I, on the other hand, laughingly allowed Marina to open a Moscow bank account for me with mine, and was presented with the passbook when I returned for my second tour. On that trip I was lucky. Pan Am had just inaugurated its New York–Moscow run. Through the kindness of its Moscow office manager, who underwent an appalling amount of maneuvering with officials at Aeroflot, Intourist and other Soviet agencies just to do me a favor, my excess rubles were accepted by Pan Am and turned into airline ticket vouchers, which meant that these rubles actually took us to the Orient, South America and several times to Europe the following year. But that, I fear, was a once-in-a-lifetime stroke of luck (particularly since neither Pan Am nor I have operated in the Soviet Union lately).

Aside from the caviar—Naomi very quickly learned the most important question in Russian, "*Yest ikra?*" "Is there caviar?" —the only other item to buy was music, when available; and during my free time I combed the music stores in every city we visited to find Soviet editions, many of which are first-class, of interesting pieces which I shipped home (and which all did, eventually, arrive). On my first trip, a good deal of this music-store browsing acquired a slightly subversive tinge that we both adored. Just before leaving the United States I'd played with Ormandy, who said that if I came across the score of the Shostakovich Thirteenth Symphony, he would be thrilled to have it: the *Babi Yar*, as this symphony is known, had been performed once in the Soviet Union and then immediately banned; it had never been played outside the country. Excited by this cloak-and-dagger assignment, I agreed with gusto to try to find it.

Soviet editions, I knew, were printed in rather small quantities, and I soon learned that something that was available in one city might be all sold out in the next. This had nothing to do with whether the music was politically acceptable or not but was a question of supply and demand (not a high-priority matter in Soviet business). Finding something even as harmless as the Scriabin sonatas might necessitate visits to several stores in several cities. I knew that the Shostakovich Thirteenth had been published and then withdrawn, but I was hoping that there might still be some copies lying around. (General inefficiency made this idea not too farfetched.) It was of utmost importance not to arouse suspicion. I adopted an air of nonchalance. In each music shop I entered I'd sashay up to the clerk and ask for a whole pile of music—all the music I was looking for—which always included two Shostakovich symphonies, one of them the Thirteenth. I read my shopping list with studied casualness. "The volume of Medtner songs; Mussorgsky's *Khovanschina*; Prokofiev, *Romeo and Juliet* . . . and, oh, yes . . . Shostakovich symphonies, the . . . uhhh, Sixth and the Thirteenth?" The Thirteenth was always "out of stock at the moment," but I became the proud possessor of scores of the other twelve of the thirteen then existing Shostakovich symphonies. I brought Ormandy caviar as a consolation prize, but he was inconsolable. (Eventually, he got what he wanted— I think it was smuggled out in microfilm—but I was not the hero of that episode.)

Nevertheless, my library of little-known Shostakovich did serve a happy purpose, and I wonder if that great composer ever could have imagined that one of my decoy purchases was responsible for a first New York performance of one of his major works. It came about in a totally unexpected way. A few years after the incident I have just described, my friend Hans Schwieger, for many years conductor of the Kansas City Symphony, was visiting us at our home. He was about to guest-conduct the Houston Symphony on a tour of the Southern and Eastern states, culminating in New York City's Philharmonic Hall. He mentioned that he was looking for an interesting work to do that would be off the beaten track, but not "too far out." I directed him toward my library of Shostakovich symphonies and suggested that he look over any that he might not know. He was particularly intrigued by the Twelfth, which he had never heard, or even seen the score of, and decided that this would fill the bill.

Thanks to Schwieger's interest in the Twelfth, I got to know the symphony quite well, as I played a number of concerts with him and the Houston Symphony on that tour, and thus was able to hear the work performed almost nightly for a period of two weeks. We traveled on chartered buses, and in addition to the unending poker game at the rear of our vehicle, there occurred occasional bursts of song (rather odd for an orchestra on tour, now that I think back on it, but they were an unusually good-natured bunch), and one of those long, arching Shostakovich melodies, running through everybody's head as it did, was often hummed in chorus, somewhat like a campfire theme, as we tooled along the highways and byways of Alabama (of all places). This symphony was full of such extended melodies.

It was also dedicated to Lenin.

One day Naomi and I were sitting in our accustomed seats on the bus behind the Schwiegers reading a local paper when, as the saying goes, we nearly dropped our back teeth. There on page four of the Gadsden *Gazette* was a little item about those crazy folks up there in New York—environmentalists (hippies, ergo Commies)—who were planning an event to dramatize their feelings about pollution, misuse of energy and so forth, to be called Earth Day. Earth Day was undoubtedly of leftist inspiration, the piece observed, because the date that had been selected—April 22—coincided with the one hundredth birthday of none other than Vladimir Ilyich Lenin. The date also coincided (although nobody but us realized it at the moment) with the New York concert of the Houston Symphony, at which this Shostakovich symphony, dedicated to Lenin, would be first performed. *What* had I done?

As our bus moved inexorably north, Naomi and I held desperate, whispered conferences. Should we break the news to the Schwiegers, now dozing so contentedly in the seats in front of us? Visions of a cordon of raging pickets around Philharmonic Hall (revenge for Jackson?) raced through our minds. To make matters worse, I wasn't even going to *be* with the orchestra in New York to take my medicine—I, the perpetrator of this foul deed, would be safely in San Francisco, playing Beethoven with Krips, on Earth Day. After chewing the matter over for a half hour or so, we took deep breaths, leaned forward and clued in the Schwiegers, who gulped nervously a few times but claimed to be amused, good sports that they were. As things turned out, nobody ever noticed. I guess only someone who had the score would be aware of the symphony's dedication, and fortunately these were in short supply.

To the best of my knowledge, that Earth Day—or Lenin's birthday—concert was the only time the Shostakovich Twelfth was played in New York. A real pity.

But back to the *ikra* and restaurants in the Soviet Union. (My digression just now was nothing compared to the detours the waitresses seemed to take en route to any table they were expected to serve.) I noticed that groups—especially Americans —eating together as a chain gang most frequently had on their plates unappetizing, grayish hunks of unidentifiable meat. Americans like steak, so they got steak. But if an American was not under the guidance of Intourist, the state tourist agency, but was on his own (or under the aegis of the Ministry of Culture, as I was); if he spoke the language, no matter how antiquely; if he could discuss with the waitress how various dishes were prepared and order anything on the menu that didn't have a line drawn through it; if he selected regional specialties, when offered—like little pork *roulades* wrapped around a kind of garlicky cream cheese in Lvov and *mamaliga* in Kishinev; and, most importantly, if he was a visiting concert performer (which had the same effect in Odessa as the appearance of a major-league baseball player in Indianapolis), he would be taken into the waitress' confidence and frankly advised of dishes to avoid (certainly beef and chicken, unless ground up into patties to circumvent their unbelievable toughness) as well as what could be really good (almost all soups, river fish, bread and milk products).

Soviet milk products were indeed exceptional. One reason, perhaps, was their freshness. Nothing seemed to be left overnight—which meant, of course, that often the day's supply was gone by noon. Whatever we did get was memorable, and the seemingly endless variety ranged from ordinary milk and buttermilk through yogurt-like manifestations such as the quite liquid *kefir* (now popular in California) and the almost gelatinous *prostokvash* to the spectacular, and creamy, ice cream. A luscious scoop of this sinfully rich stuff (sometimes served in a glass of coffee, when it became a delicacy known, with a nod to its French origin, as *cafYEH glasYEH*) went a long way toward soothing our anguished psyches. More often than not, however, it—like almost anything else—wasn't available. My friend and colleague Susan Starr told me of the response she received in one Soviet restaurant upon requesting this elusive balm. "I scrim, you scrim, vee scrim, NYET!" scrimmed the waitress, which, somehow, put everything in proper perspective.

To avoid spending the better part of the day sitting in restaurants, we devised the Buffet Ploy. The buffet (pronounced, again, as so many of these French words were, as if it were Russian: thus, *booFYETT*), or small cafeteria, existed in every hotel. In some of the larger ones, there were several. We limited ourselves to ingesting only what was available there—hard-boiled eggs; fat, but sometimes good, sausages; a hot dish or two depending upon the mood of the short-order cook; lots of black bread; tea; various kinds of buttermilk-cum-yogurt; and brandy (often swigged down from water glasses filled to the brim at breakfast time by the locals—a very understandable eye-opener)—and we saved hours.

Another way to beat the restaurant (Naomi insisted on calling it PECTOPAH, which is the way the word looks in Cyrillic) routine was to keep food in the hotel's communal fridge. When we had something perishable, we gave it to the *dezhurnaya*, who put it away for us. (A wonderfully descriptive name, *dezhurnaya*: again, Russian fractured French, meaning "of the day," with a Russian feminine ending, making it a noun. She is also an "of the night," although not the kind one might imagine.)

A *dezhurnaya* is generally a grandmotherly type who sits, concierge-like, at a desk on each floor of the hotel. Her job seems to be, in no special order, to keep and hand out room keys, take messages, see to the guests' laundry (ironing, if not washing, it herself) and act as custodian of the large, old refrigerator in the middle of her corridor, dividing the interior mentally into compartments like safe-deposit boxes, happily accepting one's bottle of milk or tin of caviar, and handing it back in pristine condition upon request. She also is the guardian of her guests' moral purity while in her establishment. It is further assumed that another of the *dezhurnaya's* duties is to report to Someone on the comings and goings of the guests (and their visitors) as and if necessary. This is in keeping with the assumption that all foreigners are followed. After a while I began to wonder if that was really so. When we were in the Soviet Union we were often left on our own because the language was no obstacle; and as Marina liked movies, it became understood that after she had finished her secretarial duties for me such as arranging practice time and other details pertinent to concerts, she could go off to a double feature and we'd wander about unescorted. And wander we did. We took incredibly long walks through just about every neighborhood in just about every city. They were generally aimless—we more or less followed our noses—and if someone was indeed shadowing us, I hope he had comfortable shoes.

My first concert in the Soviet Union took place in Donetsk. This city, our guidebook had told us, was in the coal-mining area, so of course we had a vision of what it would look like. Surprise number one. The cleanliness and neatness of Donetsk —and the other cities we saw—was astounding, especially for New Yorkers. Inhabitants regarded the dropping of even a cigarette wrapper on the street with the same distaste as if this were done in somebody's home. Bad manners! We were further startled by the profusion of trees and plant life within the city. The wide, uncrowded streets were divided by an island of greenery; tall trees had been planted at the curbs, and bushes fronted the buildings, somewhat disguising their unmitigated drabness. (An odd thing about that drabness, which was everywhere: Our eyes gradually became adjusted to it. We didn't realize how much we'd adjusted until we emerged from this gray cocoon five weeks later in the Copenhagen airport, blinking and bedazzled by the profusion of what seemed like violently vivid colors. In truth, they were perfectly normal, everyday colors, but not in the Soviet rainbow.)

Our little balcony in Donetsk overlooked a park, and on the sunny weekend morning of our first day, we looked out on an innocent scene—family groups strolling around, almost all of them lapping the ubiquitous ice-cream cone (easier to buy from park vendors than from PECTOPAH waitresses). They didn't seem to realize how miserable they were. But then again, they were undoubtedly less miserable than their parents had been during the purges, the Second World War and the German occupation; or, for that matter, than their grandparents had been during the Revolution, civil wars and famines. Later, in Kishinev, we saw a beggar—the only one we encountered. On the steps of the music conservatory sat a gypsy girl, breast-feeding her infant, with an outstretched hand. "*Pazor, pazor!* (Shame, shame!)," exclaimed the passing students. I wasn't sure whether the *pazor* was for the breast or the begging. Marina was very embarrassed—humiliated that we should see such goings-on—and hastily explained that the beggar was "a gypsy, and doesn't know how to behave."

Giving concerts for Russian audiences can be irresistible, addictive. Their much-vaunted enthusiasm is to an artist what a high-society house party on the Cap d'Antibes would be to a cat burglar. After my first appearance—it was a concerto—I went back and forth to bow the customary number of times, but the applause did not slacken in any way. I kept bowing; they kept applauding. The conductor began to look puzzled, and after a few more bows and a lot more applause he asked, "Aren't you going to play an encore?" "I didn't know it was customary at an orchestra concert," I replied, remembering when a world-famed violinist shocked the New York Philharmonic—and possibly caused them to be paid for half an hour overtime for the extra two minutes they remained seated on-stage—by bestowing an extra little goody on the audience after his scheduled performance. My conductor looked surprised, and I went out to play something. I then had to play another something, and then yet another; eventually came the realization, confirmed at all the other concerts, that if one doesn't play a half-dozen encores, or even a dozen at a solo recital, something is very wrong. Those Russian audiences expect a large number of encores as if they are part of the concert. And they deserve them: They are, as an audience, the warmest I have ever encountered anywhere, including my hometown of New York, where most of my relatives are.

These listeners also were knowledgeable—as far as the Romantic piano repertoire is concerned, at least. Playing a Chopin nocturne, I would have the feeling that the entire audience was living through the piece with me—a good feeling, particularly after many concerts I have given where I get the distinct impression that the audience (or a good part of it, anyway) is worrying that the damned thing might not be over before Johnny Carson begins.

And tremendous waves of well-wishers would come backstage. Ever since my nightly forays on Carnegie Hall as a teenager, I'd been aware of the artists' hunger for backstage ritual after almost every performance. Congratulating the performers with whom I'd by then developed at least a casual acquaintance, I began to get the feeling—confirmed later, when I was the performer—that no matter what an artist may say, he likes to have a mob scene awaiting him backstage. Even those of us who occasionally decide "not to see anyone tonight" for one reason or another would be most distressed if there was no one not to see. Nothing is more depressing than finding yourself alone in a dreary dressing room after playing your heart out and your fingers off. "Oh, we didn't want to disturb you! You must have been so tired," someone will say next day on the phone. The answer, from me, at least, is, "Never too tired to be told you liked the concert." Being alone backstage was definitely not a problem in the Soviet Union. Oddly enough, though, most of my visitors didn't want anything from me—not even an autograph. Quite the contrary. They just came to smile and show they'd had a good time. Sometimes they even brought little gifts—often picture books of various kinds—and almost always they brought flowers. Very rarely did Marina, Naomi or I leave for the hotel after a concert without armfuls of flowers trailing fallen petals after us. Many of the older concertgoers reminded me of New York Russians I knew when I was growing up; backstage, the frustrations of coping with Soviet bureaucracy during the day were diminished by these friendly and somehow familiar faces, and I always felt very much at home.

The hordes of music students who descended on the dressing room were particularly thoughtful. They would assemble in a group and always appointed a spokesmen to ask all questions, many of which were of the kind asked by music students everywhere. But the most persistent one had nothing to do either with me or with what I'd played. After all the nice things were said about my performance and my recordings (and a great deal was said about recordings—everyone seemed to know the entire catalogue. Let one disc from the West arrive in the Soviet Union, and surely, within twenty-four hours, it has multiplied into an infinite number of tapes), it was time for The Question. Always expressed with the greatest of longing, somewhat like a small child asking after a departed parent, The Question was, simply, "When will Horowitz come to play in our country?" I wish I could have given them some hope.

In most cities there were no printed programs. A few minutes before my recital was to begin, I would be approached in my dressing room by someone, usually a handsome young woman, who introduced herself as the "announcer," and asked if the program she had been sent was indeed what I would be playing. She then went into an adjoining dressing room and emerged in an evening gown. She preceded me onstage and announced what I would play for the first half of the program. This announcement consisted merely of identifying the pieces, with the movements; there were no program notes or comments of any kind. After intermission, she announced the second half, and then she left, her duties over. Between announcements she sat backstage, sometimes listening to the recital and sometimes not.

During the intermission of one of my recitals I returned to the dressing room to find my wife and my announcer sharing the sofa. The announcer, I remember, was particularly attractive, elegantly and fashionably dressed in a black velvet gown. She sat stiffly in one corner of the sofa, staring straight ahead. The wife was slouched in the other corner of the sofa, immersed, as usual, in some reading. We carried around what seemed like a year's supply of as-yet-unread Sunday New York *Times Magazine* sections, which were very handy to bring to concerts because they didn't take up much room or require much concentration and they could be jettisoned without much guilt. As I entered the room, I saw Naomi finish and jettison on the table in front of the sofa the copy she had been reading. She loved to drop these little nuggets of enlightenment in odd, unexpected places, imagining what a delightful surprise they would provide for the finder. ("Aha!" the shipwreck survivor cries as he totters onto the rockbound shore of the desert island, after eighty-three days of battling sharks in a leaky life raft. "Is that the Sunday *Times Magazine* section I see? Zounds! The September 15th issue, too—one of the ones I missed. What luck!" And he pounces on it, reading it from cover to cover before collapsing on the hot, dry sand.) Now, at last, she had her wish. Someone was going to find a nugget.

The announcer's hand crept toward the discarded magazine. She didn't speak any English, and I don't think she could read any, either; but she looked inquiringly at the magazine and then at Naomi, who, of course, handed it over with the enthusiasm of Billy Graham offering the Bible to a cannibal in Darkest Africa. "Sulzberger saves!" she cried. The announcer nodded affably and accepted the gift. (Naomi should have known better. In an airplane a few days earlier, she had tried to press Henry Luce on a seatmate who evinced curiosity in the contents of her copy of *Time*, and was devastated when—after leafing desultorily through a few pages of ads for shiny cars, television sets, panty hose and deodorants—the poor heathen had fallen sound asleep.)

In this particular Sunday *Times Magazine* there was an article by one of the Medvedevs on problems with the Soviet Government which had recently resulted in his brother's incarceration. There were several photos of the Medvedevs, and clearly visible in the background were slogans, written, of course, in Cyrillic. It would have been impossible for a Russian, seeing these photos, not to know that a political statement was being made. Naomi eyed the announcer covertly as she flipped over the pages. Unlike the sleepy gentleman in the airplane, this lady looked very carefully at each one. When she finished, she heaved a deep, sorrowful sigh, closed the magazine and looked up at Naomi with a troubled expression. She wanted to speak directly to her—no intermediary would do. She reopened the magazine. She struggled to find some way to make herself understood. Finally she spoke. Very slowly the words came out. Pointing to one of the advertisements, she asked, "Good or bad? Vat you tink? Tell me, pliss! *Da* or *nyet*? Vill vair in New York moxi-skairt?"

CHAPTER TWENTY

"And Who in Novosibirsk Is Calling Mr. Steinway?"

AT LAST OUR PLANE was approaching the runway in Novosibirsk. My neighbors awoke, astonished to find that they were still alive. The seat in front of me, bearing its now familiar head, sprang forward with a screech and I was free to move again. Then a comforting bump and thud as we touched the ground. Back to reality. My book-length reverie over, I began to swathe myself in the mufflers, glove liners, woolen caps and extra-heavy socks we had prepared for this moment. I assumed that Naomi and Marina, wherever they had been sitting on this interminable flight, were doing likewise. Finally the engines were cut, the seat-belt sign flashed off, and a stampede of lumpy bodies lumbered toward the exit.

The welcoming committee greeting us early that morning was not a little amused to see two American Eskimos descend from the aircraft, gasp for breath and, mittened paws flailing clumsily at buttons and toggles, begin to yank off layers and layers of outer garments. We soon found out that spring comes also to Siberia, and our long rambles in and around the city during the next few days were impeded neither by snow nor ice but simply by mud.

By the time I reached it, Novosibirsk was quite a different place from the town my father had visited fifty years earlier. Only a few traces of its pre-Revolutionary incarnation could still be seen. There remained on the outskirts (now suburbs) a few of the old wooden houses—almost log cabins, they were; but most of the city's two million inhabitants dwelt in cinder block. Acres of boxy, dismal, gray apartment buildings stretched far and wide over the countryside. Although these buildings looked more functional than the log cabins, I have the feeling that was as far as improvement went.

When our hosts heard that I was not the first Graffman to give a concert in Novosibirsk, we were immediately whisked to the City Museum, where an ancient gentleman with a white beard that trailed almost to the floor—the City Historian, nicknamed "Father Tolstoy"—rooted through the archives and eventually brought forth announcements and advertisements for that recital I'd been told about before leaving home. He also informed us that the building in which my father's concert had taken place was, at that time, one of the very few stone buildings in the city, and that it was still standing and still being used, only now as a restaurant. Indeed, we had a few meals there during our stay.

The auditorium in which concerts were currently being given had been built, incredibly, during the Second World War. I imagine the reason for this non-essential construction at such a time was that Novosibirsk had been designated as one of the two Siberian cities (Sverdlovsk being the other) to serve as a kind of refugee center for artists. The orchestras, opera companies, ballets and conservatories of music from Moscow and Leningrad were evacuated to them, and perhaps this explains why the Novosibirsk orchestra became one of the better ones in the Soviet Union. There was undoubtedly a tradition, albeit a short one, of high artistic standards.

Our first evening in Novosibirsk left an indelible impression. It became known as the Night of the Phone Call. Fritz Steinway (at that time one of my managers in New York) was awaiting my reply to his cable, and we had discovered, to our half-amused dismay, that it just couldn't be done. The facilities for dispatching cables in that part of the world employed only the Cyrillic alphabet. To be completely honest, we could have sent a cable in Russian which he could have had translated, but this seemed unnecessarily complicated.

"Of course, we must telephone him!" cried Arnold Katz, the conductor of the orchestra, who was looking for a diverting way to pass the evening. His eyes sparkled with anticipation. "Come, I'll help you," he offered, taking the matter in hand, as conductors are wont to do.

"Okay," I replied. "I guess we should make the call from our hotel room, so come on up."

"No," said Maestro Katz. "Not yet. First we must go to the store."

"Store?"

"Oh, certainly. We need to get some supplies. I'll tell you what. You go upstairs, and I'll get the stuff and join you presently." Puzzled, we obeyed. Soon our new friend arrived with several bottles of wine. "Now we can get down to business," he explained.

He opened the first bottle, poured out three large tumblers (Marina had gone to the movies, I think) and picked up the phone. After a while he made contact with the local operator, who in turn connected him with the long-distance operator.

"And what is your name, my dear?" inquired Maestro Katz

of the long-distance operator. (It would never do to embark upon such an adventure without proper introductions.)

"Masha," she replied.

"Oy, *Masha!* A name as beautiful as the voice! Masha, Mashinka, my dear one, my little butterfly, my jewel, my pretty white radish; do me the infinite kindness to call New York . . . What do you mean, you lovely lilac blossom, by 'no'? How can you say 'no' to Arnold Katz? . . . Ah, you are saying it will take some time? Well, how much time? . . . *TOMORROW?* Oy, Masha, Mashichka, Mashinka, that is not the way to treat our American friends. Surely you don't want them to think . . . Now, come, my dear, when is the soonest, the very, very soonest you can do it? (And, Masha, will you have dinner with me tomorrow night?) Ah, you think maybe an hour? Masha, dearest, that's more like it. So you will call them in an hour, yes? And we will meet by the stage entrance of the Philharmonic Auditorium tomorrow at seven, yes? . . . Masha, you are truly the Queen of the Telephone!"

Almost exactly one hour later our phone rang, and when I picked it up I could hear the chain of operators at work: Mashinka in Novosibirsk talking to Moscow; Moscow to London; London to New York. Finally, the New York operator in her unmistakable sing-song, sounding for all the world as if she were chewing gum: "Hallaow, hallaowww, Moscaowwww, I'm rinnnnginnnnngggg." Then the sound of a phone being picked up. The triumphant shout of the operator (ruffle of drums): "Novosibirsk is calling Mr. Frederick Steinway!" A pause at the New York end. Silence. What's happened? Have we been disconnected? After what seems an eternity, I distinctly hear male and female laughter. Then the voice of my manager's secretary. "Who," she says, attempting a dignified, businesslike voice; "Who," she tries again, Girl Friday to an international tycoon; "Who-o-o-o," she stammers, finally overcome by giggles, "*Who* in Novosibirsk is calling Mr. Steinway?"

Bright and early on the morning after my last appearance in Novosibirsk, buried under bushels of flowers, we bid a regretful farewell to Arnold Katz and drove to the airport. My next three concerts were to be in Moscow. The first of these, scheduled for the following evening, was a recital at the famous Bolshoi Zal (Big Hall) of the Tchaikovsky Conservatory. I was really looking forward to it. The Bolshoi Zal is a glorious auditorium with a distinguished history and, as I remembered from my last tour, marvelous acoustics. My most recent visit there, however, had been as a member of the audience, and even that had been unforgettable.

It had been on the last night of our last tour, a free evening, when we had decided to attend an all-Prokofiev concert. In the late afternoon a music critic who had asked to interview me came over to our hotel. (At that time we had been assigned a small suite in one of the older hotels; it had a certain charm, not the least of which was a splendid view of the Kremlin's Red Star from the seat in that little room even the Tsar has to visit.)

We spoke about many things. Our visitor, aside from the slightly disconcerting habit of using only the editorial (or royal) "we," and ending each sentence with a long string of *da*'s or *nyet*'s (depending on his point of view), was an amusing man. What was supposed to have been a half-hour session stretched on and on. Finally, I told him that we were planning to go to the concert at the Bolshoi Zal; it was time to leave, so why didn't we walk there together? That way we could talk a little longer. When I mentioned how interested we were to hear the conductor (one of the most famous of the Soviets), he made a face.

"Oh, *we* don't especially like him . . . *nyet, nyet, nyet, nyet, nyet* . . ."

"Really?" I was puzzled, because he had a great reputation. "Well then, are any of these" (and I mentioned three other well-known Soviet conductors) "more interesting, in your opinion?"

"Ooooooh, *nyet, nyet, nyet, nyet, nyet*," he replied dourly. "Although X‾‾‾‾‾ isn't a bad accompanist. But *we* really don't like him. *Nyet. Nyet, nyet, nyet, nyet, nyet.*"

"But then, who *are* the great conductors?" I persisted. "Perhaps there's somebody I haven't even heard of yet?"

"*Nyet, nyet, nyet, nyet, nyet* . . ." came his standard reply. Then he thought for a while and his eyes brightened. "Great conductors? Who do *we* think are the great conductors? Well, recently the Cleveland Orchestra and the New York Philharmonic played here. George Szell and Leonard Bernstein, that's who! *Da, da, da, da, da!*"

He agreed to walk us to the hall, and we arrived a few minutes before the performance was to begin; we raced to our seats, which is a pity, since the hall, with its elegant lobbies and corridors, is surely one of the most beautiful in the world and deserves leisurely exploration. And as with the older, landmark buildings throughout the country, it had been preserved and refurbished with the greatest of care. Soft apricot-colored velvet draperies and upholstery gave the place a mellow, even romantic atmosphere totally absent in newer halls. The auditorium itself is rectangular, shaped something like Symphony Hall in Boston (and probably dating from about the same late-nineteenth-century period), with a very high ceiling and clerestory windows just below. Under these windows are inscribed the names of the giants of Western music—tilted slightly eastward. Tchaikovsky, of course, is in the center, and surrounding him are such confreres as Bach, Beethoven, Dargomyzhsky, Mozart, Glinka and Schubert.

We were hastily ushered into what we told ourselves could have been the Tsar's box, right beside the stage; and the instant we sat down (the conductor was already on the podium) a rousing performance of *Alexander Nevsky* began. So it was not until we returned to our seats after intermission that we had a chance to nod to the only other occupant of the box, who had been seated in front of us. She was a dark-haired lady in her sixties, more smartly dressed than most Soviet women. She acknowledged our nod with a smile, but we didn't speak.

The second half of the program began with the First Piano Concerto, played by a young Soviet who was unknown to us. It's a very tricky piece, short and sassy. Prokofiev wrote it as a student, when he was about to graduate from the St. Petersburg Conservatory. Some members of the faculty, annoyed at its flip and playful quality, felt they were being poked fun at, and wanted not only to withhold Prokofiev's diploma but also to expel him for his insubordination. Quite a battle over his fate raged between the conservative and ultimately victorious liberal branches of the conservatory's faculty (among the latter, incidentally, one young lady piano teacher, Isabelle Vengerova, who staunchly held that Prokofiev should be forgiven his prank).

As soon as we heard the cadenza-like solo after the raucous opening section, we guessed we were in for a bumpy fifteen minutes. The soloist did not have the situation under control. This can happen to anybody. Horrible as such an experience is for the performer, it's also no pleasure for the innocent bystander. At the first slip, I felt my blood run cold. I saw Naomi wipe her sweating palms on her skirt and, at the same moment, heard our box companion groan in a most heartfelt manner. Thus the performance proceeded: pianist, mired in mud; me, chilled; Naomi, sweating; our neighbor, in true Russian fashion, calling upon God for help. It was evident that she, like us, knew every snare in the piece, and from her suffering we assumed that she was either the poor pianist's teacher or his mother. So when the eternal quarter hour passed and the concerto finally ended, we (in order to make her, at least, feel better) clapped wildly. We seemed to be the only members of the audience doing so; nobody else exhibited the slightest interest. After whatever applause we had incited died away, the lady turned to us with a "come off it!" look. In fluent English she asked me, "Do you play this piece?" Flustered at being cornered so boldly by someone connected with the performer, I replied, "*Da.*" "Well," she continued, still in English, "I'm awfully sorry you didn't hear it tonight." (What? What? Would a mother say something like that? She must be his teacher, then, I thought.) "Perhaps it's the first time he's played it, and he felt insecure," I suggested, again in Russian. "No," answered the lady, again in English (Naomi later called my attention to our bilingual conversation), "as a matter of fact, it's one of the few pieces in his repertoire." I was speechless. Surely she couldn't be his teacher either. Whom were we talking to? At that point, the lady, who I guess had expected to be recognized, realized our confusion, smiled wearily and said, "Oh, permit me to introduce myself. I am Mrs. Prokofiev."

That was the last time we had been in the Bolshoi Zal, and now I was looking forward to being once again on its stage. The only trouble was that our plane to Moscow still hadn't arrived. We'd come early to the Novosibirsk airport, and after checking in, sat down to await it. And sat. And sat. And sat. Eventually we were told that there would be a delay. We took a brisk walk around the airport in the dazzling Siberian sunshine and then settled down to read. (As we were later able to tell John Pope, one of the world's foremost authorities on Chinese ceramics, we are probably the only two people on this planet who studied—nay, memorized—his treatise describing the various motifs found on Chinese blue-and-white ceramics of the fourteenth century while waiting for a plane at the Novosibirsk airport.) During three more hours of sitting we learned a good deal about how to recognize, among many other patterns, four kinds of lotus panels and three kinds of classic scrolls (not to mention the diaper border), but learned nothing at all about our plane to Moscow. A jumbo plane landed and disgorged several hundred Russians carrying parasols, Japanese dolls and other Oriental trinkets (although no fourteenth-century blue-and-white ceramics that we could discern). They all joined us in what shortly became a smoky, echoing cavern of gloom.

"What's going on?" I asked one of our new companions.

"We were on our way from Tokyo to Moscow," he replied, "but there's fog in Moscow, so we were told we'd wait here until things clear up."

As Moscow is a couple of thousand miles away from Novosibirsk, this seemed an excessive precaution, but Aeroflot must have had its reasons. I began to get fidgety. This was not at all an ideal way to spend the day before an important recital. I'd

intended to have a good workout on the piano in the Bolshoi
Zal that afternoon, but after a few more hours of waiting it became clear that we would not even leave Novosibirsk until the
following morning, at the earliest. Our plane had not yet left
Moscow. After a ghastly snack at the airport *boofyett*, we were
all taken in buses to a primitive motel adjacent to the airport
to spend the night.

I told Marina to phone or wire Gosconcert in Moscow to say
that there would be no way I could play at the Bolshoi Zal the
following night. Under the best of circumstances, we'd arrive
with barely enough time to get washed and changed before the
concert, and I had no intention of walking out on that august
stage without having touched a piano for two days—not to
mention, direct from a five-hour journey on a flying cattle car.
Marina looked dubious. "I'll try to reach them," she said, "but
I don't know whether I'll be able to get anyone tonight, and tomorrow we'll probably leave before the office opens . . . I guess
I'd better send a wire and hope they get it before we arrive."

My decision turned out to have been a sensible one. By the
time we staggered off the plane in Moscow the following afternoon I certainly would have been in no condition to play that
evening. In addition—and for the first and only time—there
was no car to meet us at the airport. Of course, nobody at Gosconcert could have known when our delayed plane would arrive; and had somebody phoned Aeroflot to ask, the reply undoubtedly would have been that the plane had landed
twenty-four hours earlier, according to schedule (followed by
the sound of a receiver being slammed down). Marina called
the office, reiterated that I wouldn't—couldn't—play that night
and asked them please to send the car (there were no taxis) as
soon as possible because we were more dead than alive. Naturally, we had to wait for the car, which meant hanging around
for at least another hour. Tired, cranky and truly disappointed
at missing a concert that I'd wanted to give, I moped about the
airport and managed to pass the time by needling the Aeroflot
clerks.

A lock on one of our suitcases had been broken; so, pretending that I was dealing with a normal, capitalist airline, I brought it over to the counter.

"You see this broken lock," said I.

"We are sorry," said they.

"Could I please have the form to fill out?"

They looked blank. "Form?"

"Well, Aeroflot damaged this bag, so you have to have it fixed. Give me the claim form, please, and I'll fill it out."

A tremendous amount of buzzing, whispering, puzzled looks and searching for superiors ensued; to my amazement, one of the clerks appeared some time later with a yellowed, dog-eared sheet of paper which was precisely the form I wanted. He looked extremely relieved when I agreed it was the correct document. I filled it out with great care and then asked for a *kvitantsia*, a receipt which would entitle me to be reimbursed for the cost of the repair by Aeroflot in New York—almost like expecting the pilot of a UFO to have exact change for the George Washington Bridge. I tried to look angry, or at least stern, while playing out this scenario, but I don't know if I succeeded. The clutch of Aeroflot clerks, for their part, looked more sympathetic than annoyed or worried. I think they truly believed I'd gone crazy, which I would have if I'd been taking any of this nonsense seriously. But it was just something to pass the time—sort of like pulling the wings off butterflies, as I later found out—until our car arrived.

We were driven not to our hotel but straight to the auditorium where I was supposed to be playing scarcely two hours later. Uh-oh, thought I. Awaiting us at the entrance was a sad, elderly man, who looked like a cross between Serge Koussevitzky and a basset hound. He was Mr. Wechsler, who had been the manager of the hall for ages, I was told, and he really looked as if he carried the cares of the world on his shoulders.

"Ach," he greeted me.

I expected at least a token attempt from him to convince me to play that night—after all, the concert had not yet been called off and the audience was already beginning to gather—so I took the offensive.

"It's not *my* fault," I glowered, "that there's no way in your country to get a phone call or a wire through to anybody in authority in an emergency. You could have been informed twenty-four hours ago that the recital wasn't going to take place!"

"Ach," repeated the sad Mr. Wechsler. "But we would not dream of expecting you to play under such circumstances! That's no way to make music! No artist can perform well without rest, without practice. Do you think we don't understand that?" He looked even more hurt. "My dear, I just wanted to discuss with you when we can reschedule the recital. Then I'll tell the audience, when they come in, what the new date is. Now, go to your hotel and get some rest, and *I'll* do the worrying."

And that was more or less what happened. The recital was postponed until five days later, after my other two concerts in Moscow. As for my getting some rest, other problems intervened that evening before our heads made contact with the hotel's rather unyielding pillows.

Exhausted though we were, it was still comparatively early, and as we'd been sitting for so many hours we decided to take a walk. Crossing Red Square, I saw in the distance a poster announcing one of my concerts—the one that was to take place four days later with orchestra, at which I was to play the Prokofiev Third with Kondrashin. I could see my name and that of Kondrashin quite clearly, but whatever was below didn't seem to spell Prokofiev. We crossed the street, and with sinking hearts saw that I was announced to play, not Prokofiev, but the Brahms B-flat *and* the Chopin E minor. Shades of South America! It is true that I'd played both of these concertos about two weeks earlier, in Leningrad. But during the interim I'd been working exclusively on other repertoire—my two recital programs and several other concertos including, of course, the Prokofiev that I thought I was to be playing. The very idea of performing two such concertos in Moscow in four days' time without what I considered adequate preparation infuriated me as much as the thought of playing the recital direct from the plane that evening had done, and I spent the night imagining what terrible thunderbolts I would hurl at Mr. Aleshchenko, the head of Gosconcert, the following morning.

"Look at this! Look *here*, Aleshchenko! Here's *your* letter requesting the Prokofiev Third for this concert. Here's *my* confirmation. Here's *your* reconfirmation. So what's going on, anyway? What do you think I am, a machine? After weeks of bureaucracy, inefficiency, poor plumbing, lousy food, impossible scheduling, uncomfortable transportation, rotten hotels . . . for what, for *what*? For seeing Siberia? For seeing my father's old press clippings? Oh, sure, if anything, for the privilege of playing for those wonderful audiences. That I like to do. That's worth almost anything. But how can you expect me to do a good job if you can't even let me know what the hell I'm supposed to practice? Hah, Aleshchenko? Why should I take this from you? Not for money, certainly! Well, I've had it, see? Enough of this stupidity! You can't treat me like this and get away with it, understand? Next plane out! I'm taking the *next plane out*, you hear?"

Mr. Aleshchenko neatly sidestepped all the problems I was about to visit on him by merely being unavailable. There was simply no way to get through to him ("out of town"? "at a meeting"? "indisposed"? "liquidated"?), or, for that matter, to anyone with authority at Gosconcert. It's very hard to cancel a tour when there is nobody around to cancel it to. Marina kept trying to reach him, she assured me, but to no avail.

Meanwhile, her assistance was required on a far more urgent project. My electric razor had picked that morning to stop working, and she was needed to find a replacement, but fast. My speech to Mr. Aleshchenko wouldn't have nearly the same impact (if I ever got to see him, that is) delivered through a stubble. So Marina obligingly ran off to the vast GUM department store, where the better part of the day was spent in search and on line, trying to get me another, which she eventually did. It was slow, it was noisy (it also operated exclusively on the local current of 128 volts), but it disposed of my beard. And I soon realized that sitting around the hotel waiting for

Aleshchenko wasn't going to solve any problems, that I wasn't going to take the next plane out, and that, on the other hand, the next few days would have to be organized right down to the last second.

A practice studio at the Moscow Conservatory was put at my disposal on a round-the-clock basis. I did not make any attempt to do anything but practice. Hard-boiled eggs and tea from the conservatory *boofyett*, passed on to me at intervals during the day and night by Naomi and/or Marina became my sole nourishment, and even while I was munching or sipping my fingers kept moving on the keys. I was practicing two long recital programs plus about thirty short encores and the two big concertos. Just going over the notes superficially would take . . . well, let's say it couldn't be done the way it should be done, and leave it at that.

The following evening was my recital at the Tchaikovsky Hall, not to be confused with the Bolshoi Zal of the Tchaikovsky Conservatory—it's a completely different place at the other end of town. Unlike the Bolshoi Zal, the Tchaikovsky Hall is modern and utilitarian, and therefore not particularly memorable, either in acoustics or appearance. I recall a bleak, stony-looking auditorium and an oddly shaped dressing room which contained a small practice piano and a huge samovar, the latter manned by a motherly matron who handed me a glass of steaming tea each time I walked off the stage and stood over me until I drank down every drop. "Nice boy! It's good for you!" she kept murmuring, and I felt that at any moment she would pat my cheek.

As I was returning to the dressing room at intermission, I heard sounds of Schubert coming from the practice piano within—the famous E-flat Impromptu. What was this? Did I do something unforgivable? Was another pianist to replace me for the second half? But then my ears were assailed by a wrong note, an excruciatingly wrong note, the hysteria-producing wrong note that, once heard, could never be forgotten. Thirteen years had gone by since I'd last heard that wrong note, misread over and over by the poor girl in Auckland, and now, here it was again, in Moscow. That could mean only one thing. I flung open the door and was delighted to see Malinin. We'd missed him on previous visits, although on our last trip his wife Alya and another pianist friend, Jakov Zak, had taken us on a sightseeing spree that ranged from Tolstoy's house to the Novodevichi Cemetery (where *everybody* is buried) and culminated in what seemed like a twelve-course banquet at Zak's home.

Now the Malinins wanted us to dine with them the following night at their new apartment. They'd just moved to a five-room flat—enormous by Soviet standards, and good-sized by ours—in one of the four skyscrapers that dominated the Moscow skyline. (As with those in Minsk, these buildings—dating from the thirties and reflecting a Stalin's-eye view of the Radio City Music Hall—appeared to be identical and regarded each other fraternally from the four corners of the city.) Although eager to spend the evening with our friends in their new home, I didn't dare take any time off from the piano.

"Out of the question! Gotta practice!" I explained, but Malinin's "Out of the question! Gotta have a good meal! Can't play on an empty stomach! *I* know what's best for you!" convinced me, and the feast laid on for us—together with much healing laughter—caused our blood sugar and our morale to shoot up immeasurably. Those hours were a truce between battles.

At around midnight, Malinin drove us back to our hotel. After the requisite fifteen-minute wait for an elevator (they functioned perfectly well, but whoever designed the enormous hotel in which we were staying failed to estimate correctly how many of them would be required to serve what seemed like thousands of rooms, a miscalculation he shared with the architect of the Palmer House in Chicago), we were finally deposited at our floor, where the *dezhurnaya* looked at me suspiciously.

"There was a lady here to see you," she sniffed. "She waited for over an hour. She's gone now, but she said she would come back in a little while."

Naomi looked at me suspiciously, too; I felt puzzled, but not particularly guilty, and we continued on to our room. About fifteen minutes later came a knock on the door. The *dezhurnaya* called out, "That lady's back. Will you come out to see her?" I put on my robe and slippers and padded out into the corridor. There, under the scrutiny of the *dezhurnaya*, stood one of the Aeroflot clerks I had harangued about my damaged bag. She looked extremely uncomfortable.

"When you filled out that form the other day, I didn't know who you were," she said. "But I remembered your name, when I saw it on a poster, and I thought it would be terrible if you went back to America and . . . had trouble getting reimbursed for the repair. So I went to my superior to see if there was anything we could do." Now I began to feel somewhat uncomfortable. She continued, "Well, as I suspected, he told me that you *would* have a problem in New York because our internal Aeroflot—Aeroflot U.S.S.R.—and Aeroflot International are actually two different organizations under the jurisdiction of two completely different agencies." (In other words, I wouldn't get any satisfaction at their Fifth Avenue branch.) ". . . and you understand, of course, that we have no facilities to fix that kind of thing here" (it was one of those combination locks which, when closed, held the suitcase together) "so I then went to my superior's superior—I couldn't get to see him right away, which is why this has taken so long—and I told him the whole story. Today there was a meeting to decide what to do, and I was authorized to come and give you" (here she peered at me anxiously, as I began looking for a hole in the floor to disappear through) "ten rubles." (Breathlessly:) "Would that be satisfactory?"

I took the money, signed a *kvitantsia*, mumbled my thanks and fled, hating myself and the childish impulse that had caused me to behave so boorishly at the airport.

Earlier on that day of Malinin's dinner party I'd had the first of two rehearsals for the concerto concert, conducted by my friend Kiril Kondrashin. I'd played with him a few years before (in Monte Carlo, of all places) but we'd known each other

longer still—ever since Van Cliburn's triumphant return from
the Soviet Union in 1958, when Kondrashin accompanied him
to the United States and conducted some of the gala concerts
that Van played at that time. Everything went well at the rehearsal and I was even beginning to get over my fury at the
change of program—I hadn't forgotten the Brahms and Chopin, after all!—and beginning actually to look forward to the
concert. The following morning (ten rubles richer) I appeared
for the second rehearsal in good spirits. The orchestra was
warming up, but things seemed strangely subdued. A group of
official-looking men were standing, huddled together, near the
stage, and as I walked down the aisle I could hear voices saying,
"You tell him." "No, *you* tell him." Finally they approached
me all together, as a delegation. "We have something very sad
to tell you," they said, practically in unison. I imagined they had
discovered that it really *was* the Prokofiev Third I was to play,
after all. But no, the news was truly sad. Kiril's mother had
died the night before. Obviously, he could not conduct the
concert that evening. "Would you be willing to play with
someone else?" they asked me nervously. I shrugged; what else
could I do? With that, a grandfatherly-looking man who had
been sitting alone in the back of the auditorium was summoned. He looked at me humbly, as if to say, "I hope I'll do—
please give me a chance . . ." and turned out to be Boris
Khaikin, whose work I knew well from recordings; and who, as
it happened, had been the teacher of Kondrashin. Although I
missed playing with Kiril, Khaikin was a splendid accompanist.
He was primarily known as an opera conductor and so (as Szell
had pointed out to me many years earlier) could cope with
anything, and the concert was dispatched with no untoward incident.

The next evening was the postponed recital at the Bolshoi
Zal, and my last appearance in Moscow. The audience's enthusiasm didn't seem in any way dampened by my not having
shown up as scheduled a few nights earlier. Their affection
more than justified any inconveniences I might have endured—

even three days of hard-boiled eggs and the wiles of Alesh-chenko. When I walked onstage to begin the recital I received the kind of ovation that I would have been happy to get at the end of any concert anywhere. Then I noticed that the lid of the piano was closed. Could someone have forgotten to unlock it? That *would* be an anticlimax! But no—the piano was not locked, and when I raised the lid, there, lying on the keyboard, was a rose.

At intermission I described this touching incident to Naomi, who, backstage as usual, had been methodically working her way through our dwindling stockpile of Sunday *Times Magazine* sections. I had been very moved by this demonstration from my people, and couldn't get over the thoughtful gesture.

". . . and can you imagine," I concluded, "there, on the keyboard, was a rose!"

"My God!" screamed Naomi. "What on earth did you do?"

"Why, I put it on top of the piano."

"You touched it?" she shrieked. "Was it alive?"

"Of course it was alive!"

"And you *touched* it?"

"Naturally. I picked it up carefully, of course, to avoid the thorns . . ."

"Oh," she said more calmly. "A *rose*. I thought you said a *roach*."

Onward to Kiev, scene of my mother's childhood delights.

("We'll be back in two weeks," they'd told her, when they started on the journey that would take them away forever. They only carried a few things; all the family treasures were left for safekeeping, until their return, in the huge storage closet, *kladovka*, on shelves which in normal times were filled with jars of preserved vegetables, and jam, and pickles, and boxes of tea and bottles of wine. My mother knew this *kladovka* intimately because when she misbehaved—apparently quite often—the French lady or the German lady [never *Nyanya*, who spoiled her] would lock her in the big, dark room until she repented, or until suppertime—whichever came first. So she had plenty of opportunity to become acquainted with the contents of the storeroom, perhaps even sampling from a jar of marmalade to sweeten her incarceration. "And then, just before they went away," she told me, "they put all the silver and . . . good things in *kladovka*. Trays like this, big . . . heavy, heavy. All kinds of silver things. But Grandfather said, when he left, 'Never mind. In two weeks we'll be back.'")

Two quarter centuries later, I was back.

Kiev was still a pretty place: rolling hills, parks, sparkling river, bustling town. Although the main street had been systematically blown up by the Germans during their retreat in the Second World War, the new buildings seemed somehow less grim than most, and many of the old houses elsewhere were still standing, still in use; I imagined it was possible to get an idea of the way Kiev had looked in the old days, before it all started—the city I felt I knew so well from my mother's tales. From our hotel window I could easily see the island in the Dnieper where the dacha had stood; the Philharmonic Hall where my mother had snoozed through so many concerts, and where I was to play the following evening; the parade of streetcars, antique enough to have remained from earlier times (could it be, then, that one of them might bear tattered traces of red velvet upholstery and maybe "even a little icebox"?); and the large park, known in my grandparents' day as Merchants' Park, now Pioneers' Park. (They don't miss a thing.)

I was armed with little hand-drawn maps to lead me to the old family homes. I had the addresses too, of course; but, like the park, most of the street names had been changed to honor a different set of heroes. Naomi and I prowled about (passing the Kiev Conservatory, where at nine o'clock on a warm Sunday morning, with the windows flung wide, all secrets were exposed and I heard what sounded like an army of pianists battling what seemed like the entire piano literature of the nineteenth century), but we couldn't be sure we were heading in the right direction. We were looking for my great-grandfather's house. Finally I accosted a passerby who looked old enough to remember how things were.

"Excuse me, sir, but could you tell me—the street that was once Olghenskaya, what is it now?"

He knew what I was doing. Marina had told us that some tourists (Americans, mostly) make a sport of finding their ancestors' homes, some going so far as to ring the doorbells, asking to see the interiors. But still, he looked for a moment as if he'd seen a ghost. Then he thought a bit, replied, "Mayakovskaya," and escorted us there, looking over my shoulder at my mother's sketchy map, and watching with wistful amusement as I photographed the big old house on the corner from all angles.

There it was at last, the house of *kladovka*, where the heavy silver trays were stored. How many Soviet teeth had those ". . . good things" filled? And how many Soviet citizens now shared the drawing room where the dogs had yapped while the music teacher dozed in his yellow silk chair as my mother suffered through her piano lessons on the white Bechstein? The house looked quite the way I had imagined: ocher stucco, a house built to last for generations, permanent, solid—in spite of the crumbling balcony in front of my aunt Olga's window on the second floor. ("Oy, they *still* haven't fixed it!" my mother complained when she saw the photo I'd taken. Then, smiling, "But how the tree has grown!")

The dacha on the island, though, was gone, of course. And now there was a footbridge across the river, just about where Mikhail, singing at the top of his lungs after a night on the town, rowed out with his chickens. ("Call the hotel to send over dinner for eighteen—Mikhail won't be cooking today!") As we approached the island I could see the water lilies "all yellow and golden, so beautiful . . . beautiful they were," and the peaceful little coves where my mother had sat in the *Lilliput* and fished and daydreamed. The beach where the dacha once stood, lapped by the gentle ripples of the Dnieper, was strewn with ample Soviet bodies in various states of undress—sunbathing, cavorting boisterously, playing soccer, picnicking, licking ice-cream cones on this sunny Sunday morning.

"*Muzhiks!* Peasants! Off my property!" I commanded imperiously, to Naomi's embarrassment and Marina's delight. But nobody even looked up.

CAST OF CHARACTERS